7/29/10

Chanelle,
Great to meet you at OMB!

SECOND EDITION

An Introduction to
Enterprise Architecture

Scott A. Bernard

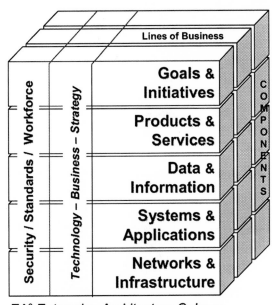

EA³ Enterprise Architecture Cube ™

This Book is Dedicated with Love
to My Wife Joyce
and Our Children
Bill, Kristin, and Katie

Table of Contents

Foreword
By John A. Zachman

I am delighted that Scott Bernard has written this book, "An Introduction to Enterprise Architecture."

We need as much focus on this critical issue as possible, especially in the academic environment and especially as we continue the transition into the Information Age. It is my opinion that this issue of Enterprise Architecture is not well understood in the ranks of General Management who see Enterprise Architecture as just an I/S or IT issue, nor in the ranks of I/S management who see it as taking too long and costing too much, nor in the ranks of academia who tend to focus on what they perceive constitutes current market demand, typically a promising technology. My opinion is, Enterprise Architecture may well be the "Issue of the Century." In fact, I felt strongly enough about this issue that I published an article by that title in the year 2000, the turn of the Century.

Exacerbating the problem, we seem to have raised a generation of people, the "web generation," who are facile with the technology, but as a result seem to think that the solution to all problems lies in technology. They are tempted to see strategy and architecture, engineering and design, modeling and methodologies as prehistoric, the preoccupation of cave men. Now, real men do Java ... or whatever constitutes the current "silver bullet," technological panacea.

I have a wise and profoundly insightful friend, Roger Greer, who was the Dean of the School of Library and Information Management at the University of Southern California. I sat on his advisory council for many years and he observed that a few decades ago, the library community became enamored with the technologies of the library and lost sight of their reason for being, which he argued was to identify problems of the community and to assemble the required knowledge to bring to bear and participate in solving the problems. Now it appears that many universities are de-committing the Library Schools because they are simply technical, storing and retrieving books. There is no conceptual substance requiring research or advanced degrees. You can learn how to store books and find them again in secondary schools. In fact, USC discontinued Roger's School because of the persistence of the technical perceptions on the part of the Administration. In fact, I was having lunch with the Dean of the Library School at the University of California, Berkley the day they de-committed that school on the same basis.

In "The Next Information Revolution" article published in Forbes ASAP August 24th, 1998, Peter Drucker observes that the present information revolution is actually the fourth information revolution. "The printing revolution (the third information revolution) immediately created a new and unprecedented class of information technologists ... who became great stars ... great gentlemen ... revered all over Europe ... courted by kings, princes, the Pope ... showered with money and honors. ... The printers, with their focus on technology (later) became ordinary craftsmen ... definitely not of the upper class. ... Their place was soon taken by what we now call publishers ... whose focus was no longer on the 'T' in IT but on the 'I.'... Is there a lesson in this for today's information technologists, the CIOs in organizations, the software designers and developers, the devotees of Moore's law?" (said Peter Drucker).

Several months ago, I saw an old friend, Gordon Everest, the originator of the "crow's feet" in logical data models. Gordon is retiring this summer because the Information Systems Department of the Business School at the University of Minnesota is being de-committed. In fact, I am afraid that the same thing may have happened at the Business School, Information Systems Department at UCLA as I have not seen any of my academic friends from UCLA for several years.

I know I have a rather radical view of this, but my observation would be the whole reason you want people with technical skills in your Enterprise is not for building and running systems. Anybody can build and run systems, the employment of the technology. The reason you want these kinds of people in your Enterprise is because they have the capability of engineering and manufacturing your Enterprise for you. That's the reason for their being, NOT simply for building and running systems.

I have some strong convictions that the raw material for engineering and manufacturing Enterprises are primitive models, not composite models. Composite models are for implementations, the embodiment of the technologies. Primitive models are for architecture, ENTERPRISE Architecture. I don't think it is possible to engineer and manufacture enterprises without building and managing primitive models. It is similar to elements and compounds. Before Mendeleyev defined the periodic table of elements, chemistry was not a science. It was alchemy, working with compounds, trial and error, unpredictable. In like fashion, I believe that until Enterprise Architects understand and manage the primitive (elementary) constructs, Enterprise Architecture is dealing with composites (compounds), technical implementations. It is not a science and is not predictable and it is not engineering and manufacturing Enterprises.

Although, Scott does not necessarily share my rather strong and radical convictions, he graciously makes reference to them several times in the body of his work, which I greatly appreciate.

In any case, I feel strongly, we must infuse these critical Enterprise Architecture ideas into the next generation, through the academic environment. We sorely need a generation of people who understand and are committed to these complex issues that will persevere and see Enterprise Architecture become a reality. If we fail to bring these longer term issues into focus and continue only to focus on technology, on implementations, short term propositions, we will not only sacrifice our legitimacy as a discipline, but from an Enterprise standpoint, may even forfeit the Enterprise's continued viability.

I was visiting a major telecommunications service provider recently in which some of the management folks got into a rather heated discussion about what was more important, to serve the customer ... or to increase the stock price. I would not argue that it is unimportant to increase the stock price, but I would suggest that this is a very short term perspective. If somebody doesn't pay attention to the customer in this very competitive industry, you may find yourself out of the game in the longer term and your stock price might not even appear anymore in the newspaper. It is not EITHER the short term OR the long term. It is the short term AND the long term.

I am not arguing that technical implementations, composites, building and running systems in the short term are unimportant, but I am arguing that if we don't pay attention to our reason for being, to engineering and manufacturing Enterprises, to primitive models, ENTERPRISE ARCHITECTURE in the longer term, we may well forfeit either our relevance as a discipline ... or sacrifice the continuing viability of the Enterprise in the process. Engineering and manufacturing Enterprises is the context within which building and running systems becomes relevant. By the way, this has profound conceptual implications for research and advanced degrees in academia.

Scott Bernard has taken a major step in intensifying the focus on these critical issues and I am particularly pleased that he has produced this work as a textbook for the academic environment.

"Introduction to ENTERPRISE ARCHITECTURE"! Our hope lies in the new generation's capacity to grasp its significance and persist in its realization.

Thank you, Scott Bernard!

John A. Zachman
Glendale, CA 2004

Preface

Intended Audience

An Introduction to Enterprise Architecture is intended to support the development of new courses on Enterprise Architecture (EA), as well as to enhance and update existing courses on business strategy and planning, information systems analysis and design, operations research, government planning, change management, knowledge management, and project management. Typically these courses are offered in graduate programs or the later part of undergraduate programs. Though it is not a prerequisite, students using this book may benefit from having prior business management and/or information technology (IT) knowledge.

EA is as much about the purpose, structure, and functioning of medium and large size enterprises as it is about the systems and technologies that support those enterprises. The concepts presented in this book are applicable to the work of executives, managers, planners, analysts, and support staff in enterprises in both the public and private sectors.

Why I Wrote This Book

An Introduction to Enterprise Architecture is the culmination of two decades of experience that I have gained through work initially as an IT manager and then as a consultant to executives in the public and private sectors. I wrote this book for three major reasons: (1) to help move business and technology planning from a systems and process-level view to a more strategy-driven enterprise-level view, (2) to promote and explain the emerging profession of EA, and (3) to provide the first textbook on the subject of EA, which is suitable for graduate and undergraduate levels of study. To date, other books on EA have been practitioner books not specifically oriented toward a student who may be learning the subject with little to no previous exposure. Therefore, this book contains references to related academic research and industry best practices, as well as my own observations about potential future practices and the direction of this emerging profession.

The response to the first edition of this book from teachers and practitioners was overwhelmingly positive, which I am most grateful for. The changes presented in the second edition include (1) adjustments to the labeling of the levels of the 'EA^3 Cube' framework to promote clarity and detailed documentation; (2) updated graphics to promote understanding: and (3) the addition of an Appendix of over fifty EA artifact examples.

Relationship to Systems Analysis and Design

This book is a suitable companion to the numerous Systems Analysis and Design (SA&D) textbooks that are in use, as it can provide an overarching context and unifying framework for the system development approaches and documentation techniques described therein. *An Introduction to Enterprise Architecture* helps to set the context for SA&D courses and related professional activities. Without the context of EA, systems development efforts throughout an organization run the risk of being disjointed and duplicative.... a phenomenon that has occurred during the past several decades. This book provides a more detailed explanation of the EA concepts that are often only summarized in SA&D textbooks, in a way that compliments, extends, and refers to foundational SA&D concepts.

It should be noted that this book identifies enterprise architecture documentation techniques at each level of a generalized EA framework and documentation methodology: the "EA^3 Cube." These documentation techniques originate from existing methods in strategic planning, business administration, and information SA&D. While this book identifies and briefly describes these documentation techniques, it does not go into detail or attempt to build proficiency in a particular technique.... that is left to the many other books on strategy, business, and SA&D, which I recommend that students refer to if additional proficiency is desired.

Relationship to Strategy and Business Planning

An Introduction to Enterprise Architecture provides a clear explanation of the relationship between strategic planning, business planning, and information technology planning. While IT resources are increasingly becoming a commodity, the importance of IT services as a business enabler continues to grow in many public and private sector organizations. In recognition of this, EA's identification of integrated IT solutions to organization-wide (crosscutting) and mission-specific (vertical) requirements is one of the focal points of this book. Strategic goals and business requirements should drive IT solutions, and EA's contribution to this alignment is another focal point of the book. Finally, this book provides specific EA documentation techniques that create strategy and business-driven views of the enterprise, which in turn can help to identify gaps in performance that IT solutions can help to close.

Relationship to Component-Based and Service-Oriented Architectures

An Introduction to Enterprise Architecture presents EA as a holistic management, planning, and documentation activity and introduces the 'EA^3 Cube' framework and implementation methodology. This approach to EA identifies distinct lines of business which encompass five sub-architecture levels and three common thread areas. The five sub-architectures address strategic initiatives; business services; information flows; systems and applications; and technology infrastructure. The three threads are security, standards, and workforce. The EA^3 Cube framework is component-based in that the "building blocks" of each of the sub-architectures are 'plug-and-play' components. These components vary widely in their purpose and nature, but are increasingly interoperable and integrated due to the standards thread that promotes non-proprietary solutions. For this reason, architecture documentation approaches (such as the non-proprietary Model-Driven Architecture, or Integrated Governance Model) can be used to populate one or more of the sub-architectures of the EA^3 Cube framework.

The EA^3 Cube framework not only recognizes and preserves the role of early architecture approaches that addressed data, applications, and networks, but also recognizes newer approaches that promote strategic scenario planning, the value of business supply chains, and web-based services. In particular, the 'Business Services' sub-architecture within the EA^3 Cube framework (the second level) exemplifies how EA can link strategy, business, and technology components across the enterprise within a "Service Bus" that encompasses platform-independent horizontal and vertical EA components. Services extend throughout the framework, but in my opinion have their origination of purpose at level two of the EA^3 Cube... being driven by strategic goals and initiatives (the framework level above the "Business Services' level), and calling for supporting information flows, systems, applications, and network infrastructure components (the framework levels below). Basic to the concept of EA components presented in this book is the idea that the "Standards" thread that enables interoperability within the Service Bus by promoting the use of EA components that are based on open-standards/protocols and non-proprietary solutions.

Organization of This Book

An Introduction to Enterprise Architecture is organized into four sections of material, a case study, and several appendices of amplifying or reference material. The case study is presented at the beginning of each section and before selected chapters to reinforce the application of the concepts in a variety of settings. The four sections are intended to sequentially develop the student's understanding of the concepts of EA, as well as methods for implementing these concepts.

Section I provides an overview and context for the book, identifies the value and risk of doing an EA, discusses the structure and changing nature of enterprises, and shows how EA helps to link strategic, business, and technology planning. Section II defines and describes what an EA framework is, presents a step-by-step methodology to implement an EA through the documentation of current and future views of resources, and describes how to communicate changes in the EA through an EA Management Plan that also can serve as a "blueprint" for modernization. Section III discusses how to use and maintain EA information in an on-line repository within the enterprise, and how governance processes can be integrated (e.g., investment planning, project management, and security). Section IV provides the author's thoughts on EA as a profession and opinions on future trends. The Appendices amplify or extend the material presented in all Sections and are intended to be primarily for student reference. A comprehensive Glossary of EA terms and acronyms are provided along with a Bibliography of additional reference material.

An Introduction to Enterprise Architecture is structured such that each Section and Chapter builds on the material previously presented. The Sections and Chapters are organized to promote understanding and a consistent, cogent flow of material by using the following design:

Sections:
➤ <u>Overview</u>. Describes the general purpose of the Section and the contribution of each Chapter.
➤ <u>Case Study</u>. An ongoing case study from the private sector that provides scenes which make the concepts of the Section and Chapters more tangible and relevant.

Chapters:

- ➤ <u>Overview</u>. Describes the purpose and key concepts of the Chapter.
- ➤ <u>Learning Objectives</u>. Lists the learning objectives for the student in that Chapter.
- ➤ <u>Introduction</u>. Provides context and introductory commentary to build student interest in the main body of material.
- ➤ <u>Discussion</u>. Provides the Chapter's concepts through descriptions, graphics, and footnoted references.
- ➤ <u>Analogy Boxes</u>. The analogy of the architecture of a house is used throughout the book to assist readers in understanding and relating the various concepts of Enterprise Architecture in a context that is common to most students. [1]
- ➤ <u>Key Term Definition Boxes</u>. Definitions of key terms are provided when they are first used to promote student understanding at the time that associated concepts are being presented.
- ➤ <u>Summary of Concepts</u>. Provides a recap of the purpose of the Chapter and its key concepts, and introduces the following Section/Chapter.
- ➤ <u>Review Questions and Exercises</u>. Provides questions that address key concepts and exercises that allow students to further explore key concepts of the Chapter and tie-in concepts from other Chapters.

Pedagogy

The design of the material and teaching approach provided in *An Introduction to Enterprise Architecture* promotes readability and applicability to real-world EA issues, including:

1. A common structure for Sections and Chapters that highlight and reinforce key learning points.
2. A Case Study to help students apply concepts to real-world situations.
3. Analogies, definitions of unique terms, and key concept extracts that are provided at the point at which new material is being introduced.
4. The consistent use of symbology in diagrams in all areas of the book.

---

[1] Spewak, Steven. <u>Enterprise Architecture Planning: Developing a Blueprint for Data, Applications, and Technology</u>. New York: John Wiley & Sons Publishers. 1992. Dr. Spewak equated the disjointedness of IT planning without enterprise architecture to the haphazard construction of the 160-room Winchester House in California over a period of 38 years without a master building plan.

5. Questions and Exercises at the end of each Chapter to test student's knowledge of the material.

6. A comprehensive *Instructor's Manual* that provides answers to review questions and exercises, comments and recommended teaching points from the author for each Section and Chapter (available separately).

General Comments

The *EA³ Cube Framework*, *EA³*, and *Living Enterprise* are registered Trademarks. All rights are reserved. Concepts for the *EA³ Cube Framework*, *EA³*, *Living Enterprise*, and the *Organizational Network Model* were generally influenced by the works of John Zachman, Steven Spewak, Talcott Parsons, and James Thompson, as is acknowledged throughout the book. The specific concepts for the *EA³ Cube Framework*, *EA³*, *Living Enterprise*, and the *Organizational Network Model* were not developed as a result of, or influenced by, any other public or private sector enterprise architecture approach or graphic. Any similarity to other EA approaches or graphics is coincidental. Of specific note; a cubic shape is generic and may be in use with other systems development, architecture, and/or business planning approaches. The uniqueness of the EA³ "Cube" is the singular combination of all of its dimensions, functions, levels, components, and other attributes. The concepts and graphics in this book were originally presented in lectures given by Dr. Bernard at various academic and professional conferences in 2002-2003 and are copyrighted by Dr. Bernard separate from this or any other publication. Permission for the use of the *EA³ Cube Framework*, *EA³*, and *Living Enterprise* is granted by Dr. Bernard for use in this printing of *An Introduction to Enterprise Architecture*.

Acknowledgements

I would like thank my colleagues and former students in the growing field of EA for their encouragement in writing *An Introduction to Enterprise Architecture*. John Zachman's Foreword is a wonderful contribution to this textbook that in my opinion gives new students to the subject of EA the best possible beginning for their studies. In my view, John Zachman is the founder of Enterprise Architecture as it has come to be known, and I sincerely thank him for writing the Foreword. John got it right when he introduced the Information Systems Architecture in 1987, and he has continued to provide on-target architecture consulting, training, and mentoring on a global basis ever since. I believe that John's emphasis on the basics, on using "primitive" EA artifacts that focus on discrete aspects of an architecture, is not in conflict with the EA^3 Cube framework or documentation methodology. My work is intended, in part, to extend that focus and to discuss the utilization of what John refers to as "composite" EA artifacts which combine several types of primitives to form specialized views of an enterprise.... views that are often helpful to managers and executives. My bottom line position is that without solid EA primitives, the composite artifacts are not possible to develop.

I would also like to thank and remember Dr. Steven Spewak who helped start the profession of EA. Steve was an inspirational mentor to me during the past few years, and he passed away in March 2004 a few months before the first edition of this book was published.... he will be sorely missed by many in our profession.

It is both exciting and challenging to be part of an emerging profession, and I salute those who endeavor to develop enterprise architectures for public and private sector organizations. To them I would say good luck, the work ahead of you will be frustrating at times, yet fulfilling as the contribution of EA to organizational success is fully realized.

One more thought. My father was a successful land developer and home builder who learned the essentials of traditional architecture on his own. There are many parallels in our lives, and this is yet another. As the head of information technology enterprises and projects, I found that I needed some way to organize the perpetual chaos of systems development and upgrade projects, ongoing operations, and more than occasional surprises. Because of this, I learned about EA, which helped to establish a reference framework for planning and decision-making.... the most valuable tool one can have in a dynamic field like IT management. Now, with greater appreciation, I enjoy being part of the growth of this new field, which in many ways is like the one that my father came to know.... a nice blessing in the journey of life.

About the Author

Scott Bernard has over twenty years of experience in information technology (IT) management, including work in the academic, federal government, military, and private sectors. Dr. Bernard has held positions as a Chief Information Officer (CIO) equivalent, IT management consultant, line-of-business manager, network operations manager, telecommunications manager, and project manager for several major IT systems installations. He has developed enterprise architectures for a number of public and private sector organizations, started an enterprise architecture practice for an IT management firm, developed his own consulting practice, and taught enterprise architecture at a number of universities, businesses, and government agencies. Dr. Bernard's areas of current research, teaching, and consulting include IT-related leadership, policy development, strategic planning, enterprise architecture, systems analysis and design, IT project management, and capital planning. In 2002, Dr. Bernard created the EA^3 Cube™ framework and methodology that is featured in this book, as well as the design for an on-line EA repository that is called Living Enterprise.™

Dr. Bernard serves as an Assistant Professor and the Director of Washington D.C. Programs for the School of Information Studies at Syracuse University. He is also a Senior Lecturer in the Executive Program of the CIO Institute and the Institute for Software Research International at Carnegie Mellon University's School of Computer Science. Dr. Bernard is a founding instructor of the Federal Enterprise Architecture Certification Institute in Washington DC. He is the founding President of the Association of Enterprise Architects, and is currently the Editor of the Journal of Enterprise Architecture.

Dr. Bernard earned his Ph.D. at Virginia Tech in Public Administration and Policy; a master's degree in Business and Personnel Management from Central Michigan University, a master's degree in Information Management from Syracuse University, and a bachelor's degree in Psychology from the University of Southern California. He is a graduate of the Naval War College, and earned a CIO Certificate and an Advanced Management Program Certificate from the National Defense University. Dr. Bernard is also a former career naval aviator who served onboard aircraft carriers and with shore squadrons, led IT programs, and was the Director of Network Operations for the Joint Chiefs of Staff.

Section I

The Concept of Enterprise Architecture

Section I presents an introduction to the subject and concepts of Enterprise Architecture (EA), as well as an overview of the purpose and value of EA for business, government, and non-profit organizations. A case study based on a fictitious business is introduced that will help the student to understand and apply EA concepts. Section I is organized as follows:

Case Study (Scene 1) - Possible Need for an EA Program

The Case Study introduces the Danforth Manufacturing Company[2] and several business and technology challenges that will cause the company to consider using EA to improve planning, decision-making, and solution implementation.

Chapter 1 - An Overview of Enterprise Architecture

Chapter 1 provides the student with an overview of the emerging profession and practice of EA. The chapter's discussion introduces the concept that EA provides a holistic view of an enterprise. This differs from the more system-centric or process-centric views that previous analysis and planning approaches have emphasized. EA is both a management program and a documentation method, and comment is made on the similarities and differences of doing EA in private and public sector enterprises.

---

[2] The Danforth Manufacturing Company that is portrayed in this Case Study is a fictitious enterprise. Any resemblance to an actual business or similar business activities is coincidental.

Chapter 2 - The Structure and Culture of Enterprises

Chapter 2 describes the structure of enterprises and why it is important to include culture in the EA documentation effort. The driving theme of this chapter is that an enterprise involves one or more social activities that involve the sharing of information. It also shows that the boundary between the structure of the enterprise and the culture is dynamic. The importance of stakeholder involvement and the management of expectations are also discussed.

Case Study (Scene 2) - Considering an EA Program

The Case Study continues with the Chief Information Officer of Danforth Manufacturing Company. The CIO makes a presentation regarding how an EA approach can help to evaluate several requests for IT systems, and coordinate their implementation.

Chapter 3 - The Value and Risk of Creating an Enterprise Architecture

Chapter 3 discusses the value and risk of creating an enterprise-wide architecture. The main concepts of this chapter are (1) that EA represents a different way of looking at resources across the enterprise, and (2) that the significant cost of creating an EA must be justified by the value that it brings to the enterprise by linking strategy, business, and technology. Another key concept is (3) that an integrated set of planning, decision-making, and implementation processes can better identify and resolve performance gaps across the enterprise, and that EA promotes this type of integrated governance. The management of change is discussed in terms of why an EA may not be accepted or used if stakeholder buy-in and participation is not achieved.

Case Study:
Danforth Manufacturing Company
Scene 1: Possible Need for an EA Program

The Danforth Manufacturing Company (DMC) develops, produces, and sells several lines of photovoltaic storage cells (solar-powered batteries) for use in various consumer, business, and aerospace products. Robert Danforth, the President and Chief Executive Officer (CEO) of DMC, has called a meeting of the Executive Committee to review several recent capital investment requests. The largest two of these was a request by Kate Jarvis, the Chief Operating Officer (COO), for a new sales and inventory tracking system and a request by Jim Gorman, the Chief Financial Officer (CFO) to invest in a new cost accounting system. Also invited to the meeting were Sam Young, the company's first Chief Information Officer (CIO) who joined the company two weeks before, and Gerald Montes, the company's Chief Counsel.

Robert Danforth was the last one to enter the executive boardroom. He smiled at his top management team and said, "Thank you all for coming by to talk a bit more about several investment requests that came out of our annual planning meeting last month. Sam, you hadn't joined the company yet, so I'm particularly interested in your thoughts today. Mainly, I want to better understand from the group why our current capabilities are insufficient and how these new systems will help bottom-line performance. Kate, why don't you go first and then we'll hear from Jim."

Kate rose and walked to an easel that held several charts and diagrams. "Gentlemen, as mentioned at the planning meeting, my request for a new Sales and Inventory Tracking System (SITS) is based on an insufficient current ability to match inventory and production information with customer orders. We are also experiencing excessive turnaround time for orders in the industrial product lines, as compared to our competition. Our sales representatives in the field are beginning to lose orders. They can't provide on-the-spot quotes based on real-time checks of available inventory and current pricing. The same goes for our representatives. They are not able to see when the custom and small job production runs are being scheduled. This would help sales in this high-profit area which we will be expanding. Our major competitor fielded this information capability almost a year ago. While I was skeptical at the time about the impact it would have on their sales, I now believe that it's a successful model for them and therefore is going to make or break us in the industrial product line."

Robert leaned forward. "Kate, this sounds quite serious. Even so, from a cost perspective I am concerned about the return on investment (ROI) for SITS. Last month you stated that initial cost estimate for the development of SITS was over three million dollars. We have tight budgets for the next two years… have you looked at ROI?" "Yes," responded Kate. "These charts show the level of investment and payback period for SITS, which I estimate to be two years, depending on how quickly and thoroughly the sales force adopts it. The lifecycle for SITS should be seven years, with positive ROI seen in years three through seven, and an average of about twelve percent per year."

Robert turned to Sam, "What do you think Sam? Isn't part of the problem here that many of our information systems don't talk to each other?" Sam grimaced slightly and said, "I think you're right, from what I've seen in my initial survey of information technology (IT) capabilities, a lot of our systems were built as individual projects based on what then were unique requirements. We now have some duplication of functionality and evidence of inefficient support for evolving business processes." Robert responded quickly, "Isn't the SITS proposal just more of the same?" "Perhaps" said Sam, "I'm hearing that Kate wants to integrate information exchanges across the sales, inventory, and production lines of business. This represents a somewhat higher-level approach to meeting several business requirements."

Robert turned to Jim, "What do you think about Kate's problem? Jim answered with a pensive look, "Well, I agree that we need to address our competition's capability. While our aerospace product line is the most profitable, the industrial product line brings in the most revenue, so there would be a significant impact on the entire company if we lose market share in the industrial product area." Robert then turned to Gerald, "So what does the Chief Counsel think?" Gerald paused for a moment and then said, "I think that we must act decisively to protect market share in the industrial product line, but I'm not sure that SITS is the answer. You might be right Robert, the proposal that Kate is making might be more of the same type of technology solution that Sam says got us in this situation."

Robert leaned back in his chair and said, "Before going further on this proposal, let's talk about Jim's investment request. I wonder if there are any parallels." Jim activated the conference room's projector and brought up a set of briefing slides. "My request is for a cost accounting system that would replace the current accounting system. As Robert mentioned, there are tight budgets the next two years, and having the ability to more readily see spending and profit generation within each line of business will help us to manage the budget more effectively. This system is one module of "WELLCO" a proven commercial enterprise resource planning (ERP) product. We can utilize this product by expanding it if other back office requirements emerge. The cost of the investment is just under $600,000. According to the vendor, the historical payback period for this cost accounting module is eighteen months, with an average annual ROI of sixteen percent during the subsequent years."

"Jim, can this new accounting capability support what Kate is looking for?" said Gerald. Jim responded, "The WELLCO module can handle some of the things Kate is probably looking for, including price and volume information in sales, inventory, and production activities, but this module is not configured to specifically support all of the information I believe she will need." "Can it be modified?" Interjected Robert. "Possibly so," said Jim, "and if not, I would think that other modules of WELLCO could handle it. Sam, help me out with this one if you can." Sam responded, "I know that WELLCO is one of the leading ERP products designed to support many front and back office functions. It might be possible to get enough functionality to support both Jim's and Kate's requirements. I am concerned that we are still looking at requirements from a program-level and systems-level viewpoint... essentially bottom-up planning. Wouldn't the company benefit more from a more strategic approach that evaluates requirements and proposed solutions across the entire enterprise in the context of our strategic goals?"

The group was silent for a moment, and then Gerald spoke. "Our annual planning retreat is where most of the company's strategic planning happens. We look at our current strategic goals and initiatives. We look at what changes are needed to keep us competitive. As you saw from the meeting last month, new proposals are also surfaced during the retreat and then followed-up on. That is to say if they merit consideration for funding and implementation." Sam asked, "Is there some model of the enterprise that is used to support these discussions?" "Well, if you mean our annual business plan, we have that" said Jim. "More than that" said Sam, "A model of strategy, business, and technology that enables you to see what we have now and what is planned for the future. Something that gives us the ability to play with the model to see what other future investment and operating scenarios would look like." "We don't have anything as fancy as that" said Kate, "Though a model like that would have helped me analyze what we could do to help the field."

Robert stood up and walked to the window. "Sam, you are new to the team, but sometimes a fresh look at a situation can provide valuable insights. What I believe you are telling us is that we lack a true top-down, strategy-driven capability to surface requirements and solutions... is that right?" "Yes" responded Sam. "DMC is not alone. Many companies have the same problem because they still support program-level decision-making. We tend to let it occur in a relative vacuum with few overarching goals and standards to guide analysis, planning, documentation, and decision-making. I am going to propose that both Kate's and Jim's proposals be reviewed through a different lens, that of an enterprise-wide architecture. If we had this type of model, we could see current capabilities, future requirements, and gaps in our ability to meet those requirements. We could also see duplicative current capabilities and future solutions. From what I have heard at this meeting we may have some overlapping requirements which probably should not be met with separate solutions if we are to optimize our financial and technology resources."

"Interesting" said Robert. "Sounds like a silver bullet, and I am wary of those" said Gerald. Robert spoke again, "Sam, would an enterprise-wide architecture really help us? If it is doable, that's great, but why haven't we heard about it before? I know there are no free lunches and where is the ROI in such an architecture?" Kate added "While I appreciate the idea, I don't have time to wait for the entire company to be modeled, I need a new capability now."

"Well," said Sam. "You are right, establishing an enterprise architecture will not be free and it will take time. Fortunately there are approaches being used by the public and private sector that support the modeling of requirements and solutions in a standardized way between multiple lines of business, which are referred to as architecture segments. So, as each segment is completed it adds to the architecture as a whole. By treating Jim's area as the company's financial segment, and Kate's area as the production segment, we can just address these areas first, thereby reducing the time for completion of the architecture part of the larger project that may implement a combined solution. We can do this by modeling only those strategic drivers, business services, and technology solutions that apply to those two segments. Eventually though, for the architecture to be the most valuable to DMC, the entire company should be modeled in its current state, and several possible future states."

"As far as ROI," continued Sam, "that is more difficult to pinpoint since the cost of doing the analysis and modeling depends on the amount of existing information and the degree of cooperation that is achieved with stakeholders. By the way, these stakeholders include our executives, managers, and support staff. But let's say that a top-down architectural analysis reveals that there are common requirements between Kate and Jim, and we can meet those requirements either through adding functionality to SITS or by buying several more modules of the commercial WELLCO product, and doing some customization. We potentially could save several hundred thousand dollars, or perhaps millions of dollars compared to doing SITS and WELLCO separately… all of which become ROI from the architecture effort. You probably haven't heard about enterprise architecture because when a company is doing it well, it can become a strategic asset that makes the company more efficient and agile. That type of capability is normally not broadcasted."

"So what's the downside?" asked Gerald. "Enterprise architecture tends to be viewed as a hostile takeover by program managers and executives who have previously had a lot of independence in developing solutions for their own requirements" said Sam. "Also, architecture brings a new language and planning processes, which like any type of change can be seen as threatening to those involved and therefore may be resisted. Strong executive sponsorship and stakeholder involvement can overcome much of this."

"Sam, the architecture approach seems to make sense, but I am not completely sold yet" said Richard. "Let's do a pilot project. I want you to work with Kate and Jim and bring me a plan and business case within two weeks to develop the part of an architecture for DMC that addresses their current capabilities and stated future requirements. We'll use this as the test for whether we want to go forward with an enterprise-wide architecture. Thank you all for your time today, see you in two weeks."

Chapter 1

An Overview of Enterprise Architecture

Chapter Overview

Chapter 1 provides an overview of the emerging practice of *Enterprise Architecture* (EA). The main concept of this chapter is that EA is a strategy and business-driven activity that supports management planning and decision-making by providing coordinated views of an entire *enterprise*. These views encompass strategy, business, and technology, which is different from technology-driven, systems-level, or process-centric approaches. Implementing an EA involves both a management program and a framework-based documentation methodology.

> **Key Term:** *Enterprise*
> An area of common activity and goals within an organization or between several organizations, where information and other resources are exchanged.

> **Key Term:** *Enterprise Architecture*
> The analysis and documentation of an enterprise in its current and future states from an integrated strategy, business, and technology perspective.

Learning Objectives

> ➢ Understand the purpose of EA.
> ➢ Understand the elements of an EA management program.
> ➢ Understand the elements of an EA documentation method.
> ➢ Understand how EA is different from other analysis and planning approaches.

Introduction

Enterprise Architecture is an emerging profession and management practice that is devoted to improving the performance of enterprises by enabling them to see themselves in terms of a holistic and integrated view of their strategic direction, business practices, information flows, and technology resources. By developing current and future versions of this integrated view, an enterprise can better manage the transition from current to future operating methods. This transition includes the identification of new goals, activities, and all types of capital and human resources (including information technology) that will improve bottom line financial and mission performance.

> *Home Architecture Analogy:* Building a room at a time without the blueprints for the whole house is analogous to developing business resources and systems without an enterprise architecture. The result is a duplication of function, inefficient information exchanges, and a lack of integration.

The strategic use of resources is increasingly important to the success of public and private sector enterprises, including extended enterprises involving multiple internal and external participants (e.g., supply chains). How to get the most from business, technology, and human resources requires an enterprise to think in terms of enterprise-wide solutions, rather than individual system development projects. Doing this requires a new approach to planning and systems development, an approach that has come to be known as Enterprise Architecture (EA). The word 'enterprise' implies a high-level, strategic view of the entire organization, while the word 'architecture' implies a structured framework for the analysis, planning, and development of all types of resources. [3]

With regard to resources, one of the greatest challenges that many enterprises continue to face is how to identify the business and technology components of strategic initiatives. A big part of this challenge is that technology, information technology (IT) in particular, has historically not been viewed as a strategic asset. As such, planning activities often have focused on the development of individual technology solutions to meet particular organizational requirements. The following equation is the 'sound bite' version of what EA is all about, and is intended to help readers remember the distinct difference between EA and other types of IT planning... that EA is driven by strategic goals and business requirements.

$$EA = S + B + T$$

Enterprise Architecture = Strategy + Business + Technology

---

[3] The term "enterprise architecture" most likely came from Steven Spewak, Ph.D. in his book <u>Enterprise Architecture Planning</u>. John Wiley & Sons, 1992.

What is Enterprise Architecture?

As an idea, EA is how to create abstract views of an organization (an enterprise) that help the people in the enterprise to make better plans and decisions. EA extends beyond technology planning, by adding strategic planning as the primary driver of the enterprise, and business planning as the source of most program and resource requirements. The place for technology planning is to provide systems, applications, networks, call centers, networks, and other capital resources (e.g. buildings, capital equipment) to meet the business requirements... which are the heart of the enterprises activities... creating and delivering those products and services that accomplish the strategic goals and initiatives of the enterprise. This is why I say that in its simplest form, the idea of Enterprise Architecture is that of integrating strategy, business, and technology (EA=S+B+T).

As a practice, EA is both a **management program** and a **documentation method** that together provides an actionable, coordinated view of an enterprise's strategic direction, business services, information flows, and resource utilization. For the purposes of this book, there will be a focus on IT resource utilization, though the concepts apply to other types of resources throughout the enterprise.

As a **management program**, EA provides:

➢ **Resource Alignment**: Resource planning and standards determination
➢ **Standardized Policy:** Resource governance and implementation
➢ **Decision Support:** Financial control and configuration management
➢ **Resource Oversight:** Lifecycle approach to development/management

EA provides a strategy and business-driven approach to policy, planning, decision-making, and resource development that is useful to executives, line managers, and support staff. To be effective, an EA program must be part of an integrated group of management policies and processes that form an overall governance structure. This governance structure includes strategic planning, enterprise architecture, program management, capital planning, security, and workforce planning, as is shown in Figure 1-1.

Figure 1-1. Governance

As a **documentation method**, EA provides:

- ➢ **EA Approach:** A modeling framework and implementation methodology
- ➢ **Current Views:** Views of as-is strategies, processes, and resources
- ➢ **Future Views:** Views of to-be strategies, processes, and resources
- ➢ **EA Management Plan:** A plan to move from the current to the future EA

The approach to EA documentation is based on the adoption of a documentation framework and related implementation methodology. Documenting current and future views of an EA helps the enterprise to identify and manage its current resources, select and implement future resources, and manage the EA transition in an effective, standardized manner. The transition from current to future architectures is an ongoing aspect of an EA program. Figure 1-2 shows an overview of the basic EA approach to visualizing the enterprise and managing EA information.

Figure 1-2: The Basic Enterprise Architecture Approach

EA as a Management Program

EA is a management program that provides a strategic, integrated approach to resource planning.   An EA program is part of an overall governance process that determines resource alignment, develops standardized policy, enhances decision support, and oversees resource development activities. EA can help to identify *gaps in the performance* of line of business activities and the capabilities of supporting IT services, systems, and networks.

Resource Alignment

EA supports strategic planning and other operational resource planning processes by providing macro and micro views of how resources are to be leveraged in accomplishing the goals of the enterprise.   This helps to maximize the efficiency and effectiveness of these resources, which in turn will help to promote the enterprise's competitive capabilities. IT resources and associated development projects within the enterprise should be reviewed to determine if they support (and conform to) one or more of the enterprise's strategic goals. If a resource and/or project is not aligned, then its value to the enterprise will remain in question. Figure 1-3 shows how IT projects (and associated resources) align with the goals of sub-enterprises, and eventually with enterprise-wide goals and initiatives.

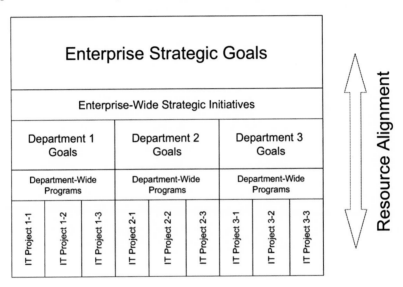

Figure 1-3: Resource Alignment

Standardized Policy

EA supports the implementation of standardized management policy pertinent to the development and utilization of IT and other resources. By providing a holistic, hierarchical view of current and future resources, EA supports the establishment of policy for:

- Identifying strategic and operational requirements
- Determining the strategic alignment of activities and resources
- Developing enterprise-wide business and technology resources
- Prioritizing the funding of programs and projects
- Overseeing the management of programs and projects
- Identifying performance metrics for programs and projects
- Identifying and enforcing standards and configuration management

Policy documents include those which can be categorized as general guidance (e.g., high-level directives and memos); specific program guidance (e.g., plans, and manuals); and detailed process guidance (e.g., standard operating procedures). By using these hierarchical categories of documents, succinct and meaningful policy is established. It does so in a way that no single policy document is too long and therefore not too burdensome to read. It is also important to understand how the various areas of policy are inter-related so that program implementation across the enterprise is coordinated. EA policies must integrate with other policies in all governance areas, so as to create an effective overall resource management and oversight capability.

Decision Support

EA provides support for IT resource decision-making at the executive, management, and staff levels of the enterprise. At the executive level, EA provides visibility for large IT initiatives and supports the determination of strategic alignment. At the management level, EA supports design and configuration management decisions, as well as the alignment of IT initiatives with technical standards for voice, data, video, and security. At the staff level, EA supports decisions regarding operations, maintenance, and the development of IT resources and services.

Resource Development

EA supports standardized approaches for developing IT and other resources. Depending on the scope of the resources involved and the available timeframe for development, various system development lifecycle methods can be used to reduce the risk that cost, schedule, or performance parameters may not be met. EA further standardized, proven approaches to project management that promote the comprehensive and effective oversight of ongoing programs and new development projects. Finally, EA supports the use of a standardized process for selecting and evaluating investment in IT resources from a business and financial perspective.

EA as a Documentation Method

References to EA began to emerge in the late 1980's in various management and academic literatures, with an early focus on technical or systems architectures and schemas for organizing information.[4] The concept of 'enterprise' architecture documentation emerged in the early 1990's and has now evolved to include views of strategic goals, business services, information flows, systems and applications, networks, and the supporting infrastructure. Additionally, documentation includes 'threads' that pervade every level of the architecture. These threads include standards, security, and workforce planning.

EA documentation is accomplished through the following six basic elements: (1) an EA documentation framework, and (2) an implementation methodology that support the creation of (3) current and (4) future views of the architecture, as well as the development of (5) an EA Management Plan to manage the enterprise's transition from current to future architectures. There are also several areas common to all levels of the framework that are referred to as (6) "threads" as shown in Figure 1-4.

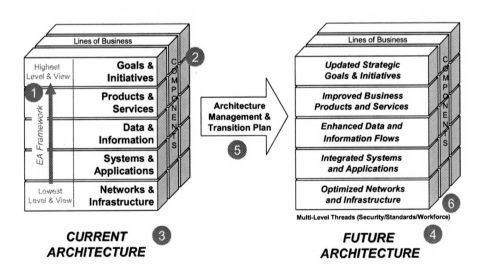

Figure 1-4: Elements of EA Documentation

---

[4] Zachman, John. "A Framework for Information Systems Architecture." *IBM Systems Journal.* Volume 26, Number 3, 1989.

EA Documentation Element #1: The Framework.

The EA documentation framework identifies the scope of the architecture to be documented and establishes relationships between the architecture's areas. The framework's scope is reflected through its geometric design and the areas that are identified for documentation. The framework creates an abstracted set of "views" of an enterprise through the way that it collects and organizes architecture information. An example that will be used throughout the book is the framework that is illustrated in Figure 1-5, which has a cubic shape with three dimensions that relate to different aspects of documenting the abstracted enterprise.

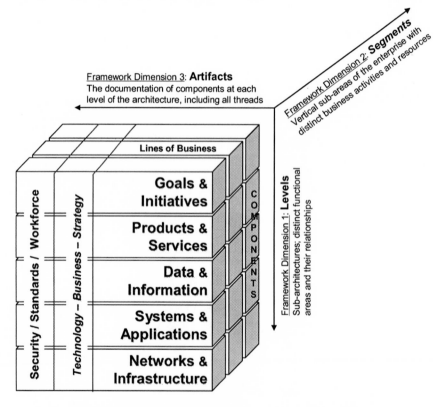

Figure 1-5: The EA³ Cube Documentation Framework

Known as the EA³ Cube™, the levels of this example framework are hierarchical so that the different sub-architectures (that describe distinct functional areas) can be logically related to each other. This is done by positioning high-level strategic goals/initiatives at the top, business products/services and data/information flows in the middle, and supporting systems/applications and technology/infrastructure at the bottom. In this way alignment can be also be shown between strategy, information, and technology, which aids planning and decision-making. Chapters 4 through 6 provide more details on EA frameworks, components, and methods.

To lower risk and promote efficient, phased implementation methods, the EA framework is divided into segments of distinct activity, referred to as *Lines of Business* (LOBs). For example, each LOB has a complete sub-architecture that includes all five hierarchical levels of the EA^3 framework. The LOB therefore can in some ways stand alone architecturally within the enterprise except that duplication in data, application, and network functions would occur if each LOB were truly independent. An architecture encompassing all five framework levels that is focused on one or more LOBs can be referred to as a *segment* of the overall EA.

Key Term: *Line of Business*
A Line of Business (LOB) is a distinct area of activity within the enterprise. It may involve the manufacture of certain products, the provision of services, or internal administrative functions.

Key Term: *Architecture Segment*
A part of the overall EA that documents one or more lines of business at all levels and threads. A segment can exist as a stand-alone part of the EA.

EA Documentation Element #2: EA Components

EA components are *changeable* goals, processes, standards, and resources that may extend enterprise-wide or be contained within a specific line of business. Examples of components include strategic goals and initiatives; business products and services; information flows, knowledge warehouses, and data objects; information systems, software applications, enterprise resource programs, and web sites; voice, data, and video networks; and supporting infrastructure including buildings, server rooms, wiring runs/closets, and capital equipment. Figure 1-6 on the next page provides examples of *vertical* and *crosscutting* EA components at each level of the EA^3 Cube framework, and Chapter 6 provides additional details.

Key Term: *Vertical Component*

A vertical component is a changeable goal, process, program, or resource (equipment, systems, data, etc.) that serves one line of business.

Key Term: *Horizontal (Crosscutting) Component*

A horizontal (or crosscutting) component is a changeable goal, process, program, or resource that serves several lines of business. Examples include email and administrative support systems that serve the whole enterprise.

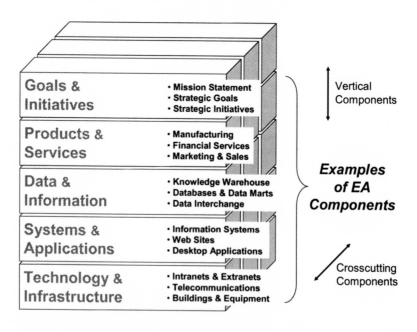

Figure 1-6: Examples of EA Components

EA Documentation Element #3: Current Architecture

The current architecture contains those EA components that currently exist within the enterprise at each level of the framework. This is sometimes referred to as the "as-is" view. The current view of the EA serves to create a 'baseline' inventory of current resources and activities that is documented in a consistent way with the future view of the EA so that analysts can see gaps in performance between future plans and the current capabilities. Having an accurate and comprehensive current view of EA components is an important reference for project planning, asset management, and investment decision-making. The current view of the EA is composed of 'artifacts' (documents, diagrams, data, spreadsheets, charts, etc.) at each level of the framework, which are archived in an on-line EA repository to make them useable by various EA stakeholders.

EA Documentation Element #4: Future Architecture

The future architecture documents those new or modified EA components that are needed by the enterprise to close an existing performance gap or support a new strategic initiative, operational requirement, or technology solution.

As is shown in Figure 1-7, the future architecture is driven at both the strategic and tactical levels in three ways: new directions and goals; changing business priorities; and emerging technologies. The EA cannot reflect these changes in the future architecture unless the enterprise's leadership team provides the changes in strategic direction and goals; unless the line of business managers and program managers provide the changes in business processes and priorities that are needed to accomplish the new goals; and unless the support/delivery staff identifies viable technology and staffing solutions to meet the new business requirements.

Figure 1-7. Drivers of Change

The future architecture should cover planned changes to EA components in the near term (tactical changes in the next 1-3 years), as well as changes to EA components that are a result of the implementation of long-term operating scenarios that look 4-10 years into the future. These scenarios incorporate different internal and external drivers and can help to identify needed changes in processes, resources, or technology that translate to future planning assumptions, which in turn drive the planning for new EA components. An example future scenario and additional details on the future architecture are provided in Chapter 8.

EA Documentation Element #5: EA Management Plan

The EA Management Plan articulates the EA program and documentation approach. The EA Management Plan also provides descriptions of current and future views of the architecture, and a sequencing plan for managing the transition to the future business/technology operating environment. The EA Management Plan is a living document that is essential to realizing the benefits of the EA as a management program. How the enterprise is going to continually move from the current architecture to the future architecture is a significant planning and management challenge, especially if IT resources supporting key business functions are being replaced or upgraded. Chapter 9 provides additional details on the development of an EA Management Plan.

EA Documentation Element #6: Planning Threads

EA documentation includes 'threads' of common activity that are present in all levels of the framework. These threads include IT-related security, standards, and workforce considerations.

IT Security. Security is most effective when it is an integral part of the EA management program and documentation methodology. A comprehensive IT Security Program has several focal areas including: information, personnel, operations, and facilities. To be effective, IT security must work across all levels of the EA framework and within all of the EA components. Chapter 11 provides more information on IT security.

IT Standards. One of the most important functions of the EA is that it provides technology-related standards at all levels of the EA framework. The EA should draw on accepted international, National, and industry standards in order to promote the use of non-proprietary solutions in EA components. This in turn enhances the integration of EA components, as well as better supporting the switch-out of components when needed.

IT Workforce. Perhaps the greatest resource that an enterprise has is people. It is therefore important to ensure that IT-related staffing, skill, and training requirements are identified for LOB and support service activities at each level of the EA framework, and appropriate solutions are reflected in the current and future architectures.

Fitting the Architecture Documentation Elements Together

While the basic elements of EA documentation provide holistic and detailed descriptions of the current and future architecture in all areas of the underlying framework, it is important to also be able to articulate these relationships in discussions and presentations with executives, managers, support staff, and other EA stakeholders. Being able to understand and relate how the architecture fits together is essential to being able to use the EA in planning and decision-making throughout the enterprise. This communication is supported through two EA program resources: the EA Management Plan and the EA Repository. As was mentioned in the previous section, the EA Management Plan is a living document that is periodically updated so that it remains relevant as the ongoing primary reference for describing where the current and future architectures are at. The EA Repository is the on-line archive for EA information and the documentation artifacts that are described in the EA Management Plan. The EA Repository is described in the next section of this chapter.

The following is an example of how to communicate about EA with stakeholders. In this example, some questions are presented about how to apply an EA framework to an enterprise, which subsequent chapters of the book answer. These are the types of questions that should be answered in the first few sessions of EA program and documentation meetings in order to promote an understanding of how the EA framework and documentation can reflect the enterprise. In the following example of how to talk about EA, the five levels and three vertical threads of the EA^3 Cube framework are used for illustration. Notice how the questions build in a way that reflects the hierarchical relationships between the levels of the EA^3 framework.

Each area of the EA^3 framework represents a functional area of the enterprise. The EA^3 framework can be used in a top-down, bottom-up, or single-component manner. To begin to use the framework in a top down-manner, a series of questions at each level should be asked in order to determine how information about the enterprise will fit within that level of the framework.

The first questions to ask relate to the strategic 'Goals and Initiatives' level of the framework. The questions are: (1) for what purpose does the enterprise generally exist (usually expressed in the mission statement) and (2) what kind of organization does the enterprise generally intend to be (often given in the vision statement)? What are the primary goals (strategic goals) of the enterprise? What then are the strategic initiatives (ongoing programs or new projects) that will enable the enterprise to achieve those goals? Finally, for this level, when will the enterprise know that it has successfully reached these strategic goals or is making progress toward these goals (outcome measures)?

Second is the business 'Products and Services' level of the framework, and it is important to first ask what are the ongoing activity areas (lines of business) that the enterprise must engage in to support and enable the accomplishment of both strategic initiatives and normal 'maintenance/housekeeping' functions? What then are the specific activities in each line of business (business services)? What are the products that are delivered in each line of business? How do we measure the effectiveness and efficiency of the line of business processes (input/output measures) as well as their contribution to strategic goals (outcome measures)? Do any of these business services or manufacturing processes need to be reengineered/improved before they are made to be part of the future architecture? What are the workforce, standards, and security issues at this framework level?

Third is the 'Data and Information' level of the framework. When the lines of business and specific business service/products have been identified, it is important to ask what are the flows of information that will be required within and between activity areas in order to make them successful? How can these flows of information be harmonized, standardized, and protected to promote sharing that is efficient, accurate, and secure? How will the data underlying the information flows be formatted, generated, shared, and stored? How will the data become useable information and knowledge?

Fourth is the 'Systems and Applications' level of the framework and it is important to ask which IT and other business systems and applications will be needed to generate, share, and store the data, information, and knowledge that the business services need? How can multiple types of IT systems, services, applications, databases, and web sites be made to work together where needed? How can configuration management help to create a cost-effective and operationally efficient 'Common Operating Environment' for systems and applications? What are the workforce, standards, and security issues at this level?

Fifth is the 'Network and Infrastructure' level of the framework and it is important to ask what types of voice, data, and video networks will be required to host the IT systems/applications and to transport associate, data, images, and conversations, as well as what type of infrastructure is needed to support the networks (e.g. buildings, server rooms, other equipment). How can these networks be integrated to create a cost-effective and operationally efficient hosting and transport environment? Will these networks extend beyond the enterprise? What are the workforce, standards, and security issues at this level? What are the physical space and utility support requirements for the networks?

The EA Repository

Providing easy access to EA documentation is essential for use in planning and decision-making. This can be accomplished through the establishment of an on-line EA repository to archive the documentation of EA components in the various areas of the EA framework. The EA repository is essentially a website and database that stores information and provides links to EA tools and other EA program resources. Figure 1-7 provides an example of how an EA repository might be designed. This example is called *Living Enterprise*™ and it is designed to support documentation that is organized through the use of the EA³ Cube framework. Chapter 12 provides additional details on the design and function of an EA repository.

Tabs: EA Management Plan | Future EA Views | EA Standards | EA Program | EA Tutorial | Site Map

Enterprise Architecture Repository

Current EA Views	Goals & Initiatives	Products & Services	Data & Information	Systems & Applications	Networks & Infrastructure	Security Solutions
High Level View	Strategic Plan	Business Plan	Knowledge Warehouse	Business Systems	Wide Area Network	Security Program
Mid Level View	Goals & Initiatives	Business Processes	Information Flows	Support Systems	Local Area Network	System Certifications
Detailed View	Performance Measures	Investment Portfolio	Data Dictionary	Application Inventory	Buildings & Equipment	Data Privacy

Figure 1-7: Example EA Repository Design – *Living Enterprise* ™

Summary of Concepts

Systems-level planning is not sufficient for the management and planning of technology and other resources in enterprises with significant size and complexity. EA is an improved approach that looks at systems holistically as well as provides a strategy and business context. EA was described as being as both a management process and a documentation method that helps enterprises with business and technology planning, resource management, and decision-making. The purpose of an EA management program was presented: strategic alignment, standardized policy, decision support, and resource development. The six basic elements of an EA documentation method were presented: the EA documentation framework, EA components, current EA views, future EA views, an EA Management and Transition Plan and multi-level threads that include security, standards, and workforce planning. An example of how to communicate the various areas of an EA framework was also provided. The following chapters of this section will describe why EA is valuable to many types of enterprises, what the risks of doing EA are, and how to ensure that EA is driven by strategic goals and business requirements.

Chapter 1 Questions and Exercises

1. What are some of the differences between enterprise architecture (EA) and a systems-level planning approach?
2. Why is EA described as both a management program and a documentation method?
3. What are the four elements of an EA management program and the six elements of an EA documentation method?
4. What are some of the EA components and documentation artifacts that would be included in current and future views at each level of the EA³ Cube framework?
5. Can EA be used by all types of enterprises? If so, why?
6. How does an EA repository support the implementation methodology?
7. Choose a real-world large-sized enterprise and determine:
   a. Is information technology seen as a strategic asset?
   b. Does an enterprise architecture program exist?
   c. Are there gaps in business/technology performance that an enterprise architecture program could help identify and correct?

Chapter 2

The Structure and Culture of Enterprises

Chapter Overview

Chapter 2 discusses the need for enterprise architects to understand the role of organizational structure and *culture* in developing an EA. Structure and culture are important to include in the EA in order to accurately reflect the true nature of organizational goals, processes, and informal structures which influence the current and future views of the architecture. Understanding structure and culture are also important in working with *stakeholders* to gain their support and manage expectations for the development and implementation of the EA program. Enterprises are types of social organizations and as such, the concepts of organizational theory presented in this chapter are applicable to the practice of EA.

Key Term: *Culture*
The beliefs, customs, values, structure, normative rules, and material traits of a social organization. Culture is evident in many aspects of how an organization functions.

Key Term: *Stakeholder*
Everyone who is or will be affected by a program, project, activity, or resource. Stakeholders for the EA program include sponsors, architects, program managers, users, and support staff.

Learning Objectives

> Understand the structural and cultural aspects of an enterprise

> Understand the differences between an organization and an enterprise

> Become familiar with models of organizations and enterprises

> Be able to tie structural and cultural aspects of the enterprise to the architecture

Introduction

Enterprise architecture is as much about people and social interaction as it is about processes and resource utilization. Understanding each of these aspects of an enterprise is essential to the development of accurate views of the current architecture and relevant, meaningful views of the future architecture.

> *Home Architecture Analogy:* An architect needs to understand the composition, preferences, and activities of the owner's family to be able to produce an effective design for their new or remodeled home. How they will use the rooms, their activity patterns, and storage needs are examples of the factors to be considered.

Insight into the "people aspect" of enterprises is also important to the development of policy, standards, and an EA Management Plan that will be accepted by the enterprise. Moving from current to future states of the EA involves changes in processes and how people will communicate. Change involves moving from what is familiar to something unfamiliar, which is uncomfortable and/or threatening to many people. Therefore, there may be resistance to programs such as EA that cause or support changes in resources and processes throughout the enterprise.

Discussion

Influences on the Field of Enterprise Architecture

EA is fundamentally an evaluation and depiction of people, processes, and resources. Some of the areas of practice and theory that have influenced the emerging discipline of EA include business administration, public administration, operations research, sociology, organizational theory, management theory, information science, and computer science. Understanding the mission, goals, and culture of an enterprise is as important to implementing an EA as the selection of analytic methods and documentation techniques. The EA approach described in this book is based on theories of how social enterprises (including enterprises) are structured and how systems and activities function within enterprises. Figure 2-1 shows the academic fields and areas of theory/practice that influence EA.

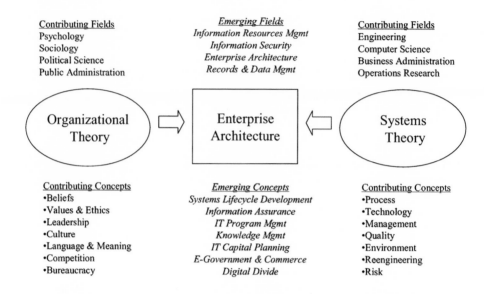

Figure 2-1: Influences on the Field of Enterprise Architecture

The Structure of Enterprises

In this part of Chapter 2 there will be some references to organizations instead of enterprises because the concepts come from established organizational theory. The concepts of organizational theory also apply to enterprises because they are types of social organizations. Organizations and enterprises are essentially complex social systems, which regardless of mission, share many similarities in their basic structure and functions.

The Parsons/Thompson Model

One of the more mature models of general organizational structure is a three-level view that was originally envisioned by sociologist Talcott Parsons in the 1950's and further developed by sociologist James Thompson in the 1960's.[5] Parsons' research identified three general levels that are common to most social organizations (technical, managerial, and institutional), based on the observation that different types of activities

---

[5] Bernard, Scott A. Evaluating Clinger-Cohen Compliance in Federal Agency Chief Information Officer Positions. Doctoral Dissertation, Virginia Polytechnic Institute and State University, April 2001.

occur at each level.[6]   Thompson built on Parsons' ideas by further identifying the different types of activities that occur at each level.[7] Figure 2-2 summarizes the Parsons/Thompson Model of social organizations.

Organizational Level	Structure *Parson's Purpose of Each Level*	Function *Thompson's Level Activities*
Institutional	Where the organization establishes rules and relates to the larger society as it derives legitimization, meaning, and higher-level support, thus making possible the implementation of organizational goals.	The organization is very open to the environment in order to determine its domain, establish boundaries, and secure legitimacy.
Managerial	Where mediation between the organization and the immediate task environment occurs, where the organization's internal affairs are administered, and where the organization's products are consumed and resources supplied.	A dynamic of mediation occurs where less formalized and more political activities occur.
Technical	Where the actual "product" of an organization is processed.	The organization is "rational" as it carries on production (input/output) functions and tries to seal off those functions from the outside to protect them from external uncertainties as much as possible.

Figure 2-2: Parson/Thompson Model of Enterprises

The geometry of the Parson/Thompson Model has been adapted by the author to resemble a series of concentric circles. This may provide a more useful image for depicting a social organization that interacts with its environment via the model's Institutional Level, facilitates internal resources via the Managerial Level, and protects a "core" of essential

---

[6] Thompson, James D. Enterprises in Action. New York: McGraw-Hill. 1967.
[7] Ibid.

processes and resources at the Technical Level. Figure 2-3 shows this spherical version of the Parsons/Thompson Model, which also is more useful in relating it to how an EA framework can document organizational functions.

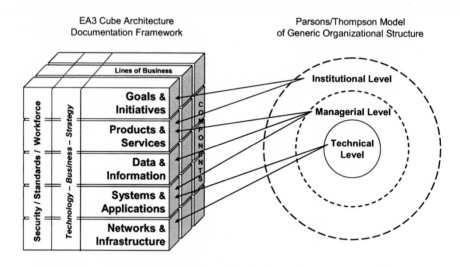

Figure 2-3: Relating Models of Organizational Function and Structure

The value of the Parsons/Thompson Model is its use as an authoritative reference for developing EA views of structure and process for an organization. Regardless of the model's wide acceptance in academia, the question of whether this fifty year old view would be relevant and useful to understanding the structure of current public and private sector organizations is answered by observing that many large and medium sized corporations and government agencies continue to be hierarchical, rule-based, and goal-oriented. These were some of the primary characteristics of the "rational" organization that Parsons and Thompson originally studied. Evidence of this still being a valid model is also seen in the rational nature of organizational charts, mission statements, strategic plans, operational plans, and business services of these types of organizations.

However, there are new types of organizations that have emerged due to technology-based changes in how people communicate and work. Global telecommunications and the Internet have made location a largely irrelevant factor in terms of where some types of work are being done (e.g., knowledge work and on-line services). Two primary changes related to organizational structure and function have resulted. First, more organizations are becoming regional or global in nature, and are relying on remote sub-groups to do significant amounts of the work. Second, more people are becoming self-employed knowledge workers who contract their services remotely to various enterprises depending on their interest, skills, and availability. Examples include people who process digitized health care forms, software developers, web site developers, distance learning instructors, financial traders, insurance salespeople, and telemarketers. Because these organizations can get certain functions accomplished remotely, their structure may become less hierarchical and more collaborative.

While it can be argued that these new networked organizations exhibit many of the structural and functional characteristics found in the Parsons/Thompson Model, there are enough differences to merit discussion of a variation of that model which may better describe how organizations operate in a more global on-line business environment.

The Organizational Network Model

New types of organizations and enterprises are appearing which are based on cooperative networks of local and remote individual workers and semi-autonomous teams who carry out key functions. In these enterprises, greater cost efficiency and more mission flexibility are achieved by removing layers of management that are not needed in a decentralized operating mode. These teams are actually sub-groups that have their own management level and technical level with core processes, and therefore will still exhibit some of the characteristics of the Parsons/Thompson Model. The difference presented here is that the organization/enterprise's structure is based on these teams and remote workers, whose goals and functions may change depending on internal and external influences.

Called the Organizational Network Model (ONM), an *Executive Team* sets policy and goals, approves resources, and evaluates results, while semi-autonomous *Functional Teams* and *Independent Workers* manage ongoing programs/lines of business, new development projects, and team-specific resources. The Functional Teams and Independent Workers receive policy, goals, and general direction from the Executive Team, yet carry out organizational functions in an independent and/or cooperative manner, depending on the goal(s). Figure 2-4 provides an illustration of the ONM.

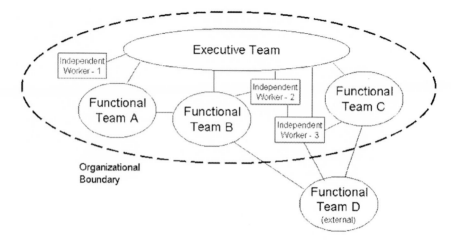

Figure 2-4: Organizational Network Model

Being less hierarchical, these "flatter" and more flexible ONM organizations can respond to changing requirements more quickly by creating, modifying, or eliminating Functional Teams and/or adjusting the number and type of Independent Workers. These types of ONM organizations and enterprises can also exist as extended supply chains or networks of teams from inside and outside the traditional organizational boundary. This includes trusted business partners and independent consultants who are allowed to share sensitive information and key resources with the enterprise as part of the activities of the Functional Teams and Independent Workers. Figure 2-5 shows how Functional Teams in ONM organizations can be related to an enterprise's Lines of Business (LOBs) in the EA[3] Cube documentation framework.

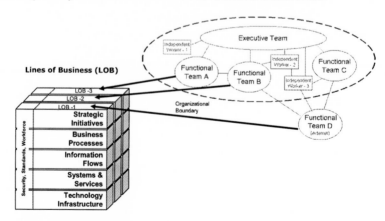

Figure 2-5: Relating Functional Teams to EA Lines of Business

Organizations and Enterprises

Organizations and enterprises are similar in that they are both types of social entities that have a culture, a formal and informal structure, goals, activities, and resources. The difference is that an enterprise can be defined as a subset of an organization or can involve multiple organizations.

Why isn't this book called *An Introduction to Organizational Architecture*? Because that would largely limit the subject to architectures that encompass an entire organization, and while those architectures are important, a more versatile concept is an enterprise, which can cover part of the organization, all of the organization, or multiple organizations.

Enterprises are normally made up of *vertical, horizontal,* and *extended* components. Vertical components (also known as *lines of business* or *segments*) are activity areas that are particular to one line of business (e.g., research and development). Horizontal components (also known as *crosscutting enterprises*) are more general areas of activity that serve multiple lines of business. Extended components comprise more than one organization (e.g., extranets and supply chains).

EA views of vertical components are complete stand-alone architectures in that they contain documentation from all levels of the EA framework. These types of vertical components are also known as "segments." When vertical segments are documented using the same EA framework, they can be aggregated into a larger architecture picture that may cover several or all lines of business. This may be a preferable way to develop the first version of an enterprise's EA as it allows them to undertake a more manageable amount of work at less initial cost (compared to attempting to do the EA for the entire enterprise all at once, without prior experience). This is called a "segmented approach" to documenting the overall EA. The segmented approach is also useful in large and/or decentralized enterprises where parts of the architecture may need to be developed and maintained by a number of different groups.

Understanding Culture

Understanding the culture of an enterprise is essential to developing realistic views of how strategic goals are established, how processes function, and how resources are used. Every enterprise is different in some way, as are the vertical, horizontal, and/or extended sub-enterprises. This is due to the culture of the enterprise being an amalgamation of the values, beliefs, habits, and preferences of all of the people throughout the enterprise or sub-enterprise.

Managing Change

Changes within the enterprise will happen regardless of the presence of an EA program, however they will happen in a more disjointed or completely independent manner without EA. The effect of the EA program is to coordinate change such that it is much more driven by new strategies and business requirements, and less by new technologies.

According to John Kotter, "To date, major change efforts have helped some organizations adapt significantly to shifting conditions, have improved the competitive standing of others, and have positioned a few for a far better future. But in too many situations the improvements have been disappointing and then carnage has been appalling, with wasted resources and burned-out, scared, or frustrated employees." [8]

People can be resistant to changes in their environment, whether it is at home or the workplace. If the EA program promotes changes in the enterprise, and if people are often resistant to any type of change when they do not have some level of control, then the EA program may be resisted by stakeholders unless something is done to increase their level of control. Increasing their level of control helps to successfully manage change, and can be accomplished in several ways, including:

- Involving stakeholders in the EA program's establishment and management.
- Regularly and effectively communicating EA activities to stakeholders.
- Allowing for stakeholder input to EA planning and decision-making.
- Managing stakeholder expectations as to what the EA program can do.

---

[8] Kotter, John P. Leading Change. Harvard Business School Press. Boston, Massachusetts. 1996.

> **Key Term: *Change Management***
> The process of setting expectations and involving stakeholders in how a process or activity will be changed, so that the stakeholders have some control over the change and therefore may be more accepting of the change.

Those who are affected by the EA program are called "EA stakeholders" and they are the ones most likely to resist the program and/or changes that are perceived to be the product of the EA program. Therefore, one of the things that the EA program manager needs to ensure is that there is stakeholder involvement in as many aspects of the EA program as is possible. This includes governance and oversight activities, the selection of an EA framework and methodology, participation in and reviews of documentation activities, and participation in the development of and updates to the EA Management Plan.

Another aspect of managing change within the EA program is regular and effective communication on program activities with all stakeholders. This includes formal documents such as an EA Program Communication Plan, the EA Management Plan, and notices regarding the periodic update of the current and future EA views. It also includes informal communication on an ongoing basis with all stakeholders to ensure that their participation and support is maintained.

The details of EA program governance are discussed in Chapter 4, but it is sufficient to say that it is important to provide "a place at the table" for as many stakeholders as can be accommodated. This increases buy-in for EA policy and decision-making, as well as the success of implementing changes called for in the future architecture.

Expectation management is yet another way to promote the success of the EA program and help stakeholders deal with change. Expectation management is about identifying realistic outputs and outcomes. It can be accomplished by collaboratively assessing the capability of the EA program to document current and future architectures, the timeframe and resources that will take, and the obstacles to acceptance by stakeholders. Expectation management is an ongoing aspect of the EA program.

Summary of Concepts

This chapter described how enterprises are types of social organizations and discussed the importance of understanding the structure and culture of the enterprise that an EA is documenting. While it is also important to understand the enterprise's processes and supporting technologies, it is the people of the enterprise who make plans and decisions about strategic direction, business activities, and resource utilization. The chapter also covered influences on the field of EA and presented two models of organizations and enterprises that can assist in the development of current and future EA views. Finally, the importance of managing change was discussed in that EA program activities may be resisted by stakeholders who feel a loss of input or control.

Chapter 2 Questions and Exercises

1. Why is it important to understand the "people side" of EA?

2. Compare and contrast an organization and an enterprise.

3. What are some of the academic fields that influence the field of EA?

4. Describe the purpose of each level of the Parsons/Thompson Model.

5. How is the Organization Network Model different from the Parsons/Thompson Model of organizations?

6. Who are stakeholders in the EA program and associated activities and might they want to resist the EA program and associated activities?

7. What are four ways to manage change with stakeholders?

8. Select a large or mid-size enterprise from business or government and describe the following:

    a. What structural and cultural aspects should be captured by EA?

    b. Who are the potential stakeholders in an EA program?

    c. What strategies for gaining stakeholder buy-in could be used?

    d. Relate strategies for managing change to various stakeholders.

Case Study:
Danforth Manufacturing Company
Scene 2: Considering an EA Program

Robert Danforth, the President and CEO of DMC, has called a follow-on meeting of the Executive Committee to review several recent capital investment requests and the suggestion to use an enterprise architecture approach to evaluate these requests and coordinate potential implementation projects. COO Kate Jarvis has requested a new custom Sales and Inventory Tracking System (SITS), and CFO Jim Gorman, has requested a new cost accounting system that is part of a commercial software package. Also invited to the meeting is CIO Sam Young, who joined the company one month ago, and who is giving a briefing on how enterprise architecture can help in this review.

"Good morning everyone" said Robert. "I'm eager to hear what you have to say about the architecture initiative. Sam, why don't you lead off, and then let's hear from Kate and Jim."

"Thank you Robert" said Sam as he handed out an 8-page document entitled *DMC Enterprise Architecture Plan – Financial and Production Segments*. "Kate, Jim, and I have spent a good deal of time together during the last two weeks and I believe that we have found several interesting things about their requirements and how an architecture approach can save us money and provide a more valuable long-term solution. We formed a working group to do the analysis and included an experienced enterprise architect and a senior systems analyst who I know from some past work, as well as several managers and staff from Kate and Jim's groups, including two sales representatives from the field. The architect, Vince Albright, provided some background on what enterprise architecture is all about and how to document and evaluate current and future views of resources and requirements. With that, the group documented the current business services and associated IT resources that might be replaced or modified by Kate's and Jim's proposals. Then, the group documented Kate's and Jim's requirements from a business process perspective and looked for areas of commonality or duplication. Finally, Vince and the systems analyst, Lily Jefferson, led the group in a scenario planning exercise that developed two plausible business and technology solutions that meet both of their requirements in an integrated manner.

Either of these integrated solutions look to be less expensive to implement than it will be to do Jim's and Kate's systems independently."

Jim then spoke to the group. "I was really impressed with what the group did in only two weeks. Sam is right about looking at these types of requirements from an architecture perspective. What I realized is that my back office support systems can have more types of direct feeds of information from Kate's line of business systems. In fact, the more we do this, the more timely and accurate the information across the company will be. The big thing here is that we eventually need to look at all of our business and technology requirements from a company-wide standpoint so that we can start to integrate and streamline our processes and capabilities."

Kate then spoke. "I agree with Jim that this was an eye-opener. There are flows of information between Jim's financial group and my business managers, but these flows and the supporting systems have been developed independently with no overarching plan in mind. Sam and his associates showed me an architecture approach and implementation process that can be completed for our respective areas within the next two months and then be used to guide the implementation of a solution that I believe will meet my requirements and those that Jim has as well. This is a win-win that can lead to more of the same. Even the sales reps were getting into the game, and provided a couple of ideas about automatically pushing sales and inventory data to them that I had not considered. I am recommending that we go with this approach to refine and select a solution so that I don't lose any more time on my competition."

Gerald leaned forward and looked at Sam. "Sam, I remember you saying that enterprise architecture links strategy, business, and technology. I am not hearing about strategy.... was that left out?" "Good question Gerald" responded Sam. "We did not go too much into company strategy because of the two-week timeframe for developing the initial architecture plan. However, that is an area that we will have to quickly address if the architecture plan for these two segments is approved for implementation. The way that I would pursue this is to identify DMC's strategic goals that relate to Kate and Jim's requirements, and ensure that the solutions align with the accomplishment of those goals. For example, I see that the company will be opening a new custom order line of business next year that builds on what we are doing on an ad-hoc basis right now. I would want to see if the solution for Kate and Jim's requirements could also be able to support similar requirements for the custom order business."

Robert then spoke. "I always want to talk about value and risk before approving any project. I am seeing value through cost savings and potential scalability of the solution. So, what is the cost of doing these segments and then the whole architecture? And, what are the risks and how do we mitigate those risks?"

"The cost of doing a complete and detailed architecture for a mid-size company like DMC may be considerable" said Sam. "And I therefore recommend this type of segmented approach to developing a company-wide architecture, where we take one line of business at a time. In the plan we developed, you will see that the cost for the first two segments is $105,000, which covers analysis, modeling, documentation, and an EA tool. There is also an $11,600 cost for documenting and applying the general architecture methodology, framework, and standards, that is largely reused in subsequent segment efforts. The analysis of these two segments should take two to three weeks, and depending on which of the two solutions is selected, the supporting documentation will take another month. So this plan delays Jim and Kate approximately two months, but saves the company well over the $121,600 cost if a combined solution is adopted."

Sam continued. "By having a standardized architecture approach, we ensure alignment in each completed segment and can also use it to guide each new development and upgrade projects throughout the company, so that architecture alignment occurs much more quickly. This approach is also a risk mitigation strategy, in that we are spreading out the cost and effort over time, involving stakeholders in the development of each segment, and incorporating lessons learned from each segment effort. Two of the most important success factors for doing an enterprise architecture are the strong support of executive leadership, and buy-in from stakeholders. If you see value in having an architecture, and have a say in how it affects you, then the architecture can become a powerful planning and decision-making tool for DMC."

Robert thought for a moment about what Sam had said and then addressed the group. "I am inclined to approve the plan to develop a standardized architecture approach and these first two segments, are there any objections?" There were no other comments. "Ok Sam, let's proceed with the plan and get together every two weeks for a progress report."

Chapter 3

The Value and Risk of Creating an Enterprise Architecture

Chapter Overview

Chapter 3 discusses the value and risks associated with creating an enterprise-wide architecture. The main concepts of this chapter are that EA represents a different way of looking at resources across the enterprise, and that the significant cost of creating an EA must be justified in terms of the value that it will bring to users of EA products in their planning and decision-making activities.

Learning Objectives

> Understand the potential value of the EA.

> Understand the risks associated with implementing an EA.

> Learn an approach for measuring the costs and benefits of an EA program.

> Understand how EA helps integrate strategy, business, and technology.

Introduction

There is both value and risk associated with the establishment of an EA program in an enterprise. On the value side, EA has the unique capability to bring together views of strategy, business, and technology that allow an enterprise to see itself in current and future operating states. EA also supports the modeling of different future operating scenarios, which may help the enterprise survive (or thrive) as it responds to changes in the internal and external operating environment, some of which can be unexpected. Additionally, an EA program establishes an integrated set of IT resource planning, decision-making, and implementation processes that can better identify and resolve performance gaps across the enterprise.

> *Home Architecture Analogy:* A set of comprehensive blueprints for building a home takes an architect a fair amount of time and money to create. Without them though, any construction that occurs is an uncoordinated activity, and the home that results may not function properly.

On the risk side, creating an EA for an entire enterprise can be time-consuming, costly, and disruptive to business services. Also, developing detailed EA documentation that covers strategy, business, and technology within each area of the enterprise can be time consuming and costly. Hiring and/or training architects and supporting analysts is one element of the cost. Another cost element is the time it takes line of business managers and support staff away from their normal work. Finally, the cost of EA documentation tools and on-line repositories has to be factored in as well. Further, there is the risk that the EA will not be used by stakeholders if they do not buy-in to the concept of EA or its perceived value.

On the value side, EA is unique in its ability to promote enterprise-wide thinking about resource utilization. EA replaces the systems-level approaches to IT resource development that have characterized the last several decades, and has left many enterprises with stovepipe and/or duplicative IT resources. EA promotes the development of more efficient enterprise-wide common operating environments for business and technology, within which more capable and flexible business services and systems can be hosted. This in turn makes an enterprise more agile and able to respond to internal and external drivers of change, which promotes greater levels of competitiveness in the marketplace.

The benefits should outweigh the costs of doing an EA, or the program should not be established. In the Case Study example, if an EA program helps DMC's executives find a combined solution to two sets of business and technology requirements, then a significant amount of money can be saved. Multiply this by several of these situations each year, and the EA program may very well pay for itself. Further, EA helps to identify existing duplication in functional capability, which can generate additional savings. Finally, EA documentation helps to identify current and future performance gaps that may not be otherwise realized, which enables the enterprise to be more proactive and cost-efficient in addressing solutions.

Discussion

Value

The value of EA is that it enhances resource-planning capabilities and supports better decision-making. This is accomplished through communication improvements in respect to current and future resources. Ideas are conveyed more rapidly while differences in interpretations and misunderstandings are reduced.

The overall value of EA will vary with the size and complexity of the enterprise, the type and number of IT-related performance gaps, duplication within current IT resources, and stakeholder acceptance. For those larger, less centralized enterprises that are regional or global in nature, EA can be an effective governance process for IT resources. For smaller more centralized enterprises, EA can help to ensure that the organization remains able to align business requirements with technology solutions, and enhance inventory, security, and configuration management activities.

Improved Planning

EA enhances both top-down and bottom-up approaches to planning. Top-down planning begins with considerations for strategy and business, which are enhanced by the holistic perspectives of the enterprise that EA provides. Bottom-up planning is also enhanced, as EA coordinates what would otherwise be disparate and separate program-level planning activities. EA also enhances strategic planning as it helps to bring together multiple perspectives of business and technology at various levels of the enterprise. Finally, EA supports program and project management by providing a baseline of reference documentation for business alignment, standards, and configuration management.

Decision-Making

EA improves decision-making by providing comprehensive views of current capabilities and resources, as well as a set of plausible future operating scenarios that reveal needed changes in processes and resources (see Chapter 8 for additional details on future scenarios). By having an on-line EA repository of information that is updated at regular intervals, decision-makers have real-time access to higher-quality information at various levels of detail.

In that the EA program links to other areas of resource governance (e.g., capital planning, project management, and security), decision-makers can obtain coordinated information on operations, support, and development activities. Chapters 10 and 11 provide additional details on the relationship between EA, capital planning, project management, and security.

Communications

EA improves communication throughout the enterprise by providing a regularly updated baseline of integrated information on strategy, business, and technology. Also, the EA program and implementation methodology bring standardized approaches and terminologies for the development and management of enterprise resources. This standard EA language and methodology is especially helpful in large, complex enterprises that are geographically dispersed, and which may have multiple social and work cultures that have promoted different ways of doing things. EA should not stifle the creativity that cultural diversity can bring, but should augment and enhance that creativity by improving the alignment of business and technology to the strategic goals and initiatives of the enterprise.

The old saying is that "a picture is worth a thousand words." Having an on-line repository of EA information is like having a 24x7 gallery of electronic documents and drawings that can be useful in a variety of activities throughout the enterprise. It is tremendously valuable if the members of an enterprise can electronically call-up the same set of EA reference materials at financial planning meetings, research and development seminars, sales and marketing reviews, and daily operations and support activities. With an updated repository of EA materials available, meetings can convey greater amounts of information in shorter periods of time, achieving higher levels of understanding based on a common set of EA terms and information.

Managing Risk

Risk is related to uncertainty, and in applied form is the potential source(s) for the failure or underperformance of a program or project. The management of risk involves lowering or eliminating the uncertainty that desired outcomes will not be realized. There are several types of risk that relate to the implementation and maintenance of an EA program, including:

Financial. Implementing an EA involves establishing current and future views of enterprise resources, an EA Management Plan, and updates to this information at regular intervals. Like any implementation project, establishing the initial set of EA information will require start-up funding that is more than what will be required for the periodic updates. Even after the EA is established, cuts in an EA maintenance budget can severely affect the program, to the point of making the EA information eventually become of little or no use if it becomes too out of date.

Lack of Acceptance. EA represents a new way of looking at enterprise resources by providing an integrated view of strategy, business, and technology that supports the   consolidation or re-engineered of these resources to produce additional value. Former approaches to program management that supported systems level planning will be replaced with EA level planning that is promoted through the EA program. This will most likely create some tensions between program level stakeholders, EA stakeholders, and other affected groups.

Loss of Key Personnel. EA is an emerging area of professional practice that requires architects, analysts, developers, and programmers. Each of these skill sets is important to the program and the loss of members of the EA team with those skills can create delays in program implementation, as well as effect implementation costs.

Schedule Delays.   As with all implementation projects, the documentation of current and future EA views as well as the creation of the initial EA Management Plan is approached as a project that has milestones and a specific schedule for completion. Delays to the schedule can come from many sources and depending on the point at which a delay occurs during EA implementation, and how long the delay is, the effect can go from being negligible to being catastrophic for the EA program.

Documentation Tools. One of the greatest challenges for a Chief Architect is to develop current and future views of the EA that are rich in detail, easy to access, and which can support modeling and decision-making types of queries. The capabilities of EA tools and supporting applications at present are such that intuitive and informative "management views" of EA information are difficult to produce with these tools. Further, because more than one software application is normally required in an EA program, tool integration is an issue that must be dealt with. As new commercial tools are introduced a Chief Architect has to consider what the effect will be on overall documentation if that product does not integrate with other tools.

Mitigating Risk

Risk mitigation plans and activities reduce the likelihood that sources of risk will emerge and negatively impact a program such as EA. Actions that mitigate risk (lower uncertainty) include strengthening executive support for the EA program, solidifying budgets, not being the first adopter of EA tools and documentation techniques, ensuring there are trained back-ups on the EA team, and using a detailed EA implementation methodology to guide the overall program. Additionally, basic program management skills address potential problems of key personnel turnover, cost and schedule overruns, performance issues, and stakeholder acceptance. Overcoming issues related to technology compatibility among EA products is achieved through the use of commercial tools that are based on open standards, and which are mature and have significant market share.

Risk identification and mitigation is not a one-time activity, it is an ongoing management review item that will assist in making an EA program successful.

Quantifying EA Program Value

How to translate value to the bottom line is one of the biggest questions executives and Line of Business (LOB) managers have about EA programs. Building a business case that includes an alternatives analysis, cost-benefit analysis, and return on investment calculation is the primary measure for evaluating the contribution to profitability and/or mission success (see the example Business Case in Appendix A). Many aspects of EA value can be quantified, including the following areas:

Shortening Planning Cycles. EA can help shorten planning cycles by providing a robust repository of on-line information regarding current and future processes and resources. While EA does not replace strategic planning or business process improvement activities, it does enhance them through contribution of useful information that that would otherwise be gathered separately.

More Effective Planning Meetings. EA information allows for the presentation of a common baseline of planning and reference information. It reduces ambiguity and increases levels of common understanding.

Shorter Decision-Making Cycles. The time it takes to gather and cross-walk strategy, business, and technology information is greatly reduced by having a repository of EA information that was developed through the use of a logical framework and archiving method. Decision-making processes can be streamlined to reflect the availability of this new resource of integrated baseline information.

Improved Reference Information. By using an EA documentation framework and implementation methodology, information on processes and resources is gathered in a standardized method using the same tools and applications. Additionally, the method for storing the information is coordinated through the use of the on-line EA repository, which requires the use of standardized data and document formats. This in turn creates the ability to perform queries for information across otherwise disparate activities and resources. It also supports a more robust data mining and business analysis capability.

Reduction of Duplicative Resources. One of the greatest contributions an EA makes to an enterprise is aiding the visualization of the value that current resources provide, where those value areas overlap, and where performance gaps exist. For example, duplicative data represents low-hanging fruit ready for elimination through the implementation of the future architecture. Subsequent improvements might then focus on the introduction of new technologies and improvements in efficiency.

Reduced Re-work. By approaching the planning and execution of new resources in a holistic manner, potential re-work that might have been created through individual program level initiatives (containing duplicative and/or conflicting capabilities) can be avoided. Also, re-work is reduced through the use of a step-by-step EA methodology and framework (see Chapters 4 and 5), that call for standard approaches to documentation that are based on mature modeling and analysis techniques.

Improved Resource Integration and Performance.   EA promotes integration through the planning and utilization of resources on an enterprise-wide basis. EA also helps to compare current and future requirements for business and technology, in order to identify performance gaps and solutions.   This result is contrasted with stovepipe program-level inputs to provide incremental improvements within individual LOBs.

Fewer People in a Process. EA supports business process reengineering (BPR) and business process improvement (BPI) activities by encouraging planning in the context of both enterprise-wide crosscutting requirements and particular LOB requirements. Quantifying this includes the elimination of parts of a process that are repetitive.   Also, streamlined processes that use resources more efficiently can equate to position requirement reductions and payroll savings.

Improved Communication. EA helps to promote a common language and central approach that can reduce misunderstandings of resource requirements and potential solutions.   This can reduce re-work. Whole processes may require repetition due to misunderstandings of different interpretations of requirements and/or solutions.

Reduction in Cycle Time. EA can help an enterprise to reduce the time it takes to plan, develop, implement, and retire resources within its business and technology operating environment. By using an EA methodology and framework (see Chapters 4 and 5), each resource is evaluated from the same holistic strategy, business and technology viewpoint, and is documented using the same set of EA tools and techniques.   Further, EA compliments capital planning and program management reviews of completed projects (see Chapters 10 and 11) so that the 'lessons learned' can be applied to subsequent efforts. In this way, the enterprise can improve efficiency and reduce the amount of time it takes to implement similar resources. For example, using an integrated enterprise architecture/capital planning/project management approach to selecting, controlling, and evaluating investments in web sites, the enterprise will be more effective and efficient in implementing each subsequent web site, and can avoid creating duplicative capabilities.

Quantifying EA Program Costs

The cost of EA should be approached from a program lifecycle view that centers on phases for implementation, maintenance, and refreshment. One way to estimate EA program costs is to look at each area of the EA implementation methodology (see Chapter 4), and identify the direct and indirect costs to accomplish each of the steps. In general, this would include the following:

- EA program administration and other enterprise administrative tie-ins
- Salary/benefits for a Chief Architect and EA team staff
- Meetings, facilities, materials, and support for stakeholder planning sessions
- Computers, applications, and web developers to establish the EA repository
- Interviews and materials to document EA current views
- Future scenario planning sessions with stakeholders
- Interviews and materials to document EA future views
- Development and documentation of the EA Management Plan
- Purchase, use, and refreshment of EA modeling applications and computers
- Regular (e.g., annual) updates to EA documentation and the online repository

The cost of establishing an initial version of the EA will be more than the cost of updating and maintaining it, due to the direct and indirect costs associated with establishing new EA processes and capabilities, and gaining stakeholder support.

The full lifecycle cost of the EA program should be established and presented to the EA program sponsor, so that there is a clear understanding of the one-time costs for implementation of the EA and the ongoing costs for EA maintenance and refreshment activities. As with any program, this budget picture should be baselined relative to the EA program activities that are approved by the sponsor, so that any approved changes to the scope of those EA activities are accompanied by a change to the budget. If this is not done, the EA program may evolve to a position of being responsible for too much relative to the resources it has available.

In that EA is an advanced analytic type of activity, most of the cost of developing and maintaining EA documentation will be the cost of labor for trained architects. The second largest cost area will be the supporting technology (hardware, software, web applications, databases, EA tools, etc.). The other major cost area will be the facility costs for the EA team's work area and meetings with stakeholders.

Those who do EA (in total or in part) for a living work under a variety of job titles, including Chief Architect, Solution Architect, Systems Architect, Data Architect, Network Architect, Security Architect, IT Consultant, Management Consultant, and a number of related analyst titles. Furthermore, there tends to be a set of classifications for senior, mid-level, and junior positions for many of these jobs. From an informal survey of EA salaries in 2003 conducted by the author, a senior enterprise architect's position can command over $100,000 per year.[9] Mid-level positions (3-5 years of experience) can earn in the range of $50,000 to $80,000.00 per year, and the junior positions for beginning architects can earn in the range of $30,000 to $50,000 per year.

As expensive as this seems, the cost to outsource these positions is even greater. The industry average for one work year is about 2,060 hours (this is Monday-Friday 8-hour days and accounts for time away for holidays and personal time off). Some federal government contract labor rates for the outsourcing of a Chief Architect and/or Senior Consultant position are over $200 per hour, which translates to over $412,000 per year. The rate for mid-level EA professionals can range from $125 to $175 per hour, so at the upper end of this range the outsourcing of one of these positions can cost over $360,050. The rate for junior EA professionals can range from $55 to $85 per hour, and at the upper end of this range the cost of outsourcing can be over $175,100.

This significant level of cost for EA labor has caused some enterprises to pause in considering the implementation of an EA program. However, when the potential savings generated by the EA program are factored in, there can be a very high return on investment, especially in enterprises where EA can reduce duplicative capabilities and help identify common solutions to otherwise separate requirements. With costs for information

---

[9] These labor cost estimates are based on commercial rates used in federal sector information technology support service and consulting contracts, as surveyed by the author in 2004-2005. The labor rates cover salary and benefits, but do not cover facilities support, desk, computer, phone, and administrative costs.

systems in the many millions of dollars, the consolidation of even a few of those systems can make the EA program more than pay for itself, as well as enable the enterprise to re-direct the funding from duplicative resources to other business requirements.

Linking Strategy, Business, and Technology

For EA to support an enterprise holistically, it must link strategy, business and technology. EA is most effective when it simultaneously supports top-down executive planning and decision-making across the enterprise and bottom-up management planning and decision-making within each LOB. In this way, EA helps to ensure that strategy drives business and technology planning. From a business perspective EA provides the context and purpose of business activities by ensuring technology is implemented only after business requirements are identified. From a technology perspective, EA provides the strategy and business context for resource planning.

Linking EA and Strategy

The EA framework and methodology organizes EA documentation in a way that allows strategy to influence business and technology planning and decision-making. This is important especially in the documentation of future EA views. By first identifying what changes are anticipated in strategic goals and initiatives, subsequent documentation of business activities and technology resources can be completed in such a way as to promote alignment, efficiency, and effectiveness. Documenting strategy involves the identification of goals, initiatives, and outcome measures.

Strategic Goals.   These are the primary objectives of the enterprise. Strategic goals typically require several years to accomplish. Changes in strategic goals are made in response in internal and external business and technology drivers and/or changes in laws and regulations.

Strategic Initiatives.   These are the business and technology activities, programs, and projects that enable accomplishment of strategic goals, such that they can effect the fundamental direction of the enterprise.

Strategic Measures.   These are outcome measures that identify when a strategic initiative has successfully met a strategic goal.   Outcome goals define when an enterprise is accomplishing its mission… when it 'wins.'

Linking EA and Business Planning

As is reflected in the design of the EA framework, strategy creates business requirements and technology supports solutions for meeting those requirements. EA documents three primary issues at the business level:

Supporting Strategic Goals. Touch points between strategic initiatives and business activities need to be clearly documented. Not all business activities are strategic, and it is important to distinguish in the EA documentation between those that directly link to strategic initiatives and those that provide general support functions for the enterprise.

Documentation of Business Activities. Documenting the creation and delivery of business products and services is important in supporting Business Process Improvement (BPI) and Business Process Reengineering (BPR) projects, and in documenting business activities to show inputs, outputs, outcomes, and other elements of influence regarding each business process. It's also important to identify how business processes are linked to one another.

Identifying Supporting Technologies. Analyzing business requirements and activities can reveal critical supporting technologies (e.g. marketing activities require sales trend analysis data, and a manufacturing process requires various types of resources including raw materials, facilities, labor, computers, data, and/or robotics). EA helps to identify and document these supporting technologies.

Linking EA and Technology Planning

Technology is a type of resource that enables information and other resource flows to support the creation and delivery of business products and services, which in turn enables the achievement of strategic goals. It is important that technology not drive business and strategy planning, especially in resource-constrained enterprises, where the expense of duplicative non-strategic technologies cannot be afforded. Bottom-up planning (e.g. where technology is the catalyst for change) is a viable use of EA; however it's not the normal process for resource implementation. It's more important for the enterprise to understand its primary directions and priorities, plan necessary business activities, and then identify the supporting resources, including IT.

Summary of Concepts

This chapter provided a detailed discussion of the value and risk of establishing an EA program. A clear articulation of the business case for EA is needed to obtain executive sponsorship and resources for EA program implementation and maintenance. Quantifying the areas of value that the EA program will contribute is important, and those include improved communication, planning, and decision-making. A total lifecycle approach to estimating costs is used to differentiate the one-time direct and indirect costs associated with program start-up and initial EA documentation from the ongoing costs of EA program management and documentation updates. Comparisons were made in the area of EA labor costs between in-house salaries and the expense of paying for external EA consulting support. In concluding the discussion of EA value, the linkage between EA, strategy, business, and technology was shown.

Chapter 3 Questions and Exercises

1. What are some of the areas of value that are generated by an EA program?

2. What are some of the risks associated with implementing an EA program?

3. How does EA help an enterprise to view its strategic direction/goals?

4. How does EA help an enterprise to view its business services?

5. How does EA help an enterprise to view technology resources?

6. What is meant by managing risk? Provide two methods to manage risk.

7. How does EA link to strategy, business, and technology?

8. Select a real-world medium- or large-sized business and identify the following:

   a. Areas of potential value that an EA program would provide. ·

   b. Areas of potential risk to the implementation and acceptance of an EA program, and strategies to mitigate those risks.

   c. How EA can help develop views of this business' strategic direction and goals; business services; and supporting resources.

Section II

Developing an Enterprise Architecture

Section II defines and describes how to accomplish and implement an Enterprise Architecture. It covers what an EA framework is, presents a step-by-step methodology to implement an EA, discusses how to document current and future views of the EA, and describes how to articulate the EA in an "EA Management Plan," which also serves as a transition and sequencing plan from the current to the future architecture.

Foundational elements of an EA program are the documentation framework and the implementation methodology. The EA documentation framework defines _what_ the EA program will document, and the EA implementation methodology defines _how_ that documentation will be gathered and used. By documenting current and future views, along with an EA Management Plan, the EA improves planning agility, helps to prioritize resource utilization, and helps to lower the risk of project failures. Section II is organized as follows:

Case Study (Scene 3) - The Importance of a Methodology

The Case Study continues the scenario at Danforth Manufacturing Company that was presented in Section I. Now that the CEO has decided to proceed with an EA program, this part of the Case Study will focus on how the EA program and implementation methodology will be implemented. The CIO has hired a Chief Architect, who describes the need for and purpose of an EA methodology.

Chapter 4 - The Implementation Methodology

Chapter 4 describes the EA implementation methodology, which is the detailed procedure for doing an EA. The EA³ 'Cube' is used as the example framework for discussing an implementation methodology. The value of adopting an EA methodology is discussed in terms of providing a detailed, comprehensive approach to EA governance and documentation, reducing the risk of producing an EA that's not useful to stakeholders.

Chapter 5 - The Documentation Framework

Chapter 5 describes the purpose of an EA documentation framework and how it establishes the scope of the EA. Several existing EA frameworks are presented as examples that have different areas of focus and relationships for EA documentation. Also, a the EA³ framework is presented in detail, as it becomes the basis for further discussion about how an EA framework can link strategy, business, and technology together to help improve resource planning and decision-making throughout the enterprise.

Chapter 6 - EA Components and Artifacts

Chapter 6 describes EA components and related artifacts. EA components are those plug-and-play 'changeable' items that provide capabilities at each level of the framework. Examples include strategic goals and measures, business services, information objects, software applications, and network hardware. EA artifacts are the descriptions of the EA components. Types of EA artifacts include text documents, manuals, guides, technical reference material, graphics, drawings, pictures, raw data, information, presentations, spreadsheets, and videos.

Case Study (Scene 4) - Developing Current / Future EA Views

This part of the Case Study illustrates how current and future EA views will be developed. The context is that of evaluating several proposed IT systems and looking for common requirements and combined solutions. Following this evaluation, two segments of the DMC architecture will be developed that cover several lines of business.

Chapter 7 - Developing Current Architecture Views

Chapter 7 covers the development of artifacts that reflect current views of EA components, within the context of the EA³ framework and the related implementation methodology. Current EA views are important to an enterprise in that they establish and/or verify what resources (including IT) are being used in the lines of business to support the achievement of strategic goals. The current EA views become a reference baseline much like an inventory that then supports planning and decision-making regarding the future architecture.

Chapter 8 - Developing Future Architecture Views

Chapter 8 covers the development of future views of EA components, again within the context of the EA^3 framework and the related documentation methodology. The future views of the EA are important to the enterprise as they encompass one or more possible future states, which represent strategies for successful performance in response to internal and external influences. The future views of the EA are developed in ways that allow them to be directly related to the EA's current views at each level of the framework, so that planned changes are evident, and various types of changes can be modeled. The chapter also provides a description of a method for developing future views that is called "scenario planning." Future scenarios can help the enterprise to envision one or more potential future business/technology operating states in a way that helps to identify areas of change that will be important to the successful attainment of strategic goals.

Chapter 9 - Developing an EA Management Plan

Chapter 9 discusses the development of an EA Management Plan, which is the document that describes how an enterprise will manage the transition of its current processes and resources to those which will be needed in the future. This transition from the current EA to the future EA is an ongoing activity, as new resources that are identified in the future EA are implemented and therefore become part of the current EA. The purpose of configuration management and version control are also discussed, along with the need to sequence implementation projects.

At a meeting of the Executive Committee several weeks before, Robert Danforth, the President and CEO of Danforth Manufacturing Company (DMC), had approved the request of CIO Sam Young to use an EA approach to evaluate two sets of IT system requirements that COO Kate Jarvis and CFO Jim Gorman had brought to the executive leadership group. Sam is now moving forward on a plan and a business case to develop an architecture for several lines of business related to Kate and Jim's requirements. These "segments" of the DMC enterprise architecture will help Kate and Jim to evaluate their recent requests for new information systems to see if there were overlapping requirements.

To properly provide leadership and resources for the project, Sam worked with DMC's Executive Committee during the past week to obtain approval to establish an EA Program that would be led by a qualified Chief Architect. The newly appointed Chief Architect reports to Sam. He selected Vince Albright, whom he had known from earlier work. Also, Sam was given a budget for this initial EA project within the EA Program, and a working area that can accommodate several people who will be hired and/or "borrowed" from other business areas for the period of the project.

This initial architecture effort is the test case for considering the development of a company-wide EA for DMC. Scene 3 describes the first meeting of the EA Working Group, which includes Sam, Kate, Jim, Vince, several line of business managers, Lily Jefferson a senior systems analyst at DMC, and several end users of DMC's current sales and finance systems.

"Hello, and welcome to the Enterprise Architecture Working Group" said Sam. We are going to develop two segments of the company's enterprise architecture, which cover several lines of business. These are lines of business that need more IT support. Before we can do that, we need to have a detailed methodology that will guide our efforts and reduce the risk that we will not be successful in developing the EA segments. I have handed out a one-page outline of an EA methodology that I used with another enterprise and it helped tremendously. The four phases of the methodology cover program establishment, methodology development, documentation activities, and maintenance. During the past several weeks, I have worked with the Executive Committee to formally establish the EA Program and bring Vince Albright on board as our new Chief Architect. Vince, congratulations and welcome. Vince was with me during the prior project that we used this EA methodology, so I am going to turn it over to him to tell us about that and guide the EA Working Group through a review to see if we want to make any changes."

"Thank you Sam" said Vince. "It is a pleasure to be at DMC and to be working with you again on an EA program, especially one that promises to bring great value to this enterprise. The first thing I would like you to know is that as Chief Architect, I will be very inclusive regarding stakeholder involvement in the development of the EA program and all EA segments. This is because I have seen that down-road acceptance can only be gained through the ongoing participation of those who will be using the EA information, and those who are impacted by the EA program. Second, I'd like to tell you briefly about my very first EA project, one where we did not use a methodology. This project started ok, but lost its way as the segments were being developed. Why? Because the EA Team did not have anything to use with participants to keep things standardized, or maintain stakeholder interest with, and we ended up with segments that did not integrate into an overall EA... so the project did not produce the amount of value that was expected, and the EA information was rarely used." "Since then, I've learned to let the business requirements drive the architecture, and to develop segments collaboratively with those who will use them, so they can ensure that the types of EA information are there when they need it.... not just the IT information we think they will need."

Vince continued. "What you received several weeks ago was the *DMC Enterprise Architecture Plan – Financial and Production Segments* report that Sam, Lily, and I developed with Jim, Kate, and several members of this EA Working Group. That report lays out the business case for this EA project, which is to evaluate the business and technology requirements for two proposed systems. To do that type of analysis, we need several segments of an overall DMC enterprise architecture, to provide reference views of the current and planned process and resources involving DMC's strategic goals, business activities, and technology capabilities. To develop these segments for the finance and production lines of business, we need a methodology. As Sam said, this methodology will help keep us on track and reduce the risk of project failure."

Jim asked, "What do I need to do to help with this methodology?" Sam answered, "Look at the outline and tell us what is not there, perhaps there is something more that you as a business executive might need to have as part of our EA Program or documentation process. Also, when we get to the modeling steps, we need to know from you, Kate, and your respective staff what kind of planning and decision-making information you need in your lines of business. We also need to know the formats you would require. From that, the EA Working Group can refine the requirements that we will use to select modeling techniques and tools. Once we get the current views established for your and Kate's EA segments, we can develop some future operating scenarios and identify planning assumptions. This is the baseline of EA information that we can finally use to evaluate your proposals for separate system. We'll see if they fit into the future architecture as proposed, or we will be able to determine if there is a better way to meet your requirements."

Vince spoke up. "Sam talked about a lot of interdependent parts there, which hopefully reinforces our comments about the value of having a methodology to guide EA activities. Also, Sam alluded to different types of EA information that we will be gathering and you may be wondering what that is and how it is organized? The short answer is that we will use an EA framework. One of the foundational elements of any EA program is the selection of an EA framework that defines the scope of the overall architecture and its sub-segments. Further, the graphic depiction of the EA framework provides a visual image of the areas of the EA and how they relate. In our project, we will review several frameworks during this meeting that are in use and select the one that best serves our needs. So, let's get on with the review of the EA implementation methodology."

The EA Working Group meeting finished its review of the EA methodology and selected an EA documentation framework. Vince called for a meeting later that week to discuss how the methodology and framework would be used to document the current and future views of the two EA segments that the project is responsible for. Sam will brief the selected methodology and framework to the Executive Committee at the next bi-monthly status meeting. The CEO had requested these meetings to stay in touch with the EA project.

Chapter 4

The Implementation Methodology

Chapter Overview

This chapter describes the EA implementation *methodology* (EA methodology), which is a detailed procedure for establishing, maintaining and using an EA *framework* and documentation approach. The EA methodology is the first step in coordinating the EA documentation approach. The value of adopting an EA methodology is that it reduces the risk of creating an ineffective EA program and/or inaccurate EA documentation.

Key Term: *EA Framework*
The EA framework is a structure for organizing information that defines the scope of the architecture (what the EA program will document) and how the areas of the architecture relate to each other.

Key Term: *EA Methodology*
The EA methodology defines <u>how</u> the EA will be implemented and how documentation will be developed, archived, and used; including the selection of a framework, modeling tools, and on-line repository.

Learning Objectives

➢ Understand the purpose of an EA methodology within the EA program.

➢ Understand the steps of an example EA methodology.

➢ Understand the relationship between an EA framework and EA methodology.

Introduction

An EA methodology is a detailed, step-by-step description of how the EA program is to be established and run, and how the documentation of the

EA is to be developed, maintained, and used. The EA methodology presented in this book is flexible enough to support the use of many of the popular EA frameworks, tools, and repositories. Figure 4-1 provides an overview of the six basic elements of EA documentation that were presented in Chapter 1. This Chapter builds on the basic elements by establishing a four phase/twenty-step methodology to establish an EA program and implement the six EA documentation elements.

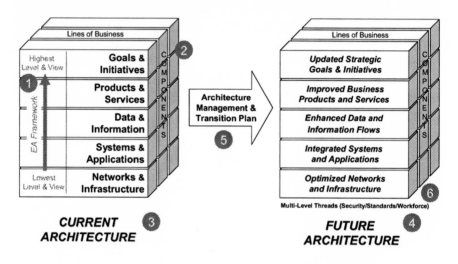

Figure 4-1: The Basic Elements of EA Documentation

Home Architecture Analogy: An EA methodology is like the standard approach that architects are taught for designing and constructing a home. There are things that must be done in a certain order for the design to be accurate and for the home to be properly constructed.

Discussion

The establishment of an EA program has many facets and one of the keys to success is to use a detailed documentation methodology to get the program started, and then to guide the EA documentation effort. The EA methodology described in this book is generalized so it can be used in a wide variety of public and private sector enterprises, and can support many types of EA frameworks, tools, and repositories. Depending on the type of enterprise, some parts of the EA methodology may need to be changed.

It is important to develop an EA methodology as one of the first steps in establishing the EA program, because it forces the enterprise to 'think through' the following important considerations:

- Which areas of the enterprise the EA will cover (scope)
- The approach to EA governance (e.g., centralized or decentralized)
- The types of EA documentation (known as artifacts) that will be needed to support business and technology resource planning and decision-making
- The EA documentation framework that best supports the needs of the enterprise
- The methods and techniques for gathering or developing EA documentation
- The software modeling tools, web applications, and databases that will be needed to automate documentation techniques and enable future scenario modeling
- How EA users will access and share EA documentation (e.g. an EA repository)
- How often EA documentation will be updated

The 20-step process presented on the following pages is an example EA implementation methodology that contains all of the general steps that would support the creation of a new, comprehensive EA program. It should be noted that the revitalization of an existing EA program will involve additional steps that will vary with each situation. Revitalization could focus on the selection of a different EA framework and implementation methodology, and/or the identification of new vertical and horizontal partitions of the enterprise that is being documented (segments and crosscuts).

Enterprise Architecture Implementation Methodology

Phase I: EA Program Establishment

Step 1:   Establish the EA Management Program and identify a Chief Architect.

Step 2:   Establish an EA implementation methodology.

Step 3:   Establish EA governance and links to other management processes.

Step 4:   Develop an EA Communication Plan to gain stakeholder buy-in.

Phase II: EA Framework and Tool Selection

Step 5:   Select an EA documentation framework.

Step 6:   Identify EA Lines of Business/Crosscuts and the order of their documentation.

Step 7:   Identify the EA components to be documented framework-wide.

Step 8:   Select documentation methods appropriate for the framework.

Step 9:   Select software applications/tools to support automated EA documentation.

Step 10:   Select and establish an on-line EA repository for documentation and analysis.

Phase III: Documentation of the EA

Step 11:   Evaluate existing business and technology documentation for use in the EA.

Step 12:   Document current views of existing EA components in all framework areas (levels/threads). Store artifacts in the on-line repository.

Step 13:   Develop several future business/technology operating scenarios.

Step 14:   Identify future planning assumptions for each future scenario.

Step 15:   Use the scenarios and other program/staff input to drive the documentation of future EA components in all framework areas. Store artifacts in the on-line EA repository.

Step 16:   Develop an EA Management Plan to sequence planned changes in the EA.

Phase IV: Use and Maintain the EA

Step 17:   Use EA documentation to support planning/decision-making.

Step 18: Regularly update current and future views of EA components, and link information in the EA repository to create high-level and detailed 'perspectives' of enterprise activities and resources in the current and future operating environments.

Step 19: Maintain an EA Repository and related modeling and analysis capabilities.

Step 20: Release annual updates to the EA Management Plan.

This EA implementation methodology addresses the establishment of a new EA program and documentation set. The revitalization of existing, but unproductive EA programs, or switching approaches, key personnel, or contracted support should be handled through the addition of Steps in Phase I and/or Phase II to address these changes. The following are more detailed descriptions of each step in the example EA methodology:

Phase I: EA Program Establishment

Phase I activities are designed to get the EA program initially started, identify key players, and communicate the EA implementation plan to the *executive sponsor* and other stakeholders in order to gain buy-in and support. These pre-documentation activities are important to ensuring that the EA program has clear goals, remains focused, and is accepted throughout the enterprise.

Key Term: *Executive Sponsor*
The executive who has decision-making authority over the EA program and who provides resources and senior leadership for the EA program.

Step 1:   Establish the EA Management Program and identify a Chief Architect.
The first step is for an executive sponsor to establish an EA program and identify a Chief Architect to lead the Program. The EA program is initially a start-up project (Phases I-III) and then an ongoing program (Phase IV). The executive sponsor must provide the Chief Architect with enough resources (e.g., budget, personnel, hardware/software, and facilities) and the authority to be able to properly establish the EA program. The Chief Architect should be accountable for EA program

resources. One of the Chief Architect's first actions should be to establish an EA team that consists of trained EA architects and representatives of various stakeholder groups.

Step 2:   Establish an EA implementation methodology.
The second step in the EA methodology is for the Chief Architect and EA team to identify all of the steps in the methodology that the enterprise needs in order to create an effective EA program.   The example EA methodology discussed in this chapter can be used as it is presented or it can be modified to meet the particular needs of the enterprise. Other methodologies from the public and private sector can be used. The important thing to remember in starting an EA is to have a detailed methodology that will guide program implementation and subsequent documentation activities, as well as reduce the risk of the EA program losing focus, effectiveness, and value.

Step 3:   Establish EA governance and links to other management processes.
The third step is for the executive sponsor and Chief Architect to co-develop an approach to EA governance that enables effective policy, planning, and decision-making within the EA management program. This approach to EA governance should include links to other management processes for strategic planning, capital planning, project management, security, and workforce planning.

Step 4:   Develop an EA Communication Plan and gain stakeholder buy-in.
The next step is to develop an EA Communication Plan that articulates the EA documentation methodology and a schedule for Phase II and III activities.   The EA Communication Plan should be written in plain language to gain stakeholder buy-in from non-technical executives, line of business managers, support staff, and other potential end users of EA documentation. The Communication Plan should include statements about the purpose and vision of the EA, examples of how the EA will bring value to the enterprise, where EA documentation will be available for access, a summary of the methodology used, and the general principles that will be used for EA development.

Phase II: EA Framework and Tool Selection

Phase II activities take place when the initial set of EA documentation is developed. This begins with the selection of an EA documentation framework that will identify the scope of the architecture, guide the techniques for the modeling of current views, develop future scenarios and associated modeling, and establish an on-line EA repository that will archive all of the EA documentation *artifacts*.

Key Term: *EA Artifact*

An EA artifact is a documentation product, such as a text document, system specification, application interface information, diagram, spreadsheet, briefing slides, and/or video clip.

Step 5: Select an EA documentation framework.

The first step of Phase II involves the selection of an EA documentation framework by the Chief Architect, with input from the EA team and stakeholders. The framework should identify the areas of the enterprise that the EA will cover, and how those areas relate. For example, the EA³ framework identifies five functional areas and three 'thread' areas to be documented, organizes different types of components, and then orients the components into lines of business. These relationships are important in conveying how the enterprise uses its processes and resources in accomplishing its goals.

Step 6: Identify the EA Lines of Business/Crosscuts and the order of their documentation.

The second step of Phase II involves the identification of vertical Lines of Business (also known as Segments) and horizontal crosscutting initiatives within the enterprise that can be separately architected, and when combined, will represent the EA for the entire enterprise. Sometimes distinct vertical LOBs are readily apparent such as functional sub-units of an organization (e.g., the Manufacturing Division, Sales and Marketing Division, Research and Development Division, Administration and Finance Division). Sometimes however, the LOB/Segment is something that makes sense within the EA and is not an established organizational boundary, so it must be identified through work with stakeholders (e.g., vertical supply chains, mission-specific capabilities). Crosscutting initiatives are those horizontal activities which function in a "common operating environment" across several LOBs. Examples of horizontal crosscuts include web services, knowledge warehouses, network infrastructure, security solutions, ERP modules, and back-office systems/applications (e.g. email, document tracking, finance and accounting, human resources).

Step 7: Identify the EA components to be documented.

Step 7 of the EA documentation methodology is to identify the EA components that will have to be documented in each functional area of the framework. For example, the EA³ framework has six functional areas (strategy, business, information, services, networks, and vertical threads). Each of these areas represents a distinct set of activities that extend across the enterprise, which are represented by EA components. EA components are plug-and-play goals, processes, measures, projects, data, services, and IT resources in the various functional areas. An EA component therefore is unique in the capability and resources that it represents within the EA framework. Each EA component is documented using information gathering methods and modeling techniques that are appropriate for the type of things that are contained in the EA component. For example, at the strategic level the enterprise's strategic goals, activities, and outcome measures are the primary items to be documented. At the business level, the line-of business services and associated measures are documented. At the information level, the flows of information, databases, knowledge warehouses, and data standards are documented. At the services and applications level, the various web services, office automation services, and software applications are documented. At the technology infrastructure level the voice, data, and video networks, as well as associated cable plants and equipment facilities are documented. For the vertical threads, IT security information, IT standards, and IT workforce information are gathered for associated activities and resources in each of the five other functional areas.

Step 8: Select documentation methods appropriate for the framework.

The next step is to select the methods that will be used to gather and develop EA documentation artifacts. For example, the following are methods for modeling in the six functional areas of the EA³ Cube framework (five levels and three threads). Appendix E provides examples of EA artifacts that can be used with the EA³ Cube and other frameworks.

Strategic Level:	Strategic Plan, Scenarios, Balanced Scorecard
Business Level:	IDEF-0 Diagrams, Flowcharts, Swim Lane Charts
Information Level:	Data Models, Object Diagrams, Data Dictionary
Services Level:	System Diagrams, Web Service Models, APIs
Technology Level:	Voice/Data/Video Network Diagrams/Documents
Vertical Threads:	Security Diagrams, Standards, IT Workforce Plans

It is important to choose documentation techniques that will provide the information that is needed for resource planning and decision-making. Therefore, the Chief Architect should consult with EA stakeholders and the EA team in selecting the methods for artifact development and what type of information will be gathered.

Step 9: Select software applications/tools to support automated EA documentation.
Once the functional areas/levels of the framework and the types of EA components are known, EA documentation and artifact modeling requirements can be established. Without doing Steps 7 and 8, it would be difficult for the Chief Architect and EA team to know the particular modeling techniques that they will have to support. For example, if object-oriented methods are being used to develop artifacts at the information level of the framework, then an EA modeling tool that has capability with the Unified Modeling Language (UML) is called for. Also, several types of EA documentation tools may be required, as there may be a requirement for a general EA modeling tool, several specialty modeling tools, and general document, spreadsheet, and graphics applications.

Step 10: Select and establish an on-line EA repository for documentation.
The last step in Phase II is for the Chief Architect and EA team to select an EA repository software application and database. The EA repository should be hosted on the enterprise's internal Local Area Network for security and ease of access to EA documentation. The EA repository is a database and file directory where all EA documentation is archived. One method to promote ease-of-use is to establish an EA web site that is the "front door" for all EA Program activities and documentation. This website's homepage can be designed to promote a clear view of the scope of the EA documentation that is available. Chapter 12 provides more information on the design of the EA repository.

Phase III: Documentation of the EA

Phase III activities are where the actual development of the EA occurs in the form of documentation artifacts. This involves analyzing and documenting the current strategy, business, information, services, and infrastructure of the enterprise. It also involves the development of artifacts that reflect changes in resources in the short-term and the development of a group of long-term future scenarios to identify possible courses of action and resource changes that would be needed in response to different internal and external influences. The activities in this phase of the EA documentation methodology conclude with the development of an EA Management Plan that summarizes the current and future views of the architecture and provides a transition and sequencing plan for short term and long term changes.

Step 11: Evaluate existing business and technology documentation for use in the EA.

The first step of Phase III is the beginning of actual EA documentation activities. Preceding activities established what would be documented, how it would be documented, and who would do the documentation. The current view of EA components is what is now being documented through the identification of what the EA components are at each level of the framework and then using existing and new artifacts to document the EA components that currently exist. In many ways this activity is like taking an "inventory" of the components (strategic goals, business services, measures, data, services, and IT resources) that already exist in the enterprise and mapping them to existing documentation.

Step 12: Document current views of existing EA components in all framework areas.

The second step of Phase III is the development of new artifacts to complete the documentation of all existing components. The documentation methods and tools identified in Step 8 are used to gather and standardize existing artifacts, as well as to develop new artifacts. These documentation artifacts are organized by levels of the framework and are stored in the EA repository that was established in Step 10. Additional details developing on the current architecture are provided in Chapter 7.

Step 13: Develop several future business/technology operating scenarios.

Prior to developing future views of EA components, it is helpful to gain a high-level understanding of the possible future directions that the enterprise could take, depending on how it responds to internal and external influences. Three or more future scenarios should optimally be developed with EA and line of business stakeholders to reflect what may occur if (1) the status quo is maintained; (2) an optimal business/technology operating environment is encountered; and (3) a high threat survival situation. There are several beneficial outcomes from the development of the scenarios. First, the enterprise is more prepared and organized to handle future situations and plan needed resources. Second, a number of planning assumptions are identified in each scenario that reveal what the priorities of the enterprise might be if that scenario is pursued. Third, the planning for future capabilities is more coordinated, as opposed to simply gathering separate inputs from line of business managers and technology managers. Separate inputs are known to perpetuate stovepipe capabilities. Chapter 8 provides additional details about how to develop future scenarios and the future architecture.

Step 14: Identify future planning assumptions for each future scenario.

Each future scenario describes, in story form, a possible business/technology operating environment that the enterprise might pursue or face. In this step, the key elements of each future scenario are analyzed to reveal what things are important to the enterprise and what changes have to occur for the scenario to become reality. For the purposes of the EA, these key elements become the planning assumptions that can then be grouped together to represent changes in each of the functional areas of the framework. One of the benefits of having the scenario and planning assumptions is that they were developed with stakeholder buy-in, which will help when future changes are implemented.

Step 15: Use scenarios, program inputs, and scheduled updates to drive documentation of future components in all framework areas.

This step involves the documentation of changes to EA components in the near term (1-2 years) and the longer term (3-5 years). These changes should be derived from the input by the leadership team (CXOs) via the operating scenarios' planning assumptions, and from program and project managers who know what the future business requirements are, as well as planned system implementations, upgrades, and retirements..   By doing it this way, the changes are more coordinated and aligned with the strategic direction of the enterprise. Future views of EA components should be developed using the same artifact documentation and modeling techniques that were used to develop the current views. This helps to more clearly identify what the changes are in each of the functional levels of the EA framework, which helps in planning and decision-making.

Step 16: Develop an EA Management Plan to sequence planned changes in the EA.
The final step in Phase III is the development of an EA Management Plan. This Plan serves to articulate how the EA was developed and provides a synopsis of the current and future views. The Plan also provides a transition and sequencing sub-plan for the near term changes, which may already be in the project pre-implementation stage. Also, a long-range sequencing sub-plan is provided that covers the potential changes associated with the future scenarios.   Chapter 9 provides more detail on the development of an EA Management Plan.

Phase IV: Use and Maintain the EA

Phase IV is an ongoing set of activities that promotes the use of EA information by all stakeholders, and establishes an annual cycle for updates.   This is where the value of the EA Program is realized, as planning and decision-making throughout the enterprise are supported. This value is maintained through regular updates of the current and future views of the architecture. Value is also gained in the maintenance of the EA repository and the maintenance of all associated software licenses for modeling and archiving.

Step 17:   Use EA documentation for resource planning and decision-making.
Upon the completion of Phase III, the current and future views of the architecture are stored in the EA repository and are ready to be used by the enterprise to support planning and decision-making.   These EA stored artifacts become a baseline of reference information that can be used in a wide variety of executive, management, and staff activities. When this is done, a greater level of understanding is developed of capabilities and performance gaps among a wider group within the enterprise. Further, by having the EA documentation in an on-line repository, this information can

be called up and referred to in meetings, which reduces the time it takes to convey an idea, increases comprehension, and reduces interpretation errors among meeting participants. For example, if in a planning meeting, one of the participants wanted to show needed improvements in information exchange within a particular line of business, EA documentation on the current and possible future views of that information flow could be called up from the repository and projected at the meeting. This, along with information on the associated business services, support applications, and networks can be referenced meaningfully. The time to convey the ideas is significantly reduced when diagrams and text are being shown to everyone at the meeting. This can stimulate more productive discussions and informed decisions.

Step 18: Regularly update current and future views of EA Components.

The information in the EA repository is valuable for planning and decision-making only as long as it is comprehensive and accurate. Therefore, it is important to regularly update the current and future views of EA components in all areas of the framework. Further, it is helpful to users of EA information if the updates are made on a regular schedule, perhaps twice a year. Also, it is important to maintain version control in between updates, so that all of the users of the EA information know that they are conducting planning and decision-making activities based on the same information. Since what is planned in the future EA views will eventually become the current architecture (at least some of it), it should be recognized that EA updates are ongoing activities that do not cease. Future EA plans will continue as an organization grows and changes. Consider a time when the enterprise no longer needs changes in future capabilities and resources. Should this occur, the EA program transitions from focusing on the establishment of the EA to maintaining the EA and seeing that it continually brings value to the enterprise.

Step 19: Maintain the EA repository and modeling capabilities.

The Chief Architect and EA team need to ensure that the EA repository and support applications/tools are kept current in terms of licensing and functionality. The requirements for archiving and modeling should be reviewed annually, and new products should be regularly reviewed to ensure that the EA team has the right application support capability. The team should be on the lookout for new improvements in tool functionality so that these improvements can be applied to the advantage of the enterprise. The costs for software purchases and license renewals should be part of the annual EA program budget.

Step 20: Release yearly updates to the EA Management Plan.
The Chief Architect needs to regularly inform EA stakeholders about the status of the EA. This is done through the annual release of an updated EA Management Plan that discusses changes that were made to the current and future views of the EA during the past year. The communication should provide a transition and sequencing plan for changes anticipated during the coming year. Also, the ongoing value of the EA needs to be communicated through the citation of examples of where EA documentation supported planning and decision-making, helped reduce duplicative capabilities, saved costs, improved alignment, and increased communication.

Summary of Concepts

This chapter presented a comprehensive methodology for the implementation of an EA program and associated documentation activities. The four phases and twenty steps of the example EA methodology are generalized so they can be used in many types of public and private sector enterprises. Phase I activities serve to establish the EA program, identify a Chief Architect to lead the program, create an EA governance capability to run the EA program in a way that integrates with other IT management processes, and issue an EA Communication Plan to gain stakeholder buy-in and support. Phase II activities serve to select an EA framework that defines the scope of the architecture, the EA components that will make up the architecture in each functional area, and software applications/tools to automate the documentation of EA components. Phase III is where the actual documentation of current and future views of the architecture occurs, as well as the development of an EA Management Plan to describe how the architecture will transition over time. The final Phase IV activities are where the EA is used throughout the enterprise to support planning and decision-making and regular updates are performed to keep the EA relevant and adding value.

Chapter 4 Questions and Exercises

1. What is an EA implementation methodology?

2. What is the role of an EA framework within the EA methodology?

3. What is the purpose of Phase I activities in the EA methodology?

4. Why are Phase III activities dependent on the completion of Phase II?

5. Compare and contrast the purpose of Phase II and Phase IV activities.

6. Can the steps of the EA methodology be changed for different enterprises?

7. Who is responsible for execution of the EA program and EA methodology?

8. How often should an EA be updated? Why?

9. Select a real-world medium or large size enterprise and provide:

    a. The phases and steps of an appropriate EA implementation methodology.

    b. The way that EA stakeholder support will be obtained.

    c. The recommended schedule for updating the EA.

Chapter 5

The Documentation Framework

Chapter Overview

This Chapter defines and describes the purpose of the EA documentation framework, provides examples of existing frameworks and discusses the EA³ Cube framework which is a generalized framework that is suitable for use in public and private sector enterprises.

Learning Objectives

> Understand the purpose of an EA framework as part of an EA implementation methodology.

> Understand how an EA framework establishes the scope of an EA.

> Become familiar with the origin of EA frameworks and several examples.

> Understand the design of the EA³ Cube framework.

Introduction

The foundational elements of an EA program are the documentation framework (EA framework) and the implementation methodology (EA methodology). The EA framework defines _what_ the EA program will document, and the EA methodology defines _how_ that documentation will be developed and used. By defining what parts of the enterprise are included in the EA, the framework defines the scope of the architecture. The design of the framework communicates the relationship of the areas of the EA that are documented.

> _Home Architecture Analogy:_ The EA documentation framework is like the structural skeleton of a home. It is the framing that defines the size and relationship of parts of the house and individual rooms.

Discussion

The EA documentation process is accomplished through an EA implementation methodology that includes (1) the framework, (2) components, (3) current architectural views, (4) future architectural views, (5) a plan for managing the ongoing transition between these views, and (6) vertical threads that effect the architecture at all levels.

Documentation, as organized through an EA framework, provides standardized, hierarchical views of the enterprise from an integrated strategy, business, and technology perspective, as is shown in Figure 5-1.

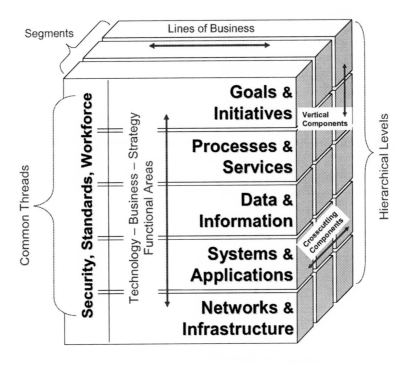

Figure 5-1: EA³ Cube Documentation Framework

The Origin of Frameworks

Information modeling and documentation frameworks emerged during the era of mainframe computing as data, software, and hardware requirements became more complex and multifaceted, and as the types of end-users increased and their locations became more distant. Reflecting the nature of that era, most early architectures were technically-oriented, often vendor and/or product-specific. Vendors of software and hardware products increasingly touted their own proprietary solutions, standards, and product lines under the banner of information or systems architectures. While this vendor-driven approach to architecture did serve to advance the capability of computing in general, it also created significant incompatibility problems for enterprises that operated a collection of IT products from multiple vendors.

In addition to the issue of product incompatibility, there was a focus on developing and operating individual information systems versus the creation of an overall IT capability within an enterprise. Furthermore, systems-level IT planning grew out of an approach to analysis and design that focused on meeting a specific set of requirements within the enterprise. For example, many enterprises introduced IT in response to a perceived need for automated support for accounting, payroll, and administrative business functions. This often grew to include manufacturing, service, and sales support. In most cases, each of these business requirements were met by individual system solutions based on proprietary vendor approaches and products. The result was a heterogeneous collection of IT resources that independently supported business areas, but could not exchange information outside of a particular system or business area. It was this scenario that gave rise to terms like "stovepipe systems" and "islands of computing capability."

This scenario was increasingly problematic to enterprises that sought to share information between lines of business and support functions. Further, the duplication in systems capability and cost of operating and maintaining a myriad of independent systems became a focal point for improvement. A desire to create interoperability, reduce costs, and increase capability was the organizational driver that changed things.

During the mid-1970's and 1980's this change came in two main areas: database and network design. First, an approach to information systems analysis and design that was based on the enterprise's information requirements came about through the introduction of standardized methods for modeling data, structure, and process. Second, the era of distributed client-server computing came into being as "dumb" mainframe terminals began to be replaced by "smart" desktop computers that could be networked in a client-server design that reached throughout an enterprise.

In the first area, an approach to database design, now known as the "structured" approach, was developed for modeling the processing and structure of data. Data Flow Diagramming (DFD) techniques allowed enterprises to identify how an information system would process data in support of a business function. The Entity-Relationship Diagram (ERD) technique allowed analysts to identify the types of data items that an enterprise wanted to collect along with the attributes and relationships of those data items. Through these two analysis methods, enterprises could design more efficient and capable "relational" databases that used procedural programming languages (e.g., COBOL, FORTRAN, C) which were capable of serving multiple information systems and business processes. Further, this shifted the analysis and design focus from proprietary solutions to generic information requirements.

In the second area, the movement from mainframe to distributed computing also served to change the way that information systems and networks were designed. While structured information modeling techniques promoted new relational database designs, networked computing promoted the hosting of these databases in multiple locations on smaller computer "servers" that could be located closer to the end-user. Information systems standards based on international and industry agreements emerged, as did new designs for the hosting and transport of the information. Important examples include the Open Systems Interconnection (OSI) Reference Model for information networks that was proposed by J.D. Day and H. Zimmerman in 1983.[10] This model has seven layers that address services, interfaces, and protocols. In 1974 the Transport Communications Protocol/Internet Protocol (TCP/IP) was proposed by Vinton Cerf and Robert Kahn [11] that led to work on a dedicated data network that connected universities and selected military and business enterprises throughout the nation (known as the ARPANET). The acceptance of TCP/IP on a broad scale in the late 1980's and early 1990's promoted the integration of telecommunications and data network infrastructures and provided the catalyst for the dramatic growth of the global Internet. Other standards for data transfer emerged in the late 1980's and early 1990's including a standard that defined "Ethernet" local area networks and 'Asynchronous Transport Mode' (ATM) networks that promoted integrated voice, data, and video transmission.

---

[10] Day, J.D., and Zimmermann, H. "The OSI Reference Model." *Proceedings of the IEEE*. Volume 71, pages 1334-1340. December 1983.
[11] Cerf, V. and Kahn, R. "A Protocol for Packet Network Interconnection." *IEEE Transactions on Communication*. Volume COM-22, pages 637-648. May 1974.

Data hosting also changed as developments in computer micro processors, hard drive storage, removable disk storage, and telecommunications interfaces all made the desktop computer, also known as the personal computer (PC), a viable candidate to support print, file, and application hosting functions. Since the early 1980's the performance capability of PCs has risen dramatically each year, while the cost of PCs has dropped. This dynamic boosted the movement away from mainframe computing to networked computing based on 'client' and 'server' PCs working together to share data and applications. Standardized approaches to application development began to emerge as a result, along with protracted competitive battles among vendors to develop products that would dominate in the new networked computing environment.

The early 1990's also saw the introduction of a new approach to designing databases. Focusing on the problem of separating structure from process in modeling relational databases, an "object-oriented" approach was developed that took advantage of new programming languages (i.e., Java, C++) that could support data objects that had attributes and behaviors. Additionally, these data objects could encapsulate (prohibit changes to) certain areas of their code to protect them from alteration. This was significant in that objects then represented reusable code whose quality in key areas was assured. Finally, the non-encapsulated areas of code offered users the ability to customize or add attributes and behaviors such that objects became a reliable and flexible building block for application and database development.

It was in this time that some of the first writing on information architecture frameworks began to emerge. In 1987 Dennis Mulryan and Richard Nolan wrote about "Undertaking and Architecture Program" [12] and in 1991 Brandt Allen and Andrew Boynton wrote an article entitled "Information Architecture: In Search of Efficient Flexibility." [13] In 1989 and 1992, John Zachman published seminal articles in the IBM Systems Journal about an idea for an Information Systems Architecture (ISA) that served to organize the documentation of information hierarchically and by function. [14] [15]

---

[12] Richard Nolan & Dennis Mulryan. "Undertaking an Architecture Program." *Stage by Stage.* Volume 7, Number 2. March/April 1987. Note: Nolan later introduced the concept of the "Balanced Scorecard" for use in IT strategic planning (with Richard Kaplan).
[13] Brandt Allen & Andrew Boynton. "Information Architecture: In Search of Efficient Flexibility." *MIS* Quarterly. December 1991.
[14] Zachman, 1989.

Zachman's work served to elevate the discussion of architectures to the level of the enterprise and stimulated additional writing on enterprise-wide information architectures that was to continue throughout the 1990s. In 1992, Steven Spewak built upon Zachman's work and developed the concept of 'Enterprise Architecture Planning' (EAP).[16] The EAP method represented a distinct departure from the technically-oriented architectures of previous years, as it focused on how IT would be used to support business functions on an enterprise-wide (enterprise) basis. It is the combined work of John Zachman and Steven Spewak that form the basis of most of the enterprise architecture frameworks that are in use today throughout business and government, including the EA³ Cube framework introduced in this book.

Examples of Enterprise Architecture Frameworks

The Zachman ISA Framework (1987 and 1992)

In the mid-1980's John Zachman observed that the data processing requirements of many of his IBM clients were becoming more complex. There was a need to show information systems from several perspectives that addressed this complexity and promoted planning, design, and configuration management. Zachman drew from both the aircraft and construction industries in developing a highly intuitive and comprehensive schema for documenting information systems architecture (ISA) in the context of several hierarchical perspectives characteristics. Zachman's ISA framework is a schema with rows and columns that functions much like a relational database in that he calls for the development of basic or "primitive" architectural artifacts for each of the 30 cells in the schema, such that none of these artifacts are repeated in other cells or combined to create what Zachman calls "composite" products. By documenting the ISA (now known as the Zachman EA Framework) in detail at each level of the EA framework, an enterprise develops multiple views of their information systems that are useful to senior executives, line managers, and support staff. Further, Zachman's approach addresses the what, how,

---

[15] John Zachman and J. Sowa. "Extending and Formalizing the Framework for Information Systems Architecture." *IBM Systems Journal.* Vol.31, No. 3. 1992.
[16] Spewak, 1992. Note: the Foreword of his book was written by John Zachman.

where, who, when, and why questions about an information system. Figure 5-2 provides the original Zachman ISA Framework.

	Data (What)	Function (How)	Network (Where)	People (Who)	Time (When)	Motivation (Why)
Scope (Contextual)	List of Things Important to the Business	List of Processes the Business Performs	List of Locations in Which the Business Operates	List of Organizations Important to the Business	List of Events/Cycles Important to the Business	List of Business Goals/Strategies
Enterprise Model (Conceptual)	Semantic Model	Business Process Model	Business Logistics System	Work Flow Model	Member Schedule	Business Plan
System Model (Logical)	Logical Data Model	Application Architecture	Distributed System Architecture	Human Interface Architecture	Processing Structure	Business Rule Model
Technology Model (Physical)	Physical Data Model	System Design	Technology Architecture	Presentation Architecture	Control Structure	Rule Design
Detailed Representations (Out of Context)	Data Definition	Program	Network Architecture	Security Architecture	Timing Definition	Rule Expectation
Functioning Enterprise	Data	Function	Network	People	Time	Motivation

Figure 5-2: The Zachman Framework

Since 1992, John Zachman has gone on to influence a number of different EA frameworks and writings on the EA, including the author's EA^3 framework and this textbook. While the basic ISA approach is evident in the current Zachman EA Framework, many new concepts have been addressed such as how IT security is an implicit element in each cell's artifact(s). Zachman has written a number of papers that are available through his website (www.zifa.com) on how his approach to EA addresses a number of old and new issues and how it is used in current work with organizations worldwide. See Appendix B (Figure B-11) for mappings of other EA approaches to the Zachman Framework.

The Spewak EA Planning Method (1992)

About the time that John Zachman was releasing his second article to expand the original ISA Framework, Steven Spewak was further extending these ideas into a planning-oriented framework that incorporated new features including a focus on business, an implementation approach that includes principles and values, a migration strategy, and ties to project management. Spewak was the Chief Architect for DHL Systems Inc. at the time of developing his "Enterprise Architecture Planning" (EAP) method. He was also the first person to prominently feature the term "enterprise" in his framework as a way to emphasize the need for architecture to move beyond individual systems planning. Spewak's definition of the term architecture is as follows:

> *"Since the aim of EAP is to enable an enterprise to share data, the term enterprise should include all areas that need to share substantial amounts of data. A good and proper scope for enterprise often equates to a business unit, division, or subsidiary because such enterprise units include all of the business functions for providing products and services to customers. Also, with responsibility and control of the bottom line, the economic benefits and justification of EAP can more easily be established".* [17]

Spewak states that EAP is a method for developing the top two levels of Zachman's Framework. The seven phases of EAP are grouped into a four-layer "wedding cake" shaped model that crates an implementation sequence, as is shown in Figure 5-3 on the next page.

---

[17] Spewak, 1992.

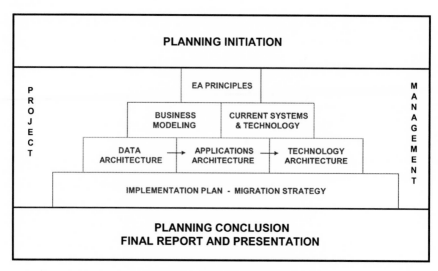

Figure 5-3: The Spewak Enterprise Architecture Planning Approach

The EA³ Cube Framework (2004)

A generalized framework for EA documentation is introduced in this book, which can be used in both the public and private sectors. The concepts used in the "EA³ Cube" framework (EA³) are founded on the works of Talcott Parsons, James Thompson, John Zachman, Steven Spewak, and the creators of the FEAF. The EA³ framework employs the generic shape of a cube, to show multiple vertical levels that are different EA documentation areas; multiple layers of depth that are distinct activity areas – referred to as lines-of-business; and multiple sub-cubes at each level that represent plug-and-play EA components.

Enterprises can implement the EA³ framework directly, or can use it as an initial baseline for the development of their own EA management and documentation approach. Many enterprises will most likely need to modify certain elements of the EA³ framework to fit their particular needs, which is encouraged as it is recognized that business, government, military, non-profit, and academic enterprises have fundamentally different cultures, economic drivers, and critical success factors. These differences may require adjustments in the framework in order to best implement an EA program that captures the current and future business and technology environment.

Common characteristics of most EA frameworks that the EA³ framework captures are that they address multiple, often hierarchical views of the enterprise and technology, and that they support integrated systems planning and implementation. The EA³ Cube framework serves primarily to organize IT resource planning and documentation activities. The framework is hierarchical to distinguish high-level views that are of value to executives and planners from the more detailed views that are of value to line managers and support staff. Figure 5-4 shows the design and key features of the EA³ framework.

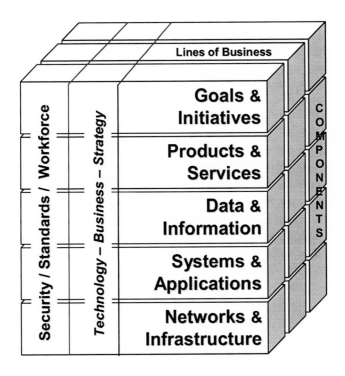

Figure 5-4: The EA³ "Cube" Documentation Framework

Hierarchical Levels of the EA³ Cube Framework

The five levels of the EA³ framework are hierarchical and integrated so that separate sub-architectures are not needed to reflect different levels or functional areas of the enterprise. The architectural areas covered at each level are arranged to position high-level strategic goals at the top, general business services and information flows in the middle, and specific support applications and the network infrastructure at the bottom. In this way alignment can be shown between strategy, information, and technology, which aids planning and decision-making.

Goals and Initiatives. This is the driving force behind the architecture. The top level of the EA³ framework identifies the strategic direction, goals, and initiatives of the enterprise and provides clear descriptions of the contribution that IT will make in achieving these goals. Strategic planning begins with a clear statement of the enterprise's purpose and/or mission, complimented by a succinct statement of the vision for success. This is followed by descriptions of the strategic direction the enterprise is taking, scenarios that could occur, as well as the competitive strategy that will ensure not only survivability, but success in terms that the enterprise must define. These overarching statements are then supported through the identification of goals and supporting initiatives that include measurable outcomes and performance measures.

Products and Services. This is the architecture's intended area of primary influence. The second level of the EA³ framework identifies the business products services of the enterprise and the contribution of technology to support those processes. The term 'business service' is used to mean processes and procedures that accomplish the mission and purpose of the enterprise, whether that is to compete in the private sector, provide public services, educate, provide medical services, or provide a defense capability. Strategic planning helps to direct and prioritize the various business services and product delivery activities in an enterprise to ensure that they are collectively moving the enterprise in the strategic direction that is set out in the Strategic Plan. Business services then need to be modeled in their current state and if change is anticipated, also modeled in the envisioned future state. Business services and product delivery processes should be eliminated if they are not adding sufficient value to the enterprise's strategic goals and initiatives. Business services and product delivery activities should be modified if change can increase value to the enterprise, be it a minor adjustment or a major shift in how that activity is accomplished. Technology is often a key enabling element in increasing value, but should not be the driving factor in the reengineering or improvement of business services and product delivery processes. It is important to review and adjust the process before IT is applied to ensure that optimal value and efficiency are achieved.

Data and Information. Optimizing data and information exchanges is the secondary purpose of the architecture. The third level of the EA³ framework is intended to document how information is currently being used by the enterprise and how future information flows would look. This level can be reflected through an IT Strategy document that ties into the enterprise's Strategic Plan and/or Business Plan. The purpose of the IT strategy is to establish a high-level approach for gathering, storing, transforming, and disseminating information throughout the enterprise. The use of concepts such as knowledge management, data mining, information warehouses, data marts, and web portals can be organized through the IT strategy. The design and functioning of databases throughout the enterprise are also documented at this level as are standards and formats for data, data dictionaries, and repositories for reusable information objects.

Systems and Applications. The fourth level of the EA³ framework is intended to organize and document the current group of information systems, and applications that the enterprise uses to deliver IT capabilities. Depending on changes at the upper levels of the EA³ framework (Business services or Information Flows) there may be planned changes to systems/applications that must be reflected in the architecture's future views. This area of the EA³ framework is also where components are a prominent feature in service-oriented architectures, as increasingly interoperable commercial applications are available to enterprises (e.g., J2EE and .NET industry standards). Large, modular applications can handle entire lines of business and/or back office functions (i.e., financial systems, manufacturing control systems, and supply chain management systems). Often referred to as Enterprise Resource Planning (ERP) systems, these commercial applications may offer modules of functionality that can be customized to allow an enterprise to reduce the overall number of applications that they operate and maintain. While ERP systems rarely provide all of the functionality that an enterprise needs for business functions and administrative support, this modular approach is reflective of a "plug-and-play" strategy that enterprises can adopt at this level of the EA³ framework to increase interoperability and reduce costs.

Networks and Infrastructure. This is the backbone of the architecture. The fifth and bottom level of the EA³ framework is intended to organize and document current and future views of the voice, data, and video networks that the enterprise uses to host systems, applications, websites, and databases. This level also documents the infrastructure of the enterprise (e.g. buildings, server rooms, capital equipment). Local Area Networks (LANs), Wide Area Networks (WANs), System Application Networks (SANs), Intranets, Extranets, Wireless Networks are all organized and documented at this level so that efficient designs can be implemented through the future architecture that reduce duplication, increase cost and performance efficiency, and promote availability and survivability. Often, an enterprise will determine that certain IT capabilities are critical to the success of the enterprise, and in these areas the architecture should reflect redundant resources in different locations such that these capabilities could continue to be available if the primary resource became unavailable.

Lines of Business within the EA³ Cube Framework

A Line of Business (LOB) is a distinct area of activity within the enterprise. LOB can also be referred to as 'vertical' mission areas. It may involve provision of services, product development/delivery, or internal administrative functions. Each LOB has a complete architecture that includes all five hierarchical levels of the EA³ framework. The LOB therefore can in some ways stand alone architecturally within the enterprise, except that duplication in data, applications, and network functions would occur if each LOB were truly independent, and crosscutting activities that reduce this duplication would not be represented. There may be cases where an enterprise would want to incrementally develop their EA due to cost or other considerations, and architecting individual LOBs is one way to do this. The LOB architectures then must be tied together so that the EA correctly represents the entire enterprise, which is what is needed for the EA to be of maximum value to executives, management, and staff.

Crosscutting Components within the EA³ Cube Framework

To avoid the inefficiencies of duplicative support within LOBs, crosscutting business and technology components are established to provide common service and product delivery capabilities, databases, application suites, and network infrastructures. Crosscutting IT services are aimed at reducing application hosting costs, increasing the sharing of information, and enabling enterprise-wide infrastructure solutions. Examples of crosscutting IT initiatives include email service, administrative services, telephone service, video teleconferencing facilities, and computer server rooms.

Planning Threads within the EA³ Cube Framework

EA documentation includes "threads" of common activity that pervade all levels of the framework. These threads include IT-related security, standards, and workforce considerations.

IT Security. Security is most effective when it is an integral part of the EA management program and documentation methodology. A comprehensive IT Security Program has several focal areas including: information, personnel, operations, and facilities. To be effective, IT security must work across all levels of the EA framework and within all of the EA components. Chapter 11 provides more on IT security.

IT Standards. One of the most important functions of the EA is that it provides technology-related standards at all levels of the EA framework. The EA should draw on accepted international, National, and industry standards in order to promote the use of non-proprietary commercial solutions in EA components. This in turn enhances the integration of EA components, as well as better supporting the switch-out of components when needed.

IT Workforce. One of the greatest resources that an enterprise has is its people. It is therefore important to ensure that IT-related staffing, skill, and training requirements are identified at each level of the EA framework, and appropriate solutions are reflected in the future architecture. An IT Workforce Plan is perhaps the best way to articulate how human capital will be employed in enabling technology capabilities, which underlie business services and information flows.

Summary of Concepts

This chapter described how an EA framework is one of the foundational elements of an EA program and implementation methodology. The EA framework establishes the scope of the EA documentation effort, and relates the areas of the architecture together. EA frameworks were first developed in the 1980's and have evolved in the public and private sectors, as well as internationally to provide support for particular approaches to EA. The EA³ Cube framework was described in detail, as part of an overall EA methodology. Chapters 6 and 7 will provide information on how to develop current and future views of EA documentation using this framework.

Chapter 5 Questions and Exercises

1. Why does an EA implementation methodology begin with the selection of an EA framework?

2. What are some of the basic characteristics of an EA framework?

3. Why are hierarchical levels of an EA framework helpful in documenting an enterprise?

4. Why is it necessary to show current *and* future views of EA documentation?

5. How does the Spewak Enterprise Architecture Planning approach relate to the Zachman EA framework?

6. Would the Federal EA Framework be useable in private sector (business) enterprises? If so, how? If not, why?

7. Choose a medium or large size enterprise and provide the following regarding the areas of the EA^3 Cube framework:

   a. List examples of documentation from the enterprise that would be appropriate at each of the five functional levels.

   b. List examples of documentation from the enterprise that would be appropriate for the three common planning threads.

   c. List examples of documentation from the enterprise that would illustrate Lines of Business.

   d. List examples of documentation from the enterprise that would illustrate crosscutting and vertical EA components.

Chapter 6

Components and Artifacts

Chapter Overview

Chapter 6 defines and describes EA components and artifacts within the context of an EA framework. Using the EA^3 framework as an example, EA components are replaceable elements within the framework that come and go with changes in strategy, business services, and new designs for resources involving information flows, applications, networks and other infrastructure. Descriptions are provided of example EA components at each level of the framework. Appendix E gives examples of each artifact.

Key Term: *EA Component*
EA components are those 'plug-and-play' changeable resources that provide capabilities at each level of the framework. Examples include strategic goals and initiatives; business services; information flows and data objects; information systems, web services, and software applications; voice/data/video networks, cable plants, equipment, and buildings.

Key Term: *EA Artifact*
An EA artifact is a documentation product, such as a text document, diagram, spreadsheet, briefing slides, or video clip. EA artifacts document EA components.

Learning Objectives

> ➤ Understand what EA components are and their role in an EA framework.

> ➤ Understand how EA artifacts describe EA components.

> ➤ See examples of EA components and artifacts throughout an EA framework.

> ➤ Understand how management views help executives understand EA components.

Introduction

While an EA framework provides an overall structure for modeling the enterprise's business and technology operating environment, EA components are the working elements of the framework at each level. In other words, EA components are "building blocks" that create discrete parts of the overall IT operational capability. EA artifacts describe EA components.

> *Home Architecture Analogy:* EA components are like the rooms of the house. Rooms can be added, remodeled, or taken away. EA documentation products are the description of each room, and can include statements, stories, pictures, and/or videos.

Discussion

EA components are the active elements of the enterprise's business and technology operating environment. EA components include IT-related strategic goals and initiatives, supply chains, information systems, software applications, knowledge warehouses, databases, websites, and voice/data/video networks, and the security solution. These EA components should function together to create a robust and seamless IT operating environment that effectively supports the enterprise's business needs. Availability, reliability, security, scalability, and cost effectiveness are key performance measurement areas for the general IT operating environment. These areas apply to each EA component, along with measures for integration and reuse.

EA artifacts are types of documentation that describe components, including reports, diagrams, charts, spreadsheets, video files, and other types of recorded information. High-level EA artifacts are often text documents or diagrams that describe overall strategies, programs, and desired outcomes. Mid-level EA artifacts are documents, diagrams, charts, spreadsheets, and briefings that describe organizational processes, ongoing projects, supply chains, large systems, information flows, networks, and web sites. Low-level EA artifacts describe specific applications, data dictionaries, technical standards, interfaces, network components, and cable plants. When these EA artifacts are harmonized through the organizing taxonomy of the EA framework, new and more useful views of the functioning of EA components are generated. This is one of the greatest values of EA as a documentation process… creation of the ability to see a hierarchy of views of the enterprise that can be examined from several perspectives.

For example, by recognizing that EA components are the building blocks of the an EA framework, and that most IT hardware and software is now commercially procured (versus being custom developed in-house), the stage has been set for a "plug-and-play" approach to IT support that must be reflected at all levels of the EA framework. Figure 6-1 provides examples of EA components and artifacts at each level of the EA[3] framework.

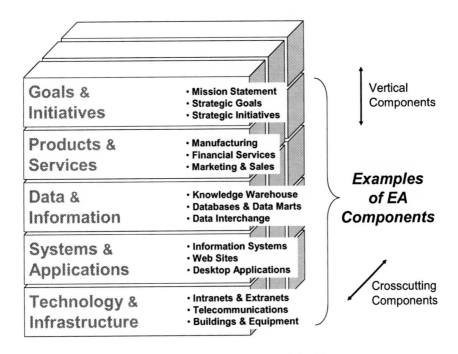

Figure 6-1: EA Components and Artifacts

The following are detailed descriptions of EA components at each level of the EA[3] framework. A more detailed description of the current view of EA components and artifacts is provided in Chapter 8, and a description of the future view of these components/artifacts is provided in Chapter 9. Appendix E provides detailed examples of each type of artifact.

EA Components at the Goals and Initiatives Level

EA Components:
- *Strategic Plan*
- *E-Commerce/E-Government Plan*

EA Artifacts:
- *Strategic Plan (S-1)*
- *SWOT Analysis (S-2)*
- *Concept of Operations Scenario (S-3)*
- *Concept of Operations Diagram (S-4)*
- *Balanced Scorecard™ (S-5)*

Large, complex enterprises often require a formalized approach to planning that accounts for changing conditions, participants, and goals. An enterprise's purpose and direction, as well as its approach to leveraging resources, are documented at the strategic 'Goals and Initiatives' level of the framework. Strategic Plans should be viewed as "living documents" which are updated periodically and which help an enterprise understand itself and adapt to changing conditions. Strategic Plans almost never are implemented without changes to the original version, because unforeseen internal and/or external events make elements of the plan unfeasible or sub-optimal for ensuring survival and maximizing success. The value of strategic planning is more in the process than in the product. By having a rational, repeatable process for dealing with the chaos and complexity of many operating environments, enterprises can better and more rapidly set a direction and goals in a formal plan that provides a common referent. The plan can be then modified periodically in response to changes in the environment.

The two EA components at this level are (1) the Strategic Plan, and (2) E-Commerce or E-Government Plan. EA artifacts at this level are the mission and vision statements, scenarios, strategies, goals, and initiative measures that are developed through the strategic planning process. While the basic mission, purpose, and/or direction of an enterprise may change infrequently; the scenarios, goals, initiatives, and measures are the flexible components of the process that can be changed as needed to reflect new mission areas, market opportunities, competitor actions, laws and regulations, economic conditions, resource constraints, and/or management priorities.

Strategic Plan

Strategic planning produces a high-level view of the direction that an enterprise sets for itself. This direction is further articulated in long-range scenarios, strategies, goals, and initiatives that serve as the baseline for short-term tactical (operational) planning that is updated annually. Strategic Plans for enterprises in dynamic and/or highly competitive environments should look three to five years into the future and be updated annually. Strategic Plans for enterprises in more stable environments should look five to ten years into the future and be updated approximately every three years.

A Strategic Plan is a composite EA artifact that should guide the enterprise's direction over a 3-5 year period in the future by providing the following items, each of which are primitive (basic) EA artifacts. Full versions of abbreviated primitive artifacts are separate artifacts.

- Provide a <u>Mission Statement</u> and a <u>Vision Statement</u> that succinctly captures the purpose and direction of the enterprise.

- Develop a <u>Statement of Strategic Direction</u> that fits the enterprise's purpose, ensures survivability, allows for flexibility, and promotes competitive success. This statement is a detailed description of where the enterprise intends to go.

- Summarize the results of a <u>SWOT Analysis</u> that is based on the statement of strategic direction and which identifies the enterprise's strengths, weaknesses, opportunities, and threats. The full SWOT analysis is artifact S-2.

- Summarize the situation and planning assumptions for several 'Concept of Operations' <u>CONOPS Scenarios</u> that support the enterprise's strategic direction. This summary should include *one current scenario* that describes at a high-level the coordination of ongoing activities in each line of business, as well as *several future scenarios* that account for different combinations of internal and external drivers identified through the SWOT Analysis. The complete scenarios are artifact S-3.

- Develop a CONOPS Graphic that in a single picture captures the essence of and participants in the current operating scenario. This graphic is artifact S-4.

- Develop a <u>General Competitive Strategy</u> for the enterprise that incorporates the current and future CONOPS scenarios and moves the enterprise in the intended strategic direction in a way that and address internal/external drivers such as culture, line of business requirements, market conditions, competitor strategies, and risk.

- Identify <u>Strategic Goals</u> that will accomplish the competitive strategy, and specify the executive sponsors who are responsible for achieving each goal.

- Identify <u>Strategic Initiatives</u> and resource sponsors for the initiatives, which are the ongoing programs or development projects that will accomplish each Strategic Goal.

- Summarize <u>Outcome Measures</u> for each Strategic Goal and Initiative, using the Balanced Scorecard™ or similar approach. The full scorecard is artifact S-5.

Because some of these areas will contain sensitive information that the enterprise will want to protect from its competitors, the full Strategic Plan should be written for internal use by decision-makers. A generalized version can then be developed for external distribution.

By using proven approaches to developing the Strategic Plan, such as the "Balanced Scorecard," enterprises are able to identify IT-related goals for the enterprise that support overall strategic goals, as well as initiatives for achieving those goals and measures for tracking progress within each initiative. Figure 6-2 shows these relationships.

Mission Statement		
Vision Statement		
Strategic Plan		
Strategic Goal #1		
Intended Outcome (s)		
Initiative 1-1	IT Component	Performance Measure(s)
Initiative 1-2	IT Component	Performance Measure(s)
Initiative 1-3	IT Component	Performance Measure(s)
Strategic Goal #2		
Intended Outcome (s)		
Initiative 2-1	IT Component	Performance Measure(s)
Initiative 2-2	IT Component	Performance Measure(s)
Initiative 2-3	IT Component	Performance Measure(s)
IT Implementation and Support Strategy		

Figure 6-2: Relationship of Strategic Level Artifacts

Mission Statement

An enterprise's Mission Statement succinctly describes the purpose and direction of the enterprise. This statement should be long enough to get the point across but provide no detail (1-2 sentences is recommended). The Mission Statement answers the "who are we" question at the level of the entire enterprise. Examples are provided below.

Mission Statement Example – Business:

"The Acme Insurance Company provides high-quality, affordable business insurance to small business owners and farmers."

Mission Statement Example – Government:

"The Orange County Highway Department provides safe and efficient roadways and bridges for pedestrian and vehicle traffic."

Vision Statement

An enterprise's Vision Statement describes in abbreviated form the competitive strategy of the enterprise. This statement should be short and memorable. The Vision Statement answers the "how are we getting there?" question at the level of the entire enterprise. The following are examples of Vision Statements from business and government:

Vision Statement Example – Business:

"In offering unbeatable value and service, the Acme Insurance Company will be the insurance provider of choice for small business owners and farmers."

Vision Statement Example – Government:

"State-of-the art planning, execution, and responsiveness will make Orange County's roads and bridges the safest and most efficient in the State."

Vision statements are more than advertising slogans, they are meant to help members of the enterprise understand the primary direction that is being pursued, and then be able to communicate that inside and outside of the enterprise.

Strategic Direction Statement

This statement establishes the strategic direction that the enterprise will pursue during the period covered by the Strategic Plan. It builds on the statements of purpose, mission, and vision, and identifies the character of the enterprise in its envisioned future state. While protecting sensitive competitive information, the statement of strategic direction should provide a guidepost for members of the enterprise to use in understanding general expectations for their contribution to survival and competitive success. It should also promote understanding among external stakeholders such that trust and perceptions of value are increased.

SWOT Analysis

One of the earliest activities the enterprise performs in developing a strategic plan is a 'Strength, Weakness, Opportunity, Threat' (SWOT) Analysis. This analysis looks at internal and external factors to determine areas that the enterprise should focus on to increase its survivability and success, as well as areas that the enterprise should avoid, or decrease its exposure to. The results of the SWOT Analysis should be summarized in the Strategic Plan, and the full SWOT Analysis is archived in the EA Repository as a separate primitive artifact (S-2). Figure 6-3 provides an example of a way to summarize and present the results of a SWOT Analysis.

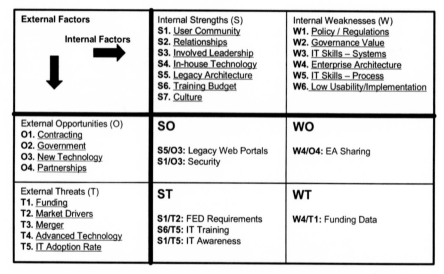

Figure 6-3: Example of a SWOT Analysis Summary Table

Concept of Operations Scenarios

Enterprises may find it helpful to develop detailed current and future 'Concept of Operations' (CONOPS) scenarios that encompass several years of operating activity, and which take into account different combinations of internal and external drivers that were identified in the SWOT Analysis. In so doing, the enterprise can evaluate the planning assumptions and expected outcomes in each scenario and evaluate the relative merit and danger of pursuing a particular course of action. Additionally, the enterprise can refine and maintain an ongoing file of information on several of the most plausible scenarios in order to be able to "bracket" a range of suitable strategies and goals for successful competition. The scenario development activity may be particularly valuable to enterprises in highly dynamic and turbulent operating environments. A summary of the scenarios and planning assumptions (matrix format) is included in the Strategic Plan, while the full version of the scenarios is a separate 'primitive' artifact (S-3). Chapter 8 provides more details on the development of future scenarios.

Concept of Operations Graphic
The CONOPS Graphic is very important to the enterprise, as it describes in one picture all of the major activities in the current CONOPS, as well as the relationship of those activities. The CONOPS graphic becomes a touchstone to help the enterprise understand what it does at a basic level.

Competitive Strategy
This area of the Strategic Plan identifies how the enterprise will achieve success in pursuing its stated strategic direction. This is done at two levels: first, a general strategy related to growth, and second, a more specific strategy related to competition and/or differentiation.

First, at a general level the enterprise establishes that it intends to grow, shrink, or stabilize. Whether it is a turnaround strategy to recover lost ground, a growth strategy to enter new markets or provide new services, or a stabilization strategy to absorb and solidify recent growth or reduction, the competitive strategy must first and foremost be flexible enough to ensure survival in the face of unplanned internal and external events, and then promote success in the goals that the enterprise decides to pursue during the period of the Strategic Plan.

Second, the competitive strategy is detailed in a statement regarding service and/or product differentiation and delivery. This area identifies one or more methods that the enterprise will pursue to achieve success in what it produces. Examples include delivering the highest quality; delivering the lowest price; having the most flexibility and/or options; being first-to-market; being a niche player; dominating market share; and acquiring competitors. These statements involve sensitive information, which the enterprise may want to hold in a separate addendum to the Strategic Plan.

Strategic Goals

The enterprise's strategic goals are those objectives that when achieved together will ensure survival and attain success, as defined in the outcome measures and performance metrics that the enterprise develops for itself. Strategic goals also serve to logically divide enterprise activities into areas that will make a meaningful and valued impact on the enterprise to move it in the direction that the Strategic Plan sets forth.

Strategic Initiatives

The enterprise's strategic initiatives are those activities which are chartered by and support strategic goals. Not all of an enterprise's activities are strategic in nature, as some activities are support functions (i.e., payroll, accounting, IT infrastructure management, and human resources). Initiatives that are strategic in nature include those ongoing programs and specific projects that accomplish one or more strategic goals. One of the questions that executive decision makers often ask when funding decisions are made for an initiative is whether there is strategic value in the planned outcome(s). Investments that have a linkage to strategic goals are said to be "aligned".

Outcome Measures

Knowing that progress is being made on strategic goals and initiatives is imperative for an enterprise's success. By definition, these are the activities that are the most important to the enterprise and therefore require regular review and refinement. By identifying goals and initiatives that can be measured, the enterprise is able to manage these activities. Measures are the most detailed EA component at the strategic level of the EA framework, and are found at each of the other levels as well.

It is important to understand the difference between "outcome" measures and "output" measures. Outcome measures identify progress being made toward some new end-state, such as better product quality, increased customer satisfaction, or more efficient processes. Output measures provide data on activities and things, such as how many cars are produced in a day, how many new customers are gained or lost each month, or how closely an activity meets a quality checklist. Outcome measures often have both quantitative and qualitative elements to them, while output measures are usually quantitative. Output measures are important for indicating progress in an initiative area, but it is the attainment of outcomes that correlate to goal attainment, and an enterprise's strategic progress. Examples of outcome and output measures are provided below.

Outcome Measure #1: Improve the factory safety environment by reducing injuries by 5 percent within one year.

Output Measure #1-1: Increase the number of safety inspections by 10 percent.
Output Measure #1-2: Require 100 percent use of safety helmets and eyewear.
Output Measure #1-3: Require accident report completion within 24 hours.

E-Commerce/E-Gov Plan

An E-Commerce/E-Government Plan is often needed by an enterprise in addition to the general Strategic Plan. This is because the general Strategic Plan usually does not address IT in sufficient detail to identify the various IT-related initiatives that may enable many of an enterprise's strategic goals. This is said in recognition that many enterprises are becoming "information centric", in that they depend on information and on IT resources to successfully accomplish key business, manufacturing, service, research, financial, human resources, and office automation functions. The E-Commerce/E-Government Plan is more like a tactical plan due to the dynamic nature of IT resources and the processes they support. The E-Commerce/E-Government Plan should provide specific program, outcome, and performance information for a two or three-year timeframe. Beyond about three years, it is difficult to predict with accuracy what new capabilities IT will be able to provide. The E-Commerce/E-Government Plan should be updated every 1-2 years.

EA Components at the Products & Services Level

EA Components:
- *Business Services*
- *Business Products*
- *IT Capital Planning Portfolio*

EA Artifacts:
- *Business Plan (B-1)*
- *Node Connectivity Diagram (B-2)*
- *Swim Lane Process Diagram (B-3)*
- *Business Process/Service Model (B-4)*
- *Business Process/Product Matrix (B-5)*
- *Use Case Narrative and Diagram (B-7)*
- *Investment Business Case (B-8)*

An enterprise's key business and support processes are documented at the Business level of the EA framework. EA components at this level include business process documentation and an IT capital planning portfolio that provides business case documentation on each investment in IT that meets operational and financial thresholds. Relationships between participants in E-Commerce and E-Government activities are often referred to as "B" for business, "G" for government, and "C" for citizen, resulting in acronyms such as B2B for business-to-business and G2C for government-to-citizen.

Business Services

Business services are those enterprise activities that directly contribute to mission accomplishment. This can be in the form of strategic initiatives to develop new or improved services or artifacts, ongoing manufacturing activities, public service delivery, and "back office" finance, accounting, administrative, and human resource functions. Business process documentation includes flow charts and modeling techniques that detail the inputs, outputs, enabling resources, and controls of an enterprise activity. It also includes the documentation of activities that completely reengineer an organizational process (called Business Process Reengineering - BPR), and activities that provide minor adjustments to a process (called Business Process Improvement - BPI).

Business Products

Business products are the tangible and intangible goods that the enterprise produces in pursuit of business and strategic goals. Examples include manufactured items, financial instruments, vehicles, structures, intellectual capital, art, music, and special events. Business product documentation is important to an enterprise as it captures and protects intellectual capital and various patent, trademark, and copyrights. Also, documentation of products is useful in BPR and BPI activities. EA artifacts that document business products contain sensitive information that should be protected when it is archived in the EA repository (see Chapter 12).

IT Capital Planning Portfolio

Because resources are limited in most enterprises, the value of making a significant investment in IT should be shown in order to identify the costs, benefits, and rate of return on capital. It may be shown in a manner to justify not using those resources on other initiatives (opportunity cost). A 'business case' for any investment is a standardized format for developing and presenting the various aspects of alternatives, cost and benefit, and return that executives are interested in. A business case should include:

- Requirement Statement
- Alternatives Analysis
- Cost-Benefit Analysis
- Net Present Value Calculation
- Return on Investment Calculation

The IT Capital Planning and Investment Control (CPIC) process is a key management activity that is designed to plan, select, control, and evaluate the enterprise's major investments in IT. The CPIC process works in concert with the EA Management Plan to move an enterprise from the current architecture to the future architecture on an ongoing basis. The use of standardized IT Project Management Plans helps make the CPIC process more efficient and more useful to project managers (see Chapter 10 for more information).

EA Components at the Data and Information Level

EA Components:
- *Knowledge Warehouses*
- *Information Systems*
- *Databases*

EA Artifacts:
- *Knowledge Management Plan (D-1)*
- *Information Exchange Matrix (D-2)*
- *Object State-Transition Diagram (D-3)*
- *Object Event Sequence Diagram (D-4)*
- *Logical Data Model (D-5)*
- *Physical Data Model (D-6)*
- *Activity/Entity (CRUD) Matrix (D-7)*
- *Data Dictionary/Object Library (D-8)*

How an enterprise uses data and information is documented at the 'Data and Information' level of the EA^3 framework. EA components at this level include documentation on the design, function, and management of information systems, databases, knowledge warehouses, and data marts. It also includes detailed documentation on the structure and processing logic of data that the enterprise is interested in.

Knowledge Warehouses

Knowledge warehouses evolved from large mainframe databases that served multiple applications and user groups across multiple systems and networks. A knowledge warehouse is a one-stop-shop for data and information about various activities and processes in the enterprise. The more types of data and information in the knowledge warehouse, the more valuable it is for analysis activities that extend beyond simple queries and report generation, but enable 'data mining' wherein all levels of the enterprise can look for patterns or new information from otherwise disparate data. This helps build new views of these activities and the enterprise.

Typically, users interact with a knowledge warehouse through a portal-like interface that enables customized access to various elements such as databases, presentations, and data, audio, and video files. A knowledge warehouse may be developed for a specific use or bought as a customizable product. Packaged versions are available from a number of vendors.

Information Systems

Information comes in three forms: data, information, and knowledge. Aggregation, meaning, and context are what differentiate each of these forms.

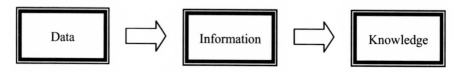

Definitions are as follows: [18]

Data: Raw facts about people, places, events, and things that are of importance in an organization.   Each fact is, by itself, relatively meaningless.

Information: Data that has been processed or reorganized into a more meaningful form for someone.   Information is formed from combinations of data that hopefully have meaning to the recipient.

---

[18] Jeffrey L. Whitten, Lonnie D. Bentley, and Kevin C. Dittman. Systems Analysis and Design Methods. McGraw-Hill/Irwin Publishers. New York. 2004. ISBN 0-07-247417-3.

<u>Knowledge</u>: Data and information that is further refined based on the facts, truths, beliefs, judgments, experiences, and expertise of the recipient. Ideally information leads to wisdom.

Information systems consist of hardware and software that work together to efficiently collect and disseminate data, as well as to enable the development and analysis of information. Information systems serve many lines of business in enterprises including administrative and financial support, manufacturing, marketing and sales, government regulation, public services, and defense systems.

Information systems originally were designed to support a particular need in an enterprise and connect to a single database. As enterprises developed more uses for information systems, greater efficiencies were achieved when several information systems shared one or more databases. This movement from "stovepipe" information system designs to more distributed and integrated designs, which span the entire enterprise and which tie together via information warehouses, is one of the driving factors in the development of the concept of enterprise architecture.

Databases

Databases are software applications that are designed to support the storage, retrieval, updating, and deletion of data elements and/or data objects. Data elements are the fundamental facts and values that are stored in databases. Data elements and their identifying and characteristic attributes are usually stored in relational databases that consist of data tables which are logically related to create a speedy, efficient, and flexible query capability. Data objects are discrete 'blocks' of code that contain attribute information about a data element as well as behaviors that create an ability for objects to interact with each other in different ways, depending on the type of triggering event.

EA Components at the Systems and Applications Level

EA Components:
- *Software Applications*
- *Web Services*
- *Service Bus and Middleware*
- *Enterprise Resource Planning (ERP) Solutions*
- *Operating Systems*

EA Artifacts:
- *System Interface Diagram (SA-1)*
- *System Communication Diagram (SA-2)*
- *System Interface Matrix (SA-3)*
- *System Data Flow Diagram (SA-4)*
- *System/Operations Matrix (SA-5)*
- *Systems Data Exchange Matrix (SA06)*
- *System Performance Matrix (SA-7)*
- *System Evolution Diagram (SA-8)*
- *Web Application Diagram (SA-9)*

The systems and applications that an enterprise uses to support its business services, product delivery processes, and information flows are documented at the 'Systems and Applications' level of the EA³ framework. One of the purposes of EA is to improve the integration and efficiency of the support systems and software applications across the enterprise. Duplication of functions and a lack of interoperability can be addressed through the establishment of technical and product standards for software. Components at this level range in size and complexity from large multi-function ERP solutions that extend throughout the enterprise to single-user desktop tools that enhance productivity.

Software Applications
Applications are software programs that provide a functional capability for "front-office" IT systems (e.g., manufacturing, sales, government services, logistics, and knowledge warehouses) or "back-office" IT systems (e.g., financial systems, human resources systems, e-mail, and office automation products such as word processors, spreadsheets, diagramming tools, photo editors, and web browsers). Enterprises often possess a myriad of applications from different vendors that are limited in their ability to function together. The selection of applications from a controlled number of vendors and/or which adhere to widely accepted standards is a method that can be used to promote the interoperability of software applications.

Web Services
Just as EA trends are emphasizing the use of plug-and-play software applications; the use of web-based IT services is significantly extending and accelerating this concept. These open-standards based web services are replacing software applications that have unique hosting and access requirements. By using the TCP/IP, SOAP, and UDDI protocols for web service management and internationally-accepted formats for information

retrieval/exchange (e.g., HTTP, HTML, J2EE, and XML), a common hosting and operating environment is created for web services. A web service is defined as any IT resource (e.g., application, program, database, or information portal) that functions through a web-based graphical user interface (GUI), such as a web browser. Web services include email, web-based ERP applications, websites, electronic commerce systems, web-based knowledge warehouses…. virtually any front or back-office function that is web-based and which operates within the enterprise on TCP/IP and SOAP compliant internal networks (Intranets). Service-Oriented Architecture (SOA) is the EA-related movement that focuses on web services.

Service Bus/Middleware
The "Service Bus" is a SOA term for a common operating environment for systems, applications, and web services that is characterized by non-proprietary open standards protocols and middleware for data exchange, software/hardware interfaces. The Service Bus is platform independent and allows any system/service to interoperate with any other system/service that is logically and physically linked to the Bus. SOA approaches promote the support of business functions through the use of shared, reusable services, which increasingly are web-based. The term that SOA approaches use for this capability is a "Virtual Enterprise Network", and the SOA term for the Service Bus is a Network Application Platform.
Middleware is a software program that links other applications together which otherwise would not be able to exchange data and information. Examples include integrating older mainframe applications and databases to those which are web-based, or enabling the sharing of data between artifacts from different vendors that may have different application programming interfaces (APIs).

Enterprise Resource Planning (ERP) Solutions
ERP solutions are marketed by vendors as one way to increase application interoperability and reduce the duplication of functions. Often based on "modules" of capability, ERPs are essentially a suite of applications offered by the same vendor that are designed to work together to create an enterprise-wide capability. ERP solutions exist for finance, marketing, human resources, payroll and accounting, and supply chain management, all of which can be interconnected to create a relatively seamless environment for sharing information. While ERPs accomplish some of the goals of EA, they fall short of providing the holistic planning, documentation, and decision-making support that EA is intended to develop and maintain. Also, ERPs normally are not able to support all of

the application requirements of the enterprise (i.e., office automation, finance and accounting, product line support, executive decision-making, e-mail). This wider yet incomplete coverage of application component requirements is one of the shortfalls of ERP solutions, which the EA program can address by establishing standards for the integration of ERP modules with other applications.

Operating Systems

Operating systems are applications that enable computers to provide basic networking and processing functions. Differences in operating systems are a large part of what distinguishes older centralized mainframe designs from newer decentralized client-server designs. Larger enterprises may operate computers that use several different types of operating systems, which may hinder the interoperability of these component resources. Commercial vendors traditionally have produced operating systems that are proprietary and are designed to limit integration to their own products; however, the proliferation of client-server network designs and the emergence of the Internet have forced vendors to offer operating systems that are increasingly interoperable.

EA Components at the Network & Infrastructure Level

EA Components:
- *Data Networks*
- *Telecommunications Networks*
- *Video Networks*
- *Cable and Wireless Backbones*
- *Security Solutions*
- *Buildings and Server Rooms*
- *Equipment*

EA Artifacts:
- *Network Connectivity Diagram (NI-1)*
- *Network Inventory (NI-2)*
- *Capital Equipment Inventory (NI-3)*
- *Building Blueprints (NI-4)*
- *Network Center Diagram (NI-5)*
- *Cable Plant Diagram (NI-6)*
- *Rack Elevation Diagram (NI-7)*

The Technology Infrastructure level of the EA^3 framework functions to integrate and connect the enterprise's IT resources at the application and information levels. Seamless integration of voice, data, video, and transport (cable/wireless) resources is one of the keys to creating an operationally effective and cost-efficient IT infrastructure.

Data Networks

Data networks are designed to transport data and information in coded digital form between various computers that support storage, retrieval, updates, and processing for end-users. These networks have a logical design that identifies how data and information will flow between systems, applications, databases, and websites. The network also has a physical design that consists of a data transmission "backbone", an information hosting environment, and external interface points (unless it is a stand-alone system). The network backbone often consists of commercially procured routers, switches, hubs, security equipment, backup power units, equipment racks, and cable. The hosted network environment includes commercially procured computers for storage, processing, and end-users, as well as commercial software for business and office automation requirements and custom-developed software that is designed to support unique requirements. Data networks within an enterprise, referred to as Local Area Networks (LANs) or Internal Networks (Intranets) normally interface with a telecommunications network to connect to the global Internet. Enterprise-specific External Networks (Extranets) are also known as Wide-Area Networks (WANS).

Telecommunications Networks

Telecommunications networks are designed to transport voice signals in coded form (analog waves or digital electron/photon flows) between end-users. These networks also have a logical design that identifies how voice signals are transported between network components and a physical design that identifies the types of equipment involved in signal processing and transmission. This includes hardware, software, cable plants, cellular/wireless nodes, microwave repeaters, and relay satellites. Telecommunications networks exist at a local level to support parts of an enterprise or an entire enterprise. These are known as "Public Business Exchange" (PBX) systems which are commercially available from a number of vendors. Telecommunications systems that are regional, national, or international in nature often involve multiple sub-networks that interface at numerous points to increase coverage, routing, and reliability. Because of the ubiquitous presence of telecommunications networks, the rapid development of the Internet on a global basis has been made possible in large part due to the conversion of voice transmission capacity to dedicated data transmission, as well as the addition of significant amounts of new capacity from existing and new commercial providers. The co-transmission of digital voice and data signals is now commonplace, and new standards have arisen to support this on most telecommunications networks (e.g., ISDN and Voice-Over-IP).

Video Networks

Video networks are designed to transport video image signals in coded form (analog waves or digital electron/photon flows) between production sites and viewing sites. Like the other types of networks, video networks have logical designs to show the flow of image signals and physical designs to identify production, transmission, and receiving equipment. National and international standards have emerged that promote the transmission and reception of video signals on a global basis. Video networks can be as small as peer-to-peer computer-based applications or video teleconferencing (VTC) equipment that operates within an enterprise or between several users, or as large as a regional, national or international television network.

As with voice networks, digital coding of video signals supports the co-transmission of this information on the same network backbone that transports voice and data. This seamless integration of voice, data, and video transmission capabilities brings new capabilities for information exchange within and between enterprises. Future architectures will often call for this type of integration, with applications and equipment that will support it.

Transmission Backbones

The transmission capability of an information network (voice, data, or video) has its foundation in connectivity between network equipment. This connectivity can be provided through various media including cables (copper or glass fiber), wireless cells (short-range radio waves), transmission towers (medium range microwaves), and/or satellite links (long-range up-link and down link of VHF, UHF, or EHF radio waves). These "backbones" of interconnectedness are what allow the electrons and/or photons to flow in a super fast stream of binary (on or off) code or in analog waves that are translated into data, voice signals, and/or video signals. Improvements in hardware, software, and cable media have allowed for the near instantaneous transmission of millions of binary elements called bits (one binary element) and bytes (a group of 8 binary elements). The ability to now transmit billions of bits and bytes of digital information has allowed for the development of sophisticated applications and databases that bring new capabilities for people and enterprises to communicate in robust ways that include information in the form of data, images, and sound.

Management Views of EA Artifacts

EA management views are high-level composite graphics that depict multiple aspects of EA components in a simplified or more attractive big-picture format than that which is normally produced by EA tools. Without management views, the basic (primitive) EA artifacts may consist primarily of technical models that do not hold the interest of EA executive sponsors and users, therefore putting the EA program at risk. The purpose of management views is to lower this risk by:

- Gaining and maintaining EA executive sponsors and resources
- Communicating high-level management-friendly views of EA
- Showing the boundaries of the enterprise being documented
- Combining EA and other IRM artifacts into actionable information for managing and decision-making

EA management views can help various types of users to both understand and share EA artifacts. For example, members of the EA team who are modeling data in several information systems can develop a management view to show how information from those systems is used between various LOBs, and in so doing gain the support of managers in those business areas. In addition, management views can help to translate EA artifacts that are in technical modeling or analytic formats into views that are easier to understand by those who are not trained in that documentation methodology.

Summary of Concepts

This chapter described the purpose of EA components and artifacts within an EA framework. Using the EA³ framework as an example, EA components were described as replaceable elements within the framework that come and go with changes in strategy, business services, and new designs for IT resources involving information flows, applications, and the technology infrastructure. Descriptions were provided of the types of EA components that exist at each level of the framework. Chapters 7 and 8 will focus on current and future views of the EA artifacts that describe EA components at all levels of the framework.

Chapter 6 Questions and Exercises

1. What are EA components and how do they relate to a framework?

2. What are EA artifacts and how do they relate to EA components?

3. What parts of an enterprise's Strategic Plan could be viewed as EA components?

4. What parts of the E-Government/E-Commerce Plan could be viewed as EA components?

5. Why can an enterprise's business services be viewed as EA components?

6. Why can an enterprise's information flows and data objects be viewed as EA components?

7. Why can an enterprise's software applications and networks be viewed as EA components?

8. What is a web service, and upon which protocols is it based?

9. Why are national and international standards important to EA components?

10. Which elements of an IT security program can be viewed as EA components?

11. List several hypothetical EA components at each level of the EA^3 framework for a large automobile manufacturing company.

    a. Compare and contrast the use of the term "component" in the context of how it is used in this chapter with the use of the term in the software and application development industry.

    b. Obtain the Annual Report of a Fortune 500 corporation and list potential EA components at each level of the EA^3 framework.

CIO Sam Young and Chief Architect Vince Albright are leading an EA Working Group through the development of architecture segments that cover several lines of business at DMC. These segments of the overall DMC enterprise architecture will help COO Kate Jarvis and CFO Jim Gorman work together as they evaluate requirements and plan solutions for new information systems. Scene 3 had covered the need for a detailed implementation methodology, and this scene describes the approach the Working Group will take in documenting the current and future views of these segments of the DMC EA.

"Thank you for coming to today's meeting of the Enterprise Architecture Working Group" said Sam. We are going to talk about the method for developing current and future views of the two segments of the company's enterprise architecture we are developing. These segments cover manufacturing and production, which are the lines of business identified by Kate and Jim that require more IT support. At the last meeting we developed the detailed implementation methodology that will guide our efforts and reduce the risk that we will not be successful. Vince Albright, our Chief Architect, will describe the documentation of current and future views."

"Thank you Sam" said Vince. "In accordance with our implementation methodology, we will be using the EA[3] framework to organize and guide the documentation of current and future views of these segments of the DMC architecture. Following the framework's structure, we will gather existing artifacts of information on the lines of business in the following order: strategic goals and initiatives, business services, information flows and data elements, systems and support services, and the network infrastructure. These documentation artifacts come in many forms including reports, policy memos, manuals, spreadsheets, briefing slides, diagrams, and video files. By organizing these artifacts in the online EA repository into categories that match the levels and areas of the framework, we can establish links between the information to produce robust new views of the lines of business. This also establishes a baseline of EA information for future planning and decision-making."

Vince continued. "As for documenting the future views, we will start by establishing several future operating scenarios with Jim, Kate and their staff members. These scenarios are short stories about possible future activities in a variety of friendly and hostile business climates. The scenarios help us to identify important planning assumptions about their future line of business activities, depending on the environment. Once the most probable scenario is selected, we will use the planning assumptions to guide discussions in our Working Group, and decisions by Jim and Kate on what they want to invest in to best position themselves for success in the future. Finally, we will identify how these decisions cause changes to the current EA at each level of the framework, and will document those changes in new artifacts that are saved in the EA repository in a separate future EA section."

Over the next several weeks, the EA Working Group gathered existing or developed new documentation artifacts for the current views of the two EA segments at each level of the EA framework. The Group then developed several future operating scenarios from which future view artifacts were developed. Chapters 7 and 8 provide more details on the development of current and future EA views.

Chapter 7

Developing Current Architecture Views

Chapter Overview

This chapter covers the development of current views of the EA, within the context of a documentation framework and implementation methodology. The current architecture is actually a collection of EA artifacts that document existing EA components throughout the enterprise. Current EA views are important to an enterprise in that they establish or verify what resources (including IT) are being used in lines of business to support the achievement of strategic goals. This becomes a reference baseline much like an inventory that then supports planning and decision-making regarding the future architecture.

Learning Objectives

 ➤ Understand how current views relate to the EA implementation methodology.

 ➤ Understand how current views relate to the EA documentation framework.

 ➤ See examples of current views of EA components and artifacts.

Introduction

The current view of the EA is intended to show the IT resources that are presently active in the enterprise's IT operating environment. This is also known as the "as-is" view of the EA. Depending on the amount of prior EA planning, these IT resources may or may not be aligned with the enterprise's strategic goals and business services. If little EA planning has occurred, then a significant amount of duplication in function may be present. As is shown in Figure 7-1, current views of the EA provide an enterprise with documentation of existing strategic goals, business services, information flows, IT systems/services, and technology infrastructure, as well as the common "thread" areas of security, standards, and workforce planning.

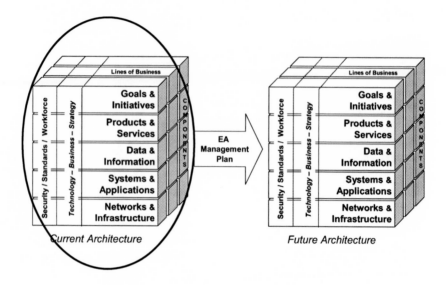

Figure 7-1: The Current Architecture

Discussion

Documentation of the current EA is important to an enterprise because it provides a set of baseline reference information/artifacts for planning and decision-making. Also, by completing the documentation of current EA components at all levels of the framework, a view of the enterprise emerges that reveals associations, dependencies, and performance gaps between the enterprise's business requirements and current capabilities. Selected examples of how artifacts showing current EA components can be developed are discussed as follows. Appendix E provides examples of all of the artifacts that are recommended in using the EA^3 Cube for documentation of an enterprise in the public or private sector..

Home Architecture Analogy: Having a completed current EA is like having a full set of blueprints for an existing home. It provides an authoritative reference source for future planning and decision-making, as well as a historical archive that may be required for audit or research purposes.

Strategic Level EA Artifacts – Current View

EA Components:
- *Strategic Plan*
- *E-Commerce or E-Government Plan*

EA Artifacts:
- ***Strategic Plan (S-1)***
- ***SWOT Analysis (S-2)***
- ***Concept of Operations Scenario (S-3)***
- ***Concept of Operations Diagram (S-4)***
- ***Balanced Scorecard™ (S-5)***

Strategic planning produces a high-level view of the direction that an enterprise sets for itself. This is documented in the general Strategic Plan and accompanying E-Commerce or E-Government Plan where the role of IT is described in more detail. The enterprise's strategic direction is further articulated in EA artifacts that include long-range scenarios, goals, and initiatives that serve as the baseline for identifying short-term tactical (operational) goals. Strategic Plans should look five to ten years into the future and be published every two to three years. The current view of strategic level artifacts should be updated only as changes to the Strategic Plan and/or E-Commerce/E-Government Plan are formally published. This preserves the authoritative nature of the artifacts at this level and represents what is currently endorsed as policy by executive leadership. These artifacts include:

Strategic Level Artifact – Current Strategic Scenario
Some enterprises choose to develop and maintain future scenarios of how the business and technology operating environment might function under different sets of internal and external influences (see Chapter 8 for more details on future scenarios). In the current view of the EA, the desired artifact related to scenario planning is the scenario that has become the current planning context for the enterprise, and contains the current planning assumptions. In other words, of the several future scenarios that are periodically developed through the strategic planning process, one eventually is selected as representing what the enterprise is going to do. When implemented, this selected future scenario becomes the current operating scenario. Periodically comparing the current strategic scenario to several potential scenarios that are maintained in the EA's future views can be a valuable strategic planning activity.

Strategic Goals

All of the enterprise's current strategic goals are artifacts that should be documented in the current EA. Of particular interest though, are IT-related strategic goals, which are those that rely on some element of IT to help to move the enterprise in the strategic direction described in each of several scenarios. These IT-related goals should be thoroughly documented in terms of related initiatives and outcome measures. These IT-related goals must meet several criteria to be of strategic value: (1) achieve some element of the enterprise's purpose, (2) result in an outcome within a scenario that is discernable and measurable, (3) not reduce the enterprise's flexibility so much that other scenarios cannot be pursued and/or threats to enterprise survival cannot be addressed, (4) have enterprise support for implementation. Examples of strategic goals that have an IT element are provided below:

"Improve global communications availability, quality, and cost." (The IT element is the voice, data, and video infrastructure).

"Improve product quality and availability" (The IT element is the data on product manufacturing, quality control, inventory levels, and retail outlet re-order levels).

Strategic Initiatives

Each strategic goal that the enterprise identifies is pursued though strategic initiatives. Initiatives include such activities as mergers and acquisitions, research and development projects, system implementation or integration projects, process redesign and improvement, new market entries, product consolidation, business alliances, and service improvement to internal and external customers. Progress in achieving strategic initiatives must be measurable so that the enterprise can manage the resources given to that initiative and know whether success has been achieved. Strong executive support, sufficient resources, and program management skills are needed for an initiative to succeed.

IT-related strategic initiatives are those which relate to IT-related strategic goals in a way that enhances information flows, improves/integrates supporting systems, services, and/or applications, or optimizes the network infrastructure.

Examples of IT-related strategic initiatives that are tied to example strategic goals are provided as follows.

Example Strategic Goal #1: *Improve marketing and sales information.*

- Strategic Initiative #1-1: *Begin sales data mart within six months.*

- Strategic Initiative #1-2: *Consolidate marketing systems in two years.*

- Strategic Initiative #1-3: *Increase customers by eight percent in a year.*

Performance Measures
Each strategic goal should be stated in a form that includes a measurable and meaningful outcome. Each supporting strategic initiative should include measurable and meaningful outcome and output measures. Outcome measures describe an intended future state. Output measures describe levels of activities or items that contribute to the attainment of an outcome.

> Example Outcome Measure: *"Improve competitiveness by being no lower than #3 in national market share across all product lines within one year."*

> Example Output Measure: *"Increase the availability of products in retail outlets by ten percent within six months."*

Business Level EA Artifacts – Current View

EA Components:
- *Supply Chains*
- *Business Processes*
- *IT Capital Planning Portfolio*

EA Artifacts:
- ***Business Plan (B-1)***
- ***Node Connectivity Diagram (B-2)***
- ***Swim Lane Process Diagram (B-3)***
- ***Business Process/Service Model (B-4)***
- ***Business Process/Product Matrix (B-5)***
- ***Use Case Narrative and Diagram (B-7)***
- ***Investment Business Case (B-8)***

Process Documentation
One method for modeling business processes is known as the Integration Definition for Function (IDEF) technique. Developed in the mid-1970's for modeling complex military projects, IDEF-0 uses Inputs, Controls,

Outputs, and Mechanisms (ICOM) to show the parts of an activity within an enterprise, as is illustrated in Figure 7-2.

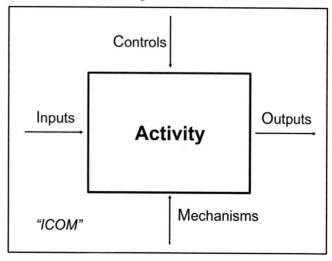

Figure 7-2: IDEF-0 Activity Modeling

<u>Inputs</u>:   Items that initiate/trigger the activity and are transformed, consumed, or become part.

<u>Controls</u>: Guide or regulate the activity; usually indicate when/ how a process will be performed.

<u>Outputs</u>: The results produced by the activity; the reason for which the process was performed.

<u>Mechanisms</u>: Systems, people, and equipment used to perform the activity.

IDEF-0 activity modeling is suitable for business process documentation in that it provides both high level context views, and more detailed views of each step in the activity in a format that can be further decomposed and interrelated with other processes to show linkages. IDEF-0 modeling is useful in showing linkages between steps in a process as well as internal external influences, but does not indicate a particular time sequence for the overall set of activities.

Another method for showing business processes is a "swim lane" diagram that shows activities in horizontal rows, so as to identify areas of responsibility for those activities. Figure 7-3 provides an example of a swim lane diagram.

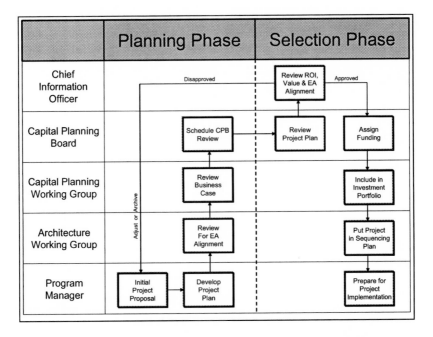

Figure 7-3: Example "Swim Lane" Diagram of a Process

In this example of a swim lane diagram, the various stakeholders in an enterprise's IT Capital Planning and Investment Control (CPIC) process are shown during the Planning and Selection Phases. See Chapter 10 for more details on the CPIC process.

A third method for showing business processes is a traditional flow diagram that includes events, decision-points, and sequenced flows of the activities and decision points in a business process. Figure 7-4 on the next page provides an example of a flow diagram of a simple business process.

The drawback of flow diagrams, in comparison to IDEF models is that the regulatory controls on inputs/outputs are not shown, nor are the mechanisms that are needed to perform the activity.

The drawback of flow diagrams, in comparison to swim lane diagrams is that the particular roles of the various participants in the process are not identifiable.

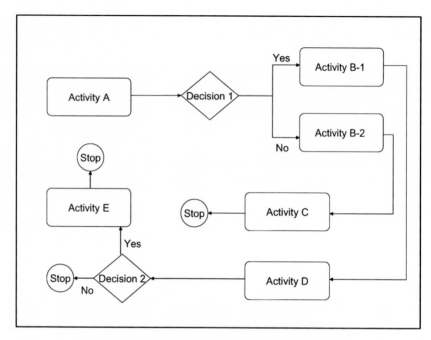

Figure 7-4: Business Process Flow Diagram

It is important for an enterprise to maintain descriptions and models of all of its key business services. This not only aids in reengineering and improvement activities, but also supports design and analysis work related to business process reengineering/improvement activities, as well as the development of future architecture views.

Business Level Artifact – Project Management Plans

The Project Management Plan (PMP) is a standard format document used by project managers, project sponsors, and the project team to improve the conceptualization, documentation, tracking, oversight, and execution of project work throughout the enterprise. The PMP should be used in new IT system, application, database, or infrastructure projects, as well as upgrade efforts in the same areas. In small-scale, quick-turnaround projects some of the elements of the PMP can be minimized, but none should be eliminated. By establishing project documentation in each area of the PMP, project managers will have more control over cost, schedule, and performance goals, and the resultant IT resource is more likely to add value to the enterprise by being in alignment with strategic direction, investment policy, and architecture.

The PMP should be tailored to identify the business need being addressed by the project as well as how the project will be accomplished. The amount of information and level of detail included in the sections of the PMP should be determined by program characteristics such as size, complexity, and enterprise. It is important to include supporting documents in appropriate sections of the PMP, such as the IT Strategic Plan, a Work Breakdown Structure, business case documentation, the Technical Standards Reference Model, training plans, and test plans.

The PMP documents the overall management concept and approach used to achieve program objectives. The project manager prepares and issues the PMP during the Planning Phase of the capital planning process (See Chapter 10). The PMP is the common link between the Project Manager and all others involved in the project. The Project Manager uses the PMP to schedule and direct the entire system development process, while higher levels of authority use the PMP as a baseline for planning activities. Many participants may see a project only via a PMP. The PMP should be updated at each project milestone as a prerequisite for proceeding to the next phase in the project life cycle. At a minimum, the PMP should cover the following areas (additional details are provided in Chapter 10):

- Executive Summary
- Project Requirements
- Strategic Alignment
- Architectural Alignment
- Business Case
- Project Controls
- Project Enterprise
- Security and Privacy
- Appendices

Business Cases
A business case is an analysis of the requirements and value of making a particular investment. In the context of EA, developing a business case for investments in IT helps to ensure that maximum value is generated from new development projects, as well as ongoing operations and maintenance activities. In addition, the routine development and review of business cases for IT investments helps to promote strategic alignment and architectural alignment such that the

components and products of an EA are more integrated (Appendix A contains an example business case from the DMC Case Study).

There are six areas to an investment business case: (1) statement of the requirement, (2) an alternatives analysis, (3) a cost-benefit analysis, (4) a risk analysis, (5) a calculation of the return on the investment "ROI," and (6) selection of an alternative with comments and recommendations on implementation.

Statement of the Requirement: This part of the business case clearly and succinctly establishes what the business requirement is, and should avoid making any recommendation on solutions, including technology. This part of the business case should describe the current situation and what need is not being met (a gap in performance).

Alternatives Analysis: This analysis looks at several (preferably three or more) alternatives to meeting a business requirement. The requirement may be to upgrade an existing component in the EA, develop a new component, or for the provision of support services such as help desk or systems administration functions. The alternatives can differ in the recommended process, technical solution, type of personnel to be employed, facilities to be used, etc. The chosen alternatives should represent the full scope of options that could be used to meet the requirement. One of the alternatives can be the "status quo" which recommends doing nothing different from what the current situation is.

Cost-Benefit Analysis: This analysis identifies and compares the costs and benefits of each alternative for meeting an IT requirement. Costs include the total of direct and indirect expenses incurred. Benefits include those that are tangible (measurable) and intangible (not directly measurable). The benefits must exceed costs for an alternative to be viable and should add significant value to the enterprise.

Risk Analysis: This analysis identifies the risk for each alternative. Risk is the identification of sources of uncertainty in a project and/or obstacles to success. Areas of risk for IT projects include being the first adopter of a new technology, budget reductions, loss of key personnel, insufficient testing or training, and schedule delays. "Mitigating" risk is the term commonly used to refer to the strategy identified to lower the probability that a particular risk will occur. Risk mitigation strategies should reduce uncertainty, prevent obstacles to success, or provide responses to overcome obstacles should they occur. An example of this is to have trained back-ups for key positions, or using open standards products to avoid being locked into one vendor.

Return on Investment: This "ROI" calculation is done for each alternative and is calculated by dividing total quantified benefits (in dollars) by total quantified costs (in dollars). It is the percentage return on the originally invested capital. For multiple year calculations, the ROI should be discounted using Net Present Value (NPV) methods. NPV discounts future levels of funding in order to take into consideration inflation and other rising costs over the lifecycle of the alternative (e.g., a 3% discount factor is applied each year). ROI is calculated as a percentage by dividing quantified benefits in dollars by quantified costs in dollars over the total lifecycle of the alternative. ROI is one of the factors that executives use to determine the merit of investing in a proposed project and also to compare that merit to other investments/projects that cannot be done if that particular alternative is implemented (opportunity cost). Enterprises often establish a minimum acceptable ROI level in order to enforce evaluating the "opportunity cost" of the investment, which considers whether the amount equal to the cost of the IT investment would be better spent on another investment. Some IT investments can produce very high ROI levels if significant savings in personnel costs and/or cycle times are achieved.

Alternative Selection Statement: This statement documents the selection of the best alternative based on all aspects of the business case. This includes types of costs, types of benefits, the risk mitigation strategy, and ROI. The rationale for selecting an alternative and rejecting others should also be documented for future reference.

Information Level EA Artifacts – Current View

EA Components:
- *Knowledge Warehouses*
- *Information Systems*
- *Databases*

EA Artifacts:
- ***Knowledge Management Plan (D-1)***
- ***Information Exchange Matrix (D-2)***
- ***Object State-Transition Diagram (D-3)***

- *Object Event Sequence Diagram (D-4)*
- *Logical Data Model (D-5)*
- *Physical Data Model (D-6)*
- *Activity/Entity (CRUD) Matrix (D-7)*
- *Data Dictionary/Object Library (D-8)*

Documenting information flows involves the development of data models that show the structure and flow of data in the enterprise's business services and supporting IT systems/services. Data can be modeled and analyzed using "traditional" and/or "object-oriented" methods, depending on how the resulting documentation is intended to be used. For example, if the intended use is with relational databases and/or third-generation procedural programming languages (i.e., C, FORTRAN, or COBOL) then the use of traditional methods (i.e., Entity-Relationship Diagrams and Data Flow Diagrams) is called for. If the intended use of data is with object-oriented databases, fourth generation object-oriented (OO) programming languages and associated object-oriented diagrams that use the Universal Modeling Language (UML) are called for (e.g.., Java, C++, ADA, and Smalltalk). This OO approach also uses what is called the Common Object Reuse Brokered Architecture (CORBA).

Data Structure and Data Flow Diagrams

Modeling Information Structure. The "traditional" approach to information systems development is based on the modeling technique called Entity Relationship Diagramming (ERD). ERDs are used by IT systems analysts and programmers to identify the "things" (data entities) that an enterprise wants IT systems to capture, as well at those external entities that a system interfaces with. ERDs also provide data entity descriptions, attributes, relationships, and the rules for the frequency of those relationships. In that enterprise architecture seeks to provide an enterprise-wide view of all IT resources, it is important that ERDs show not only what is in each system, but also how systems interface with each other. ERDs are not decomposed per se, but they can serve to show several systems, or parts of large complex systems. Figure 7-5 on the next page shows an example of an ERD diagram for a hypothetical real estate tracking system.

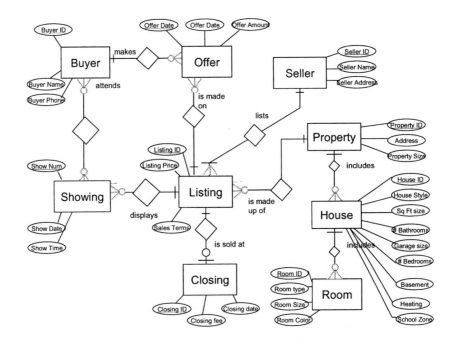

Figure 7-5: Example Entity-Relationship Diagram

Modeling Information Flows. Data and information flows are documented in traditional and object-oriented methods, depending on how the resulting documentation is intended to be used. The traditional method of documenting data flows was developed in the early 1970's and centers on the use of Data Flow Diagrams (DFDs). DFDs should reflect the processes that transform data within an information system. Transformation can involve the creation, update, deletion, or reading of data. An Entity/Activity Matrix[19] can help analysts and programmers to move from ERDs to DFDs as they design how an information system will function in support of enterprise requirements. DFDs can be decomposed from a very high "context" level, to a basic process level, to several sub-levels that examine each process in greater and greater detail. Figure 7-6 on the next page provides an example of a high-level DFD for a hypothetical highway maintenance tracking system.

---

[19] Also known as a "CRUD" matrix, as it shows how data is used in an information system as it is Created, Read, Updated, or Deleted.

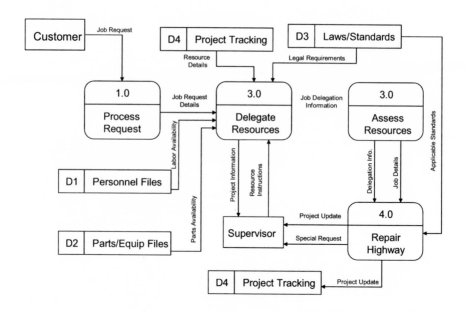

Figure 7-6: Example Data Flow Diagram

Object-Oriented (OO) approaches to modeling data structure and process together were developed in the mid-1980's by Ivar Jacobson, Grady Booch, and James Rumbaugh. Their combined efforts produced what is now known as the Uniform Modeling Language (UML). Objects are specific sequences of code in fourth generation programming languages that represent something in the business requirements domain that an IT system must create, use, or interact with. Objects are like entities in that they have a name and attributes, and link to other objects according to rules for frequency. One might say that objects "know things about themselves." Objects are unlike entities in that the code for objects also contains behaviors (also known as methods), which are triggered by events that are also identified in the code… one might say that objects also "know how to do things." Beyond knowing things about themselves and knowing how to do things, there are three defining characteristics of an object: polymorphism, inheritance, and encapsulation:

- Polymorphism: Multiple object behaviors invoked by triggering events.
- Inheritance: Attributes that carry over between parent and child objects.
- Encapsulation: Hidden code that protects object attributes and behaviors.

The concept of objects allows analysts and programmers to take a more intuitive approach to designing information systems, applications, databases, and websites. Also, because objects are specific sequences of code they can be reused, which saves programming time and increases quality and performance. For example, an "invoice" object developed for a sales system might be reused across several lines of business in an enterprise that has multiple product lines and billing procedures. The basic functionality of the invoice object is both protected and inherited in all systems, with additional custom features and behaviors being added as they are needed.

Object-oriented analysis and design activities begin with the documentation of business requirements in the form of a narrative Use Case. Four basic types of diagrams are then used to describe the Use Case, each of which is an EA artifact that should be maintained at the Information level of the EA framework: (1) Use-Case Diagram; (2) Class/Object Diagram; (3) Object Sequence Diagram; and (4) Object State-Transition Diagram. Use Case Diagrams show a static (snapshot) overall view of the activities (use cases) and actors in an information system, and how information will be exchanged. Class/Object Diagrams show a static view of the things that interact in each Use Case in the information system, and how the object's behaviors will perform those interactions. Object Sequence Diagrams show how groups of objects exhibit behaviors in response to a specific event called a trigger. Note that the same Object can exhibit different behaviors in response to different events. The State-Transition Diagram shows the entire lifecycle of a particular Object, in terms of how event triggers can invoke different behaviors.

Data Dictionary / Object Library
Data Dictionaries are repositories for the data entities and attributes that an enterprise collects and stores in databases. Standards for the format of data are documented in the Data Dictionary, as are dependencies and rules for relationships and dependencies among data entities that are identified in Entity Relationship Diagrams.

Object Libraries are repositories for reusable objects. From a technical perspective, it is the discrete pieces of programming code that actually make up an object, and that are being stored in the Object Library as a complete reusable unit. Object-oriented programming languages (i.e., JAVA, ADA, Smalltalk, C++) develop code segments that are distinct in their identity and function, and which are reusable in that the object can be integrated into other applications with little customization. Commercial software developers increasingly create applications using an object-oriented approach so that they can maintain the application more efficiently by adjusting or adding/deleting individual objects. Vendors also are increasingly selling objects that are common to financial, manufacturing, and administrative applications. These commercial objects and those custom developed by the enterprise should be archived in the Object Library. Other information products developed in platform independent languages should also be included in the Object Library. These include EA artifacts such as web pages and web service components that are developed in object oriented languages and saved in compatible formats such as HTML, XML, J2EE, and ebXML.

System & Service Level EA Artifacts – Current View

EA Components:
- *Software Applications*
- *Web Services*
- *Service Bus and Middleware*
- *Enterprise Resource Planning (ERP) Solutions*
- *Operating Systems*
-

EA Artifacts:
- *System Interface Diagram (SA-1)*
- *System Communication Diagram (SA-2)*
- *System Interface Matrix (SA-3)*
- *System Data Flow Diagram (SA-4)*
- *System/Operations Matrix (SA-5)*
- *Systems Data Exchange Matrix (SA06)*
- *System Performance Matrix (SA-7)*
- *System Evolution Diagram (SA-8)*
- *Web Application Diagram (SA-9)*

The current view of IT systems and applications should function to show an accurate picture of the software applications, front/back office services, and operating systems that the enterprise currently has active in its IT operating environment. In that many of these IT resources were developed in an independent manner, the completed current view of the support applications level of the framework may show (1) a lack of integration in areas with requirements for exchanges of information, (2) duplications of function, (3) little or lots of vendor diversity, and/or (4) where business requirements are not being met.

System Level EA Artifact – Application Programs

The various types of software applications that an enterprise uses to support business, office automation, and other functions are often varied in their design, programming languages, interface points, and source vendors. It is sometimes helpful to develop a graphical view of these support applications to show what is present, and the general types of functions being supported. Figure 7-7 is an example of the type of diagram that can show an overview of the enterprise's current "suite" of systems, applications, and supporting network protocols.

E-Commerce Service	Supply-Chain Management Service	Public Web Portal	E-Government Service	Web Services
HR Module	Payroll Module	Inventory Module	Sales Module	Enterprise Resource Planning System/Applications
CAD Drawing Application	Data Mining Application		Scheduling Application	Back-Office Business and Office Automation Systems/Applications
Project Tracking Application	Graphics Application	Photo Editing Application	Document Tracking Application	
Office Automation Application Suite (Word Processing, Spreadsheets, E-Mail, etc.)		Web Browsers	Database Application	
Desktop - PC Operating System	File Server Operating System		Database Server Operating System	Desktop & Server Operating Systems
Print Server Operating System	Web Server Operating System		Security Firewall Operating System	
Ethernet	Frame Relay & VPN	Asynchronous Transfer Mode (ATM)	ISDN	TCP/IP	Network Transport Protocols (voice, data, video)

Figure 7-7: General View of Systems and applications

Additional descriptions and views can focus on specific types of support applications to show specific functions and interfaces. As was shown in Figure 7-8, it may be beneficial to show a "hierarchy" to the applications such that operating systems are at the base, office automation and business applications are in the middle, and web applications are on top.

An Application Programming Interface (API) is a series of functions that software applications use to make other applications and operating systems perform supporting actions. In other words, APIs define how applications will interact at the Systems/Services level of the EA. For example an API for a program can be used to open windows, files, and message boxes and perform more complicated tasks, just by passing a single instruction. API descriptions should describe both internal function and external connectivity so that a picture of activity and interrelationships is created.

System and Service Interface Diagrams

IT systems are distinct collections of applications, databases, operating systems, and hardware that meet specific business or technology requirements of the enterprise. These systems increasingly are required to directly and indirectly interface with other IT systems to enable information sharing across the enterprise. The use of non-proprietary industry and international standards for software and hardware solutions enables these interfaces. System Interface Diagrams (also called Node Connectivity Diagrams) are physical and logical depictions of how and where these interfaces occur. Additional documentation on the type of supporting standards and protocols is needed to complete the documentation of system and service interfaces.

As was described in Chapter 6, a Service-Oriented Architecture (SOA) approach is used to describe and document IT systems and web services within the Systems/Services level of the EA^3 framework, and can be considered to be a sub-architecture of the EA^3 framework. Web services are based on the TCP/IP (HTTP) information exchange protocol and open standards information formats such as HTML, XML, and J2EE (.NET is a proprietary protocol owned by Microsoft ®). Web services are therefore platform independent, and can exchange information with any other web services in the common operating environment, which is referred to as the Network Application Platform (NAP) Service Bus.

Web service interfaces within the NAP Service Bus are defined by the Simple Object Access Protocol (SOAP), which is an extensible XML messaging format. SOAP is an industry standard that was developed in the late 1990s by Microsoft® and several other Windows product vendors, which the World Wide Web Consortium (W3C) adopted as an international standard. SOAP interfaces consist of an envelope, header and body, and utilize a transport binding framework to define HTTP bindings, and a serialization framework for XML encoding.

Universal Description, Discovery, and Integration (UDDI) is a standard format and method for registering and discovering web services. UDDI is a web "meta-service" that functions as a registry by using SOAP messages to find web services. The UDDI registry organizes web service information into four categories: business entity, business service, binding template, and service type. Additionally, a Web Services Description Language (WDSL) is used to describe the web service found by the UDDI registry. Figure 7-8 shows a general view of web services and the roles of SOAP, the UDDI Registry, and WDSL.

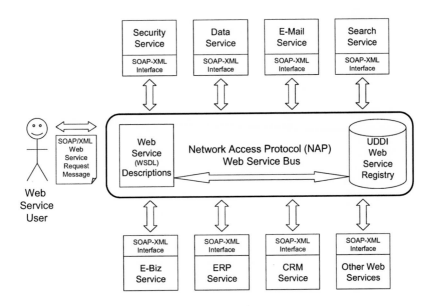

Figure 7-8: General View of Web Services

Technical Standards

IT applications should be selected based on technical standards and protocols from industry, national, or international bodies which have no bias toward particular vendors or products. Standards for APIs, service functionality, and software/hardware integratability should be documented to assist in decision-making regarding the selection of new applications and the operations and maintenance of existing applications. The WSDL web service descriptions and NAP Web

Service Bus interface documentation are some of the additional artifacts that need to be gathered.

Infrastructure Level EA Artifacts – Current View

EA Components:
- *Data Networks*
- *Telecommunications Networks*
- *Video Networks*
- *Cable Plants*
- *Security Solution*

EA Artifacts:
- ***Network Connectivity Diagram (NI-1)***
- ***Network Inventory (NI-2)***
- ***Capital Equipment Inventory (NI-3)***
- ***Building Blueprints (NI-4)***
- ***Network Center Diagram (NI-5)***
- ***Cable Plant Diagram (NI-6)***
- ***Rack Elevation Diagram (NI-7)***

Network Documentation

At the infrastructure level of the EA, networks, backbone routers/switches/hubs, equipment rooms, wiring closets, and cable plants should be described in detail using both text documents and diagrams that show logical and physical design. Each of the enterprise's voice, data, and video networks should be documented such that analysis and decision-making regarding current operations and maintenance is supported. Figure 7-9 on the next page provides an example of this type of documentation.

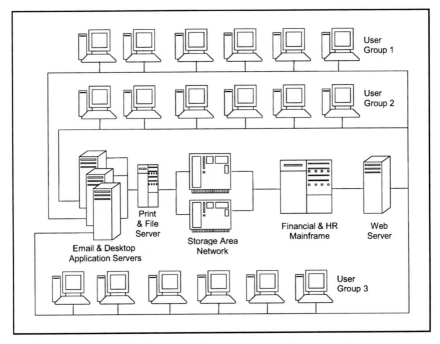

Figure 7-9: Example Network Design Diagram

Technical Standards

Technical standards for voice, data, and video networks should be identified to provide a reference for the analysis and support of current infrastructure resources as well as the planning for future resources. Standards from national and international bodies should be used to encourage the selection of vendor products that will better integrate with other existing and future products. Network technical standards are also provided in the form of policies, technical specifications, and Standard Operating Procedures.

Security Documentation

Each network and IT system that is supported by the technology backbone must be tested and certified for security vulnerabilities. This is done so that an effective level of business support is maintained, and that an overall IT security solution is established for hosted applications, services, databases, and websites. The related EA artifacts include the development of system/network security plans, vulnerability test reports, disaster recovery and continuity of operations plans, and certification and accreditation review results (see Chapter 12 for additional details).

Configuration Change Requests

There should be a standard method for requesting changes to the EA artifacts, so that configuration control over the current and future EA views can be maintained. Using an EA Change Request (EACR) form is one way to have a standardized format and process for updating EA documentation. Making the EACR form an electronic template helps promote use by all stakeholders, as does the archiving of pending and approved EACRs in the EA repository's database.

Hardware/Software Inventories

One of the functions of the EA is to provide a repository for periodic inventories of the enterprise's software and hardware assets. Maintaining an inventory of these IT resources helps to determine what levels of investment will be needed for operations, maintenance, and training as well as major technology upgrade and replacement projects. Using automated inventory systems and bar code labels assists in maintaining an accurate inventory as resources are brought into and retired from the IT operating environment.

Summary of Concepts

This chapter provided descriptions and examples of EA artifacts that document the current state of components at all levels of the EA framework. The collection of current artifacts represents the "as-is" view of the EA. This is important to the enterprise because it serves as an integrated inventory of reference information for resource planning and decision-making. The current views of EA components also show how strategic goals, business services, and technology resources are effectively aligned, and performance gaps can also be revealed. Chapter 8 will discuss the development of future views of the architecture, and Chapter 9 will describe the concept of an EA Management Plan that serves to manage the ongoing transition between the current and future states of the enterprise's EA.

Chapter 7 Questions and Exercises

1. What is the purpose of current views of EA components?

2. How do artifacts relate to EA components?

3. Provide some examples of artifacts at the Goals & Initiatives level of the EA^3 framework.

4. What is IDEF-0 modeling and how can it be used to document EA components at the Products & Services level of the EA^3 framework?

5. What are the differences between traditional (ERD and DFD) data modeling techniques and object oriented data modeling techniques (UML)?

6. Provide some examples of artifacts at the Applications & Services level of the EA^3 framework.

7. Is vendor-supplied documentation on software and hardware products important to retain as EA artifacts? Why?

8. What are some of the EA artifacts that would be desired at the Network & Infrastructure level of the EA^3 framework?

9. Find a public or private sector enterprise and identify the following current EA components/artifacts at each level of the EA^3 framework:

    a. Identify current strategic goals, initiatives, and outcome measures.
    b. Identify current LOBs, business services, and associated activity/flow diagrams.
    c. Identify current information flows and data documentation in each LOB.
    d. Identify the current IT systems and applications that support information flows for each LOB.
    e. Identify the current IT infrastructure and networks that host IT systems and applications.

Chapter 8

Developing Future Architecture Views

Chapter Overview

This chapter covers the development of future views of the EA, within the context of a documentation framework and implementation methodology. The future views of the EA are important to the enterprise because they capture one or more possible business and technology operating scenarios, which supports planning and decision-making. These future operating scenarios are based on assumptions of capability and strategies for successful performance in response to internal and external influences. The creation of future view artifacts is accomplished by using the planning assumptions in the scenarios and the same documentation and modeling techniques as were used to develop the current view artifacts. This allows future view artifacts to be directly related to current view artifacts at each level of the framework, so that potential and planned changes are evident, and various types or combinations of changes can be modeled.

Learning Objectives

> ➢ Understand how future views relate to the EA documentation framework.

> ➢ Understand how future views relate to the EA implementation methodology.

> ➢ Understand how scenario planning helps the development of future views.

> ➢ See examples of future views of EA components and artifacts.

Introduction

The future view of the EA documents the IT resources that will be active in the operating environment several years in the future. This is also known as the "to-be" view of the EA, as opposed to the "as-is" view that documents current IT resources and was described in Chapter 7. Depending on the amount of EA planning that has occurred previously in the enterprise, future IT resources may or may not be aligned with the enterprise's strategic goals and business services. If little EA planning has occurred, then a significant amount of duplication in function may be present and the future view of the EA should show how that duplication will be eliminated.

> *Home Architecture Analogy:* Having future EA views is like having a full set of blueprints for the modification of an existing home. It provides an authoritative reference for the architect and homeowner to use in discussing the changes to the home.

As is shown in Figure 8-1, future views of the EA provide an enterprise with documentation of identified changes to strategic goals, business services, information flows, support applications, and network resources.

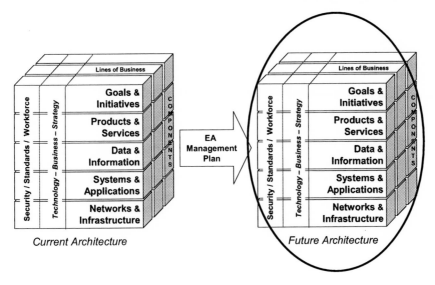

Figure 8-1: Future Architecture Views

Discussion

The development of future EA views is important to an enterprise because it supports resource planning and decision-making. Also, by completing the documentation of the future EA at all levels of the framework, a view of the potential future enterprise emerges that reveals changes in priorities, processes, and resources. This serves to promote communication about these potential changes throughout the enterprise.

In developing the future EA, each level of the framework is documented with artifacts to show components that are approved for implementation, or are in the idea/planning stages. The potential changes to existing EA components include new or updated strategic goals and initiatives, business services, information flows, systems, support applications, and networks. Initiatives that are in the very early stages of consideration can be left out of future views until they have firm backing from sponsors, strong business cases, and viable technical solutions. This avoids cluttering future EA views with initiatives and updates that have little chance of being implemented, and which over time will detract from the perceived value of the EA as an authoritative reference for planning and decision-making. Candidate initiatives are better documented in a special section of the EA Management Plan (see Chapter 9).

Developing CONOPS Scenarios

Concept of Operations (CONOPS) scenarios have been used as a military planning tool for millennia. Similarly, the ability to envision several potential courses of action is key to winning many types of recreational games. Using chess as an example, anticipating how an opponent might react to your moves is part of what makes for a chess master. Top levels of play involve being able to think through several alternative scenarios of moves and counter-moves that create a dynamic balance between acting and reacting.

Similarly, an enterprise should continuously monitor the internal and external operating environment and make tactical and strategic moves so as to simultaneously avoid catastrophic situations and pursue opportunities to maximize mission success. Large enterprises in the public and private sector have used future scenarios for a number of years to support their planning, including Royal Dutch Shell, the World Bank, and the U.S. Federal Railroad Administration.

The role that future scenarios can play in the development of EA future views is that of identifying a range of operating options and planning assumptions for the enterprise. Developing several scenarios that capture a variety of good and bad operating environments helps the enterprise to think through its probable responses (defensive moves) and initiatives (offensive moves) in advance. It also helps to identify the resources and capabilities that will be needed for those responses/initiatives.

CONOPS Scenarios can be quite detailed, and are used to document both the current operating environment, and a number of plausible future operating environments. Enterprises should identify a range of internal and external factors from the SWOT Analysis in deciding which future CONOPS scenarios to document. Having a number of future scenarios is helpful to an enterprise because it is impossible to predict which particular internal/external factors will come into play to create either a helpful or hostile operating environment.

One of the most effective formats for developing a shortened version of a CONOPS Scenario that is easy to share and use in the enterprise was developed by Dr. Robert Neilson.[20] This type of scenario takes the form of a short story which is told through the eyes of a central character who is involved in future events that reveal the internal and external drivers of the business and technology operating environment at that time. These drivers are then related to specific planning assumptions in three areas of change: process, people, and technology. Neilson states that stories are easy to remember, and the highlighting of planning assumptions reveals the resources and capabilities that will be needed if that scenario is implemented.

The enterprise's need for detailed strategic plans is not replaced by scenarios, rather, scenarios can serve to summarize and energize the essence of several courses of action that are called for in the strategic plan, and make them more memorable. Table 8-2 provides an example CONOPS scenario involving the fictitious Case Study enterprise, Danforth Manufacturing Company.

---

[20] Neilson, Robert. "Strategic Scenario Planning at CA International." *Knowledge Management Review*, Issue 12, January/February 2000.

Making a Sale in 2008
Future Challenges for DMC

Jeff Linder, Vice President of Industrial Sales for Danforth Manufacturing Company (DMC) had just finished a presentation at the 2008 National Highway Safety Conference along with Richard Danforth, DMC's CEO, who had teleconferenced in on the big display screen behind the podium.[1] As Jeff was leaving the main conference room, Andrea Newman, Director of Safety and Transportation for the State of Tennessee, asked Jeff if they could talk for a few minutes about the new line of solar-powered highway and street lights that they had just given a presentation on. [2, 3]

"Thanks for taking a minute to talk Jeff. I want to tell you about a situation we have in Tennessee and see if your new product line can help" said Andrea as they found a table in the refreshment area.[4] "No problem, thanks for asking" Jeff said. Andrea pulled up a document on her tablet computer and said "Jeff, here is a report that shows an increasing number of serious accidents in rural areas of Tennessee involving passenger cars and agricultural equipment or commercial trucks. We've attributed it to the growth of suburban communities further out in the countryside that then depend on two-lane country roads for commuting into the city.[5] When you put slow tractors and trucks together with cars that are in a hurry at all hours to get somewhere, you have a recipe for disaster." "Isn't this problem being seen in other places around the country?" asked Jeff. "Yes, and one of the contributing factors that is consistently coming out of investigations of the night-time accidents is the lack of good lighting on these country roads.[6] I am thinking that your highway grade solar lighting can help us provide more night time visibility on high-risk rural roads without having to invest in the supporting electrical infrastructure." [7, 8]

DMC Future Scenario (continued)

Planning Assumptions
8. Increased cost benefit of solar powered lighting.
9. Continued incorporation of additional product features to expand customer base.
10. Global use of PDAs for employee communication.
11. Integration of sales, marketing, and production information.
12. Accurate customer quotes on the fly.

Jeff thought for a minute before responding. "You know, the new line of highway lights has options to incorporate 911 emergency call boxes and Global Positioning System (GPS) equipment that can connect to both State and local level first responders.[9] This might be useful in also improving response times should an accident occur in spite of the improved lighting." Andrea nodded and said, "Yes, I doubt that better lighting will solve the entire problem, but it will help people see each other better, and these other options can improve accident response times, which will also save lives. What is the pricing like on these units?"

Jeff pulled his Personal Digital Assistant (PDA)[10] out of his pocket and connected to DMC's marketing and sales database at headquarters via a satellite Internet link.[11] "Andrea, these units are $11,300 each, including the GPS and 911 features." Andrea took notes and responded, "If I can get permission to conduct a pilot test in a couple of months can you provide the lights?" Jeff asked "How many miles of road?" "About four miles in the particular area I'm thinking of" said Andrea. "Ok, the suggested density for the new unit is 18 per mile, so that would be 72 units total. I can give you our 10 percent early-adopter discount, so the total would be $732,240. Let me check what the shipping time would be." Jeff sent a high priority email to Bob Green, Vice President of Manufacturing. Bob was in the factory when he received Jeff's email on his PDA, and after checking the DMC Production Scheduling System, responded two minutes later that a special order for 72 units could be completed and shipped 35 days from when the order is received. Jim relayed this information to Andrea, who said, "Wow, that was fast. I have all the information I need to propose the pilot project. I will get back to you in the next week. Thanks." [12]

Table 8-2: Example CONOPS Scenario and Planning Assumptions

Updating Future EA Views – Version Control

At some point the new components and artifacts in the future view of the EA become implemented and therefore should be documented as part of the current view of the EA. These ongoing changes to the EA represent a challenge in terms of how best to show at any given time what is current and what is planned. Perhaps the simplest and most effective way to approach this is to 'freeze' the current and future views of the EA at regular periods (e.g., twice each year). This promotes clarity and supports EA version control. Using this example, changes to current and future views are collected for four to five months and then are published in the sixth month as a new release of the enterprise's EA. EA stakeholders come to expect the new releases and know that they can then rely on the information not changing in the EA repository for the next few months. Special releases can be made if a there is an important change in the middle of the normally static period. Without this type of version control, the EA repository becomes a free-for-all whereby no one is sure when and where changes will appear, and this will detract from the perceived value of EA information.

The following are examples of how new or upgraded EA artifacts would be documented in the future view of related EA components at each level of the EA³ framework. Appendix E provides examples of each artifact.

Strategic Level EA Artifacts – Future View

EA Components:
* *Strategic Plan*
* *E-Commerce or E-Government Plan*

EA Artifacts:
* *Strategic Plan (S-1)*
* *SWOT Analysis (S-2)*
* *Concept of Operations Scenario (S-3)*
* *Concept of Operations Diagram (S-4)*
* *Balanced Scorecard™ (S-5)*

EA components and artifacts at the Strategic Level of the EA³ framework serve to articulate the general direction and priorities that the enterprise intends to take along with the goals, initiatives, and measures that define success. The E-Business or E-Government Plan then serves to provide more detailed descriptions of how IT initiatives will support the enterprise's Strategic Plan, with a focus on strategic goals and key business services. Updated plans should be published every few years to reflect the changes in direction and priorities that the enterprise intends to take. The future view of these plans can serve as draft documents where potential changes that have executive sponsorship are recorded until the official publication of the new plans. The future view of these EA components should link to the future view of all related EA artifacts, such as strategic goals, scenarios, initiatives, and performance measures (described below).

Strategic Scenarios
Strategic scenarios can be added or deleted from the Strategic Plan's future view in response to changes in the internal and external operating environment. To promote comparison and analysis, potential future scenarios should be documented in the same way that the current scenario is documented: as an integrated narrative and set of high-level planning assumptions regarding enterprise priorities, performance, resources, and risks.

Strategic Goals
While the current view of IT-related strategic goals represents high-level EA artifacts that are documented in the enterprise's current Strategic Plan, the future view of these EA artifacts represents changes to those goals, or new goals that are not yet formally adopted and published as part of the Plan. New strategic goals also serve to direct the development of future operating scenarios, which should capture the priorities and direction of those new goals.

Strategic Initiatives
The current view of IT-related strategic initiatives serves to create an awareness and appreciation for the role that IT plays in supporting key business and administrative processes throughout the enterprise. It also supports high-level resource planning, also known as "capital planning and investment control (CPIC) process (see Chapter 9 for additional details). The future view of IT-related strategic initiatives is intended to show the changes that are being planned to existing initiatives as well as new initiatives that will be introduced in coming years. This is especially valuable to enterprises that have highly structured planning and budget processes.

Performance Measures

Changes to strategic goals and initiatives in the future views will require new or modified outcome and output measures of success.

Business Level EA Artifacts – Future View

EA Components:
- *Supply Chains*
- *Business services*
- *IT Capital Planning Portfolio*

EA Artifacts:
- ***Business Plan (B-1)***
- ***Node Connectivity Diagram (B-2)***
- ***Swim Lane Process Diagram (B-3)***
- ***Business Process/Service Model (B-4)***
- ***Business Process/Product Matrix (B-5)***
- ***Use Case Narrative and Diagram (B-7)***
- ***Investment Business Case (B-8)***

Enterprises continually change their business services in response to a number of influencing factors including new customer requirements, different competitive strategies, new technologies, and changes in resource availability. These factors (also known as drivers) are documented at both the Strategic Level and the Business Level of the EA³ framework. The documentation of drivers at the Strategic Level often centers on those influencing factors that originate in the external operating environment, while the documentation of Business Level drivers often focuses on influencing factors that originate in the internal operating environment. EA components at the Business Level may extend beyond the internal operating environment (i.e., supply chains involving external suppliers), but they are fundamentally internal management processes. Future views of related EA artifacts primarily reflect approved changes to these business services and associated implementation activities.

There are four general types of changes to business services that occur: (1) the introduction of a completely new process, (2) elimination of an existing process, (3) major reengineering of an existing process, and (4) minor improvement of an existing process. Effective management at the Business Level requires that these changes be coordinated so that the performance of the enterprise does not decline. Therefore, reviews of existing business services should be performed periodically by line-of-business managers to identify those which may be obsolete, duplicative, or not adding sufficient value to the achievement of strategic goals. Resulting decisions to eliminate or change existing processes, or add new processes, are what get documented in the future view of Business Level EA components and artifacts.

Process Documentation

Similar to the approach to documenting future views at the Strategic Level of the EA³ framework, only those potential changes to business services that have executive sponsorship should be documented at the Business Level. This maintains value in the future view and promotes the use of this information for planning and decision-making.

Documenting approved changes to business services helps to maintain "upward alignment" in the EA³ framework with strategic goals and initiatives. It also promotes "downward alignment" in the EA³ framework to ensure that EA components and artifacts at the lower three levels are properly adjusted to best support the anticipated process changes. The enterprise should be consistent in how current and future business process are documented (e.g., IDEF-0 models, swim lane diagrams, and/or flow-charts) so that analysis and planning is best supported.

Project Plans

The Project Management Plan (PMP) is a living document that promotes proven, standardized approaches to implementing new or upgraded IT resources. The current view of the PMP is developed in the requirements planning stage of the project lifecycle, with updates being made as changes in requirements, solutions, or resources occur. A future view of a PMP may not be needed with certain EA component development approaches, also known as Systems Analysis and Design Methods (SADMs) that promote the development of the entire system capability in one effort (e.g., the "waterfall" or "rapid application development" methods). However, those SADM approaches that promote the incremental (phased), or evolutionary (spiral) development of EA components may benefit from having a future view of the PMP to show the implementation of system modules that are envisioned at some future time. The phased implementation of large ERP projects with several modules would be an example of where having both a current and future view of the PMP would be beneficial. PMPs are maintained on systems throughout the lifecycle, until the system is disposed.

Business Cases

The investment business case is the part of the PMP that documents the value of the investment to the enterprise. The business case is unique in that it ties directly to the enterprise's budget and financial planning process, and as such usually requires a review at least annually. The initial approval of the business case centers on an identification of benefits that exceed costs (both quantitative and qualitative). Approval also focuses on a determination that the rate of return on the capital invested (ROI) meets meaningful, measurable targets established by the enterprise, such that another use of those funds is not warranted (opportunity cost). The business case should then be reviewed annually to determine if sufficient benefits continue to be generated to merit continued investment. If they are not, the investment should be cancelled or modified such that sufficient ongoing value is created. Chapter 9 provides additional details on business case development and evaluation as part of the IT capital planning process.

Information Level EA Artifacts – Future View

EA Components:
- *Knowledge Warehouses*
- *Information Systems*
- *Databases*

EA Artifacts:
- **Knowledge Management Plan (D-1)**
- **Information Exchange Matrix (D-2)**
- **Object State-Transition Diagram (D-3)**
- **Object Event Sequence Diagram (D-4)**
- **Logical Data Model (D-5)**
- **Physical Data Model (D-6)**
- **Activity/Entity (CRUD) Matrix (D-7)**
- **Data Dictionary/Object Library (D-8)**

Future views of EA components and artifacts at the Information Level of the EA³ framework reflect changes that are anticipated in the collection and flows of information that are needed to support changes in business services (upward alignment) or changes that are anticipated at the Systems/Services Level or the Technology Infrastructure level of the EA³ framework.

Data Models

Traditional views of data models that show structure (Entity-Relationship Diagrams) and process (Data Flow Diagrams) can be developed to show future changes either as separate documents or through the use of special notation that can be integrated into current views (e.g., the use of dashed lines and symbols to show future data entities, flows, stores). Whichever approach is taken, the important idea is to provide a future view of data structure and process in a way that is directly comparable to the current view so that areas of change can be easily identified.

Another "traditional" data modeling artifact that merits the development of a future view is the Activity/Entity Matrix (also called a CRUD Matrix). This matrix maps activities occurring at the IT system boundary to the data entities that are affected. This mapping enables the data analyst and enterprise architect to see where and how data is Created, Read, Updated, or Deleted (CRUD). By identifying who in the enterprise is responsible for (owns) the activity, the logical owner of the data and the processes that transform the data can also be identified. Having current views of the CRUD Matrix and knowledge of future changes in business services enables the development of a future view of the CRUD Matrix, which identities potential changes in the ownership of data and which may lead to discussions of changes in data standards and formats. IT system consolidation, upgrade, or replacement activities that seek to improve the efficiency of data handling or increase the cost-effectiveness of the new system will benefit from a detailed analysis of current and future views of the CRUD Matrix.

Object-Oriented Data and System Models

Object-Oriented (OO) views of future system activities (Use Cases), data process/structure (Class and Object Diagrams), data transformation (State Transition Diagrams), and information flows (Sequence Diagrams) should be developed in the same way that the current views of these same EA artifacts were developed so that an easy identification of changes can be made.

One of the most powerful reasons for adopting an OO approach to data modeling and IT system analysis and design is that objects can be modified with minimal effort to reflect changes in requirements or use in different scenarios. Object reuse lowers the cost of systems upgrade projects, and supports the use of modular applications that are object-based (e.g., Java applications). Developing future views of how information in the form of objects will be stored differently helps analysts, programmers, and architects to produce better logical and physical data models, promotes application interoperability, and supports plug-and-play EA components that are based on open standards or a particular vendor product line.

Data Dictionaries / Object Libraries

Data Dictionaries provide taxonomies and standard formats for the data entities that are used in the enterprise's various IT systems. Data Dictionaries do not store actual data, they just provide a list of entities, attributes, data field formats, and standards. These standards help to promote system interoperability and the consolidation of databases. The future view of a Data Dictionary would show the changes in data standards and formats that are anticipated to be needed as a result of system/application/database changes.

Object Libraries are similar in concept, except that they store both the formats/standards and the actual modules of code that constitute an object. Since one of the basic features of objects is encapsulation (protection of parts of the code module from alteration) the object library can store distinct objects just as a book rests independently on the shelf among other books until pulled off the shelf and checked out of the library. Various versions of an object can be separately stored for use in different systems and applications (e.g., an invoice object that provides different types of invoices that are custom tailored for different product lines).

Systems/Services Level EA Artifacts – Future View

EA Components:
- *Software Applications*
- *Web Services*
- *Service Bus and Middleware*
- *Enterprise Resource Planning (ERP) Solutions*
- *Operating Systems*

EA Artifacts:
- ***System Interface Diagram (SA-1)***
- ***System Communication Diagram (SA-2)***
- ***System Interface Matrix (SA-3)***
- ***System Data Flow Diagram (SA-4)***
- ***System/Operations Matrix (SA-5)***
- ***Systems Data Exchange Matrix (SA06)***
- ***System Performance Matrix (SA-7)***

- *System Evolution Diagram (SA-8)*
- *Web Application Diagram (SA-9)*

The Systems/Services level of the EA^3 framework is organized around integrated "plug-and-play" components that are based on open standards, and reusable objects of code that underlie and enable a component-based and service-oriented approach to EA, as is promoted in the EA^3 framework. Various EA artifacts are used to document the future components at the Systems/Services level, including program code and technical documentation on releases and upgrades; interface diagrams; and standards.

Application Interface Descriptions

Descriptions of application software programs and their interfaces in the future view provide an understanding of what will change from what is currently in operation as well as what new functional capabilities will have to be integrated. Application Program Interfaces (APIs) are a feature of most commercial software programs and are where the designed interface points in the programming code are located. These APIs define the extent of interoperability and may include open standards if maximum integration with a wide variety of other products is desired by the vendor. Conversely, APIs may be proprietary and limit interoperability to products from a specific vendor (e.g., interfaces between modules of an ERP product). The EA artifacts at this level are the technical description of APIs and lists of API standards.

Application Interface Diagrams

Interface diagrams in the future view show the changes to existing system, service, and application interface points. These interface points are where information exchanges occur, and infer connectivity which is shown in more detail at the Technology Infrastructure Level of the EA. Interface diagrams are also important to show how component applications will interact the enterprise's common operating environment, including how web-based services exchange information through the NAP Web Service Platform. In the case where these applications are commercial products from different vendors, these interfaces can identify where compatibility must be present and as such help to establish future requirements for integration.

Standards

Technical standards documentation in the future view shows the international, national, local, and industry standards that changes to commercial and custom-developed services, systems, and applications must meet. This includes APIs and other interoperability or performance requirements, WSDL descriptions of web services in the UDDI Registry are an example of the technical standards that need to be identified for future implementation if a Service-Oriented Approach to this level of the EA^3 framework has not yet been adopted by the enterprise.

Infrastructure Level EA Artifacts – Future View

EA Components:
- *Data Networks*
- *Telecommunications Networks*
- *Video Networks*
- *Cable Plants*
- *Security Solutions*

EA Artifacts:
- ***Network Connectivity Diagram (NI-1)***
- ***Network Inventory (NI-2)***
- ***Capital Equipment Inventory (NI-3)***
- ***Building Blueprints (NI-4)***
- ***Network Center Diagram (NI-5)***
- ***Cable Plant Diagram (NI-6)***
- ***Rack Elevation Diagram (NI-7)***

The Technology Infrastructure level of the EA framework documents components such as the enterprise's voice, data, and video networks, as well as the security solution that protects them. In that one of the goals of EA is to promote the integration of these networks into one seamless technology backbone, the future view of EA artifacts at this level documents changes to this infrastructure.

Network Documentation
Documentation of the enterprise's IT networks in the future view show changes to the integrated voice, data, and video infrastructure components. The enterprise's LAN, WAN, and other networks are shown mainly in diagrams and technical specification documents. These EA artifacts should focus on changes to cable plant(s), wireless, telephone and data wiring closets, network backbone hardware and software, servers, desktop and portable computers, peripherals, and remote access resources.

Technical Standards

IT network technical standards documentation in the future view shows changes to national, international, and commercial standards that are being used to guide changes to the enterprise's technology backbone. This includes changes to standards that are reflected in models of networks, including the OSI model and TCP/IP model. It also includes standards for telephony, wireless communications, and remote video conferencing.

Security Documentation

Future views of security documentation shows the expected changes and updates to security standards, plans, testing, and certification of each IT system and network component of the EA, as well as related security documentation for applications and databases.

Configuration Changes

The future view of EACRs consists of an archive of approved, but yet to be implemented EA Change Requests. These EACRs document the technical and operational impact of changes to EA components at all levels of the EA. See Chapter 9 for more information on EACRs.

Hardware/Software List

The EA artifact in this area of future views is a list that documents anticipated changes in the quantity and type of IT hardware and software products that will be used in EA components throughout each of the levels of the EA framework

Summary of Concepts

This chapter provided examples of EA artifacts that document future views of EA components at all levels of the EA^3 framework. The use of future scenarios is one way to identify possible future operating environments and planning assumptions which the future EA views can then be based on. The same documentation techniques should be used in developing both current and future views of EA components so that changes are easier to highlight and compare. Chapter 9 will describe the purpose and composition of an EA Management Plan, which provides a description of the ongoing transition between current and future views of the EA.

Chapter 8 Questions and Exercises

1. How far into the future should the EA future views attempt to provide documentation?

2. Why is the same documentation technique used in the current and future view of an EA component?

3. What is the relationship between the enterprise's Strategic Plan and EA future views?

4. How can the ongoing transition between current and future EA views be managed?

5. How can Business Process Improvement (BPI) and Business Process Reengineering (BPR) activities be reflected in future views at the Products & Services level of the EA³ framework?

6. How can changes in information flows and data structures be reflected in future views at the Data & Information level of the EA³ framework?

7. How can changes in applications and functionality be reflected in future views at the Applications & Systems level of the EA³ framework?

8. How can changes in voice, data, and video networks be reflected in future views at the Networks & Infrastructure level of the EA³ framework?

9. Develop a future scenario for an enterprise that describes changes in processes, human factors, and technology. Identify the planning assumptions that underlie these changes.

10. Find a public or private sector enterprise and identify current EA components and artifacts at each level of the EA³ framework

Chapter 9

Developing an
Enterprise Architecture Management Plan

Chapter Overview

This chapter discusses the development of an EA Management Plan, which is the document that describes how an enterprise will manage the transition of its current processes and resources to those which will be needed in the future. This transition from the current EA to the future EA is an ongoing activity, as new resources are implemented and therefore become part of the current EA. The purpose of configuration management and version control are also discussed, along with the need to provide a sequence for implementation projects.

Learning Objectives

> Understand the purpose of an EA Management Plan.

> See an example format for an EA Management Plan.

> Understand the types of content that go into an EA Management Plan.

> Understand the purpose of summaries of the current and future architecture.

Introduction

The EA Management Plan documents the enterprise's performance gaps, resource requirements, planned solutions, a sequencing plan, and a summary of the current and future architecture. The Plan also describes the EA governance process, the implementation methodology, and the documentation framework. It is a living document that is updated at regular intervals (e.g., annually) to provide clear version control for changes in current and future views of EA components and artifacts throughout the framework. The EA Management Plan should be archived in the on-line EA repository to support easy access to the information and to promote the linkage of EA to other IT management processes.

Discussion

The enterprise's EA is in continual transition as IT implementation and upgrade projects are completed. Large and mid-size enterprises often have many IT projects underway at any given time, which requires an overarching level of coordination, prioritization, and oversight. As is shown in Figure 9-1, the EA Management Plan provides this coordination and supports oversight for changes to the enterprise's EA, between the current and future views.

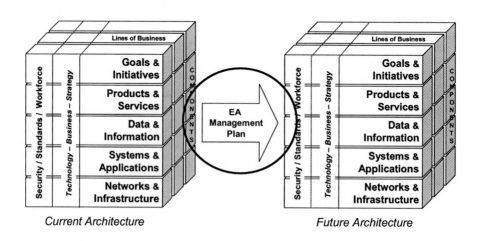

Figure 9-1: The Role of the EA Management Plan

Home Architecture Analogy: The EA Management Plan is like the architect's project plan, which summarizes the work and shows the design, approach, timeframe, and sequencing of work for the remodeling of a home.

EA transition and the management thereof are documented in an EA Management Plan, which has several sections as is shown in the example format provided in Figure 9-2 on the next page.

```
        Enterprise Architecture Management Plan

Part 1.  EA Program Management
    1.1     Governance and Principles
    1.2     Support for Strategy and Business
    1.3     EA Roles and Responsibilities
    1.4     EA Program Budget
    1.5     EA Program Performance Measures

Part 2.  EA Current Architecture Summary
    2.1     Strategic Goals and Initiatives
    2.2     Business services and Information Flows
    2.3     Systems and applications
    2.4     Technology Infrastructure
    2.5     IT Security
    2.6     EA Standards
    2.7     Workforce Requirements

Part 3.  EA Future Architecture Summary
    3.1     Future Operating Scenarios
    3.2     Planning Assumptions
    3.3     Updating Current & Future Views
    3.4     Sequencing Plan
    3.5     Configuration Management

Part 4.  EA Glossary and References
```

Figure 9-2: Example Format for an EA Management Plan

EA Management Plan: Part 1. EA Program Management

EA as a management program supports policy development, decision-making, and the effective/efficient use of resources. The EA Program Management section documents the activities associated with administering EA as an ongoing program.

1.1. <u>Governance and Principles</u>: This section documents the way that policy and decision-making will occur within the EA program. It is also where the underlying principles of the EA program are articulated.[21] EA

---

[21] The concept of "EA Principles" was first proposed by Steven Spewak in his book <u>Enterprise Architecture Planning: A Blueprint for Data, Applications, and Technology</u>. John Wiley & Sons. 1992.

governance is perhaps best described through a narrative that provides EA program policy and an accompanying flow chart that shows how and when decisions are made on EA issues such as IT investment proposals, project reviews, document approvals, and standards adoption/waivers. EA principles articulate the enterprise's values as they relate to the EA. These principles then guide the EA program's establishment and management. Examples of EA principle are (1) the degree to which the enterprise promotes the open sharing of information, (2) an emphasis on stakeholder participation, (3) the recognition that IT is normally a means and not an end in itself, (4) an emphasis on using commercial products that are based on open standards, and (5) a recognition that EA adds value for planning, decision-making, and communication.

1.2. <u>Support for Strategy and Business</u>: This section emphasizes that one of the main purposes of the EA program is to support and improve the enterprise's strategic and business planning, as well as to identify performance gaps that EA components can help close. By showing how EA components are being currently used, and identifying useful new processes and technologies at each level of the framework, improvements in performance can occur that are captured in the future EA views. For EA components to be viewed as a strategic asset and EA be viewed as part of the strategic planning process, business executives must see the value of the EA program in supporting the outcomes that matter to them. It is therefore important to show the linkage of the EA program to the accomplishment of the enterprise's strategic goals, as well as to clearly show how EA components support line of business activities.

1.3. <u>EA Roles and Responsibilities</u>: This section documents the roles that stakeholders in the EA program will play, and what the responsibilities associated with those roles will be. This is where the players on the EA team are also identified. A table format is an effective way to show roles and responsibilities, as is exemplified in Figure 9-3.

EA Team Position	EA Team Role	EA Responsibilities
Sponsor	Executive Leadership	Be the champion of the EA program. Provide resources. Assist in resolving high-level EA issues.
Chief Information Officer (CIO)	Executive Leadership and Decision-Making	Facilitate the establishment and ongoing operation of the EA Program. Lead the resolution of high-level EA issues. Integrate EA and other governance.

EA Team Position	EA Team Role	EA Responsibilities
Chief Architect	Program Management	Manage the EA program and documentation process. Select and implement the EA framework and documentation methodology. Identify EA standards and manage EA configuration management sub-process.
Line of Business Managers	Requirements Identification	Participate in EA program decision-making. Promote the identification of IT-related requirements and EA solutions for each LOB.
Solutions Architect	Problem Solving	Collaboratively identify solutions for IT-related problems within LOBs. Support EA documentation.
Systems Architect	Analysis and Design	Provide technical analysis and design support for systems-related EA component selection and implementation. Ensure that IT systems meet integration and interoperability requirements. Support EA documentation.
Data Architect	Analysis and Design	Provide technical analysis and design support for database-related EA component selection and implementation. Ensure that databases meet integration and interoperability requirements. Support EA documentation.
EA Tool Expert	Application and Database Support	Maintenance of EA Software Application. Maintenance of EA repository and information.
End-User Representative	Requirements Identification / QA	Identify end-user requirements for EA components. Provide feedback on the effectiveness of solutions.
Webmaster	Website Support	Maintenance of EA website, associated content, and links to other websites as needed.
Research Analyst	Requirements Analysis	Document and verify LOB and end-user requirements. Assist in EA component design and documentation activities

Figure 9-3. Example EA Roles and Responsibilities Matrix

1.4. <u>EA Program Budget</u>: This section documents the budget for the EA program by fiscal year and over the total lifecycle, so that the total cost of ownership (TCO) is identified. While EA program is ongoing, a lifecycle period of five years is recommended to be able to calculate TCO. In general, the costs to be included are those for EA program start-up and operation, salaries and work facilities for the EA team, the initial documentation of the EA, periodic updates to the EA, development of the EA Management Plan, EA tool purchase and support, and EA repository development and maintenance. The initial estimate of these costs represents the "baseline" for EA program funding. Spending during the lifecycle should be tracked against this baseline to promote effective management of the EA program. If changes in the scope of the EA program occur, a corresponding change in the funding baseline should also be made.

1.5. EA Program Performance Measures: This section documents how the effectiveness and efficiency of the EA program will be measured. As was described in previous Chapters, there are two types of measures: outcome and output. Outcome measures identify progress being made toward some new end-state, such as better EA component integration, increased application end-user satisfaction, or more effective IT investment decision-making. Output measures provide data on activities and things, such as how many databases exist, how many e-mail are sent each day, or how closely an IT project is meeting baseline estimates for cost/schedule/performance. Outcome measures often have both quantitative and qualitative elements to them, while output measures are usually quantitative in nature. While output measures are important for indicating progress in an initiative area, it is the attainment of outcomes that correlate to goal attainment, which is the most important thing to an enterprise. It is important to be able to measure the attainment of outcomes, so that the positive effects (added value) of the EA program can be identified. Examples of outcome and output measures for the EA program are provided below.

EA Outcome Measure #1:   Reduce IT project planning average costs by ten percent within one year.

EA Output Measure #1-1: Number of IT projects planned that year.
EA Output Measure #1-2: Prior three year's average cost of IT project planning.
EA Output Measure #1-3: Prior three year's average # of project scope changes.
EA Output Measure #1-4: Current year's average cost of IT project planning.
EA Output Measure #1-5: Current year's average # of project scope changes.

EA Management Plan: Part 2.
Summary of Current Architecture

One of the purposes of the EA Management Plan is to show an overview of the linkage between current EA components and products at each level of the EA³ framework. In this way, the present role of IT within the enterprise is better understood and can be further analyzed from either a top-down, or bottom-up perspective. The objective of this part of the EA Management Plan is not to duplicate the extensive documentation described in Chapters 4 and 5, but to provide an integrated view of how the components and artifacts work in support of each other. This also sets the stage for Part 3 of the EA Management Plan, which discusses future changes in EA components and artifacts to achieve improved performance and/or efficiency. The following are examples of how current EA components and artifacts can be described at each level of the EA³ framework.

2.1. Strategic Goals and Initiatives: This section identifies how the EA program and specific EA components support the attainment of the enterprise's strategic goals and initiatives. This section builds upon comments provided in the Strategic Plan, and is included to more clearly show which EA components and strategic initiatives are involved in each strategic goal area. A general description is then provided of how IT components support each goal and initiative at the *Strategic Initiatives* level of the EA³ framework. Figure 9-4 provides an example format for an artifact that maps EA components to the enterprise's strategic goals and initiatives.

Strategic Goal	Strategic Initiative	Supporting EA Component(s)
Be #1 in Product Service	New Customer Service Website	New Service Website, Service Database, Product Parts Database, Customer Database, PCs and Laptops, Sales Database
	Upgrade of Customer Service Database	Service Database, Customer Database, e-Billing Application, Sales Database
Increase Safety	New Assembly Line Safety Features	Robotics Controllers, Production Scheduler, Safety Database

Figure 9-4: Mapping EA Components to Strategic Goals/Initiatives

2.2. <u>Business services and Information Flows</u>: This section identifies and emphasizes the role that EA plays in supporting business process analysis and improvement, as well as identifying and optimizing information flows within and between these processes. It also re-affirms the EA principle that EA components are a means to enable effective business services, and should not be procured unless there is a strong business case that supports investment. Within this section, the enterprise's main LOBs should be listed along with the key business services and associated information flows in each LOB. A general description is then provided of how IT components support each key business process at the Business services level of the EA^3 framework.

Detailed diagrams of information flows and data structure are also provided using the various types of artifacts that populate the Information Flow level of the EA^3 framework (e.g., Entity Relationship Diagrams, Data Flow Diagrams, and Object-Oriented Diagrams). As shown in Figure 9-5 on the next page, a table format can be effective in creating an artifact that maps the relationships between LOBs, key business services, information flows, and supporting EA components.

Line of Business	Key Processes	Information Flows	Supporting EA Component(s)
Sales	Marketing	Daily marketing and sales data pushed to data mart. Periodic summaries.	Sales Data Mart Web Site, Sales & Inventory Database, Laptops, Remote Access Extranet
	Invoicing	Receipt and processing of customer orders. Customer invoicing.	Customer Database, e-Billing System, Sales Database
	Commissions	Recording and payment of sales commissions, in conjunction with base salary payments.	Sales Force Tracking Database, ERP-Payroll Module and Database
Manufacturing	Production Runs	Tracking of product manufacturing and inventory levels.	Robotics Controllers, Scheduling Application, Inventory Database
	Supplier Parts Orders	End-to-end supply chain management with internal and external customers.	Supplier's Extranet Web Portal, Parts Inventory Database
Administration	Payroll	Recording of work hours data, salary data, and payment information for bi-monthly payroll and Mo/Qtr/Yr Summaries.	ERP - Payroll Module and Database
	Accounting	Integrated management of data for the General Ledger, Working Capital Fund, Accounts Payable, and Accounts Receivable	ERP – Accounting Module, Customer Database, e-Billing Application, Sales Database g Module.
	Human Resources	Employee benefit participation and claims information.	ERP – HR & Benefits Module and Database, External Supplier of 401K Plan's Database
	Office Automation	Email transmission and archiving, document and file management and archiving, print, copy, and fax transmissions.	Bundled COTS Application for Word Processing, Spreadsheets, Web Page Creation, and Presentations

Figure 9-5: Mapping EA Components,
Lines of Business, and Information Flows

2.3. Systems and applications: This section identifies how current EA components and artifacts at the Systems and applications level of the EA³ framework support the information flows that are required for LOBs throughout the enterprise. The discussion should summarize how well this "suite" of commercial and custom developed IT systems and front/back office services provide the functionality the enterprise needs for LOB operations and office automation. This can range from large scale, multi-module ERP solutions, to commercial applications and databases, to small custom-developed websites.   Comments should focus on degree of integration, potential scalability, user satisfaction, and any reliance on proprietary solutions.

2.4. Technology Infrastructure: This section discusses the voice, data, and video EA components and artifacts that make up the Technology Infrastructure level of the EA³ framework. The discussion should focus on how well these internal and external networks, systems, and cable plants integrate to create a "seamless" infrastructure. Comment should also be made on how well the infrastructure currently handles the transport of voice, data, and video information, in terms of reliability, scalability, and cost-efficiency.

2.5. IT Security. This section discusses the general approach to IT security at all levels of the EA framework. IT security should be part of any strategic goal or initiative that depends on accurate, properly authenticated information. High-level descriptions are provided on how security is built into business services and the control of information flows, as well as the design and operation of systems, services, and networks. Specific IT security information should not be part of the EA Management Plan because it could reveal vulnerabilities. This type of information should be documented in a separate IT Security Plan that only certain people in the enterprise have access to (see Chapter 11).

2.6. EA Standards. The standards section documents the Technical Standards Reference Model (TSRM), which provides EA standards for voice, data, video, and IT security that are used during EA component development. The TSRM can also provide a list of preferred vendors and products that meet the technical standards that an enterprise adopts. EA standards are a key element of the configuration management (CM) process and come from international, national, local, government, industry, and enterprise sources. Selected standards should include standards for voice, data, and video technologies from leading standards bodies throughout the world, including the Institute of Electrical and Electronics

Engineers (IEEE), the National Institute of Science and Technology (NIST), the International Enterprise for Standardization (ISO), the European Committee on Standardization (CEN), and the Federal Enterprise Architecture's Reference Models (see Appendix B). An example of the format for a TSRM is provided in Figure 9-6.

Standards Area	ISO/CEN Standard	IEEE Standard	NIST Standard	Local Standard	Products
Voice					
Data					
Video					
Security					

Figure 9.6: Example Technical Standards Reference Model

The following examples of international EA standards from ISO and CEN:

- ISO 14258 (1998): Concepts and Rules for Enterprise Models.
- ISO 15704 (2000): Requirements for Enterprise Reference Architectures and Methodologies.
- CEN ENV 40003 (1991): CIM-Systems-Architecture Framework for Modeling.
- CEN ENV 12204 (1996): Constructs for Enterprise Modeling.

2.7. Workforce Requirements. This section describes the approach to IT workforce planning and training that the enterprise uses in human capital management. People are often the most valuable resource an enterprise has, and IT workforce plans should detail training requirements for EA component operations support and new development projects at all levels of the framework.

EA Management Plan: Part 3.
Summary of Future Architecture

3.1. Future Operating Scenarios. In this section, the future operating scenarios are presented along with a narrative description of the purpose of the scenarios and the spectrum of operating environments that the scenarios respond to. For example, three scenarios are presented with an opening narrative that explains that they represent:

- Scenario 1: Continuing with the status quo.

- Scenario 2: An aggressive business strategy in a good market environment.

- Scenario 3: A defensive business strategy during a market down-turn.

Each scenario has planning assumptions built into it, as was described in Chapter 8, that highlight changes that will need to occur in processes, people, and technology. Lastly, in this section, a description is provided of the selected course of action for the enterprise (e.g., Future Scenario 2 will be pursued because a good business environment is forecast for the next several years).

3.2. Planning Assumptions. The planning assumptions from the scenarios are further discussed in terms of what they mean to the priorities of the enterprise as it implements the future EA. The assumptions identify new capabilities and resources that will be needed if the enterprise is to be successful in each scenario. This section then focuses on the selected scenario and the planning assumptions that will underlie that course of action. Continuing the example from above, if Future Scenario 2 is being pursued, then several new e-commerce systems may need to be built and new manufacturing capacity supported. The planning assumptions that were identified in Future Scenario 2 become the guideposts for decisions about how to change the current EA, which needs to be described.

3.3. Updating Current and Future Views of the EA. Documentation of planned changes in processes and resources is what creates the future views of the EA at all levels of the framework. Using the EA^3 framework as an example, these updates should be accomplished in a "top-down" manner, to preserve the emphasis on strategy and business, and to maintain the logic of the documentation's relationships. Therefore, these updates would begin with to the enterprise's strategic goals and initiatives.

Changes to the enterprise's strategic plan are made periodically or in response to a significant new internal or external business or technology driver. Most strategic plans are intended to last several years, with associated goals, initiatives, and measures changing very little. Changes in the EA³ framework at this level therefore may be minimal if it is not time to update the strategic plan. Goals, initiatives, and measures should be considered as exchangeable EA components. This means that a goal or measure can be added, dropped, or modified without nullifying the entire strategic plan.

A similar approach is used to review and update the enterprise's business services at the second level of the EA³ framework. It is important to ensure that the current views of business services are complete and can show how they support the accomplishment of current strategic goals. The changes in business services then can be made considering any changes in strategic goals, initiatives, and measures that may be planned and documented at the top level of the EA³ framework. Also, documentation at the Business Process Level of the EA³ framework should show future planning for more effective, cost-efficient, and technically integrated processes.

At the third level of the EA³ framework, the development of future views enables proactive planning to improve information exchange within the enterprise, and promotes the establishment of standards for the format of commonly used data entities/objects which further promotes EA component interoperability. Planning at this level of the EA³ framework first considers the information-related requirements of the level above, business services. Once these are identified, cross-cutting information flows between processes, as well as flows within single processes can be identified and documented using whatever methodology is selected for use in the EA³ framework (either traditional structured methods or object-oriented methods). Finally, planning for information flows looks downward in the EA³ framework at the Systems/Services level and the Technology Infrastructure level.

Documenting changes to the flow of information within and between business services (and new data standards) will enable EA planners to select EA components at these two lowest levels of the EA³ framework that best support the information flows and data standards. A focal point for the discussion in this Section is to identify any current performance gaps that exist at the higher levels of the EA[3] framework and map them to current EA components and products. The future view of the Systems/Services level of the EA[3] framework should show which EA components will be changing and in what timeframe (see the Sequencing Plan). EA components at this fourth level of the EA should increasingly be selected for their interoperability as well as performance and scalability.

At the Technology Infrastructure level of the EA[3] framework, future changes will reflect EA components (hardware and software) that will provide a more robust, reliable, and secure voice, data, and video backbone transport capability. Interoperability, cost-effectiveness and open standards are additional factors to be considered.

3.4. <u>EA Sequencing Plan</u>: The Sequencing Plan section of the EA Management Plan documents the tasks, milestones, and timeframe for implementing new EA components and artifacts. Large and mid-size enterprises often have many new development, upgrade, retirement, or migration projects underway at any given time and these require coordination to establish the optimal sequencing of activities. Sometimes there are dependencies between projects that also require proper sequencing. For example, an improvement to the capacity of the data infrastructure may be required before additional systems and/or databases can be effectively hosted so that maximum performance can be attained. Another common example is the consolidation of EA components (IT resources such as systems, applications, and databases) to improve both performance and overall cost effectiveness. Figure 9-7 on the next page provides an example of a sequencing diagram that shows EA component consolidation activities.

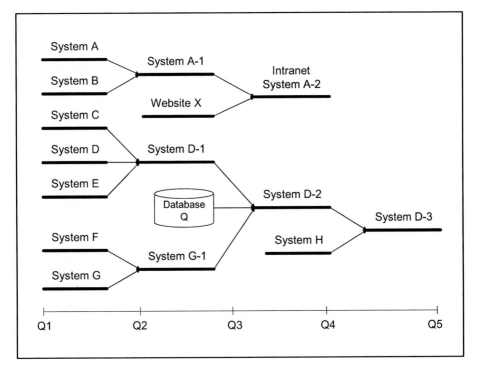

Figure 9-7: Example EA Sequencing Diagram

3.5. <u>EA Configuration Management</u>: The EA Configuration Management (CM) section of the EA Management Plan serves to support the sub-process by which changes to the EA are managed and the standards in the TSRM are applied. Changes to the EA include the addition, upgrade, retirement of EA components or artifacts. CM ensures that (1) a standardized process is used in reviewing proposed changes, (2) technical standards for voice, data, and video are followed or waived, (3) there is a documented waiver process, (4) waivers have specific time limits, so that EA standards are eventually realized, (5) there is enforcement for EA documentation version control. The CM process should be overseen by the Chief Architect, and be supported by an Architecture Working Group that includes stakeholders from throughout the enterprise. The CM process works through the submission, review and approval/rejection of an EA Change Request (EACR) form by any stakeholder, as shown in Figure 9-8 on the next page.

**Enterprise Architecture
Change Request Form**

Date Submitted: _____
EACR Control #: _____

Submitted By: _____

EAF Level: *Strategic   Business   Information   Application   Technology*

Description of Requested Change : _____
_____
_____
_____

Justification: _____
_____
_____

Group(s) Affected: _____
_____
_____

Description of Supporting Documentation (attach to EACR): _____
_____
_____

- -

EACR Action (Completed By Chief Architect)

Approved   Not-Approved   Waiver Granted Until (date: _____)

Include in EA Version _____   Publication Date: _____

EAF Standard Area: *Documentation   Voice   Data   Video   Security*

EAF Standard(s) Affected: _____

Reason for Non-Approval or Waiver: _____
_____
_____
_____

Chief Architect: _____   _____
                             Signature   *Date*

Figure 9-8: Example EA Change Request Form

EA Management Plan: Part 4.
EA Glossary and References

This part of the EA Management Plan is where a Glossary of EA terms is provided along with an Acronym List. There should also be a bibliographical list of reference books and articles that might provide additional background or that help the reader's understanding of the EA Management Plan. Because the EA is still an emerging area of professional practice, the Acronym List and Glossary are helpful in creating a common set of terms and definitions for use throughout the enterprise.

Summary of Concepts

This chapter provided a description of the purpose, format, and content of an EA Management Plan. This Plan describes the EA management process, implementation methodology, and documentation framework, as well as summaries of current and future views of the EA. It is a living document that is updated at regular intervals to provide clear version control for changes in current and future views of EA components and artifacts at each level of the framework. The EA Management Plan should be archived in the on-line EA repository to support easy access to the information and promote linkage of the EA program to other IT management processes.

Chapter 9 Questions and Exercises

1. What is the purpose of an EA Management Plan?

2. What is an EA Change Request and how is it used within the Configuration Management process?

3. What is the purpose of the Sequencing Plan?

4. What is the role of a Chief Information Officer in the EA program?

5. What is the role of a Chief Architect in the EA program

6. How do technical and product standards contribute to the EA program?

7. Why are standardized terms important to an EA program?

8. What are summaries of current and future views an important part of the EA Management Plan? Who is the intended audience of the EA Management Plan?

9. How can an EA Management Plan show "gaps" in enterprise performance?

10. Develop a flow chart for EA governance in a public or private sector enterprise. Show where policy development and decision-making occur, as well as interfaces to other management processes, including capital planning, project management, and security.

11. Develop a Sequencing Plan for the implementation of a major commercial Enterprise Resource Planning (ERP) product that has software modules for finance, accounting, payroll and benefits, manufacturing, inventory, and sales. Show how existing stovepipe systems in each of these areas would be replaced by the ERP.

12. Develop an EA Roles and Responsibility Matrix for a public or private sector enterprise of your choice.

Section III

Using an Enterprise Architecture

This section discusses how to use and maintain Enterprise Architecture information within the enterprise; and how related governance processes can be integrated.

Case Study (Scene 5) - Linking EA to Other Management Processes

The Case Study continues the scenario at Danforth Manufacturing Company (DMC) that was presented in Sections I and II. This scene describes how the EA information will be used in the company's capital planning process to support investment decision-making. It also talks about how the EA information supports project management and security planning.

Chapter 10 - The Role of Investment Planning and Project Management

Chapter 10 introduces the concepts of the capital planning and investment control (CPIC) process and its relationship to enterprise architecture and project management. The four phases of the CPIC process are described (plan, select, control, and evaluate). The chapter also introduces the concepts of project management and how they relate to enterprise architecture.

Chapter 11 - The Role of Information Technology Security

Chapter 11 introduces the concepts of IT security and how they relate to enterprise architecture. Four elements of an IT Security Program are described: information security, personnel security, operational security, and physical security. Additionally, EA artifacts related to IT security are discussed, including system security plans, risk assessments, test and evaluation reports, continuity of operations plans, disaster recovery plans, and system certification and accreditations.

Chapter 12 - The Enterprise Architecture Repository and Support Tools

Chapter 12 discusses the purpose and functionality of the on-line EA repository. The design of an example repository (Living Enterprise™) is described, as well as the relationship of a repository to the underlying EA documentation framework. The chapter also provides a mapping of EA component documentation techniques to the areas of the EA repository, and discusses the role of EA support tools.

The Case Study continues the scenario at Danforth Manufacturing Company (DMC) that was presented in Sections I and II. The CIO and Chief Architect have now completed a project with the sponsors of two lines of business who currently have requirements for IT systems. The sponsors, CFO Jim Gorman, and COO Kate Jarvis, had their teams work with the EA Working Group to develop EA segment documentation for the financial and production lines of business. These segments represent the first parts of the company's architecture. This scene describes how the EA segment documentation will be used in the company's new capital planning process that will support IT investment decision-making. This scene also includes a discussion about how the EA artifacts support project management and security planning activities. Upon Sam's recommendation, Jim agreed to lead a new Capital Planning Working Group, and DMC's CEO Robert Danforth acknowledged that the Executive Committee's would serve as the company's Capital Planning Board with final investment decision approval.

CIO Sam Young opened a day-long workshop for DMC's EA Working Group, which included members of the newly formed Capital Planning Working Group. "Today's workshop will be a bit different because we are going to use the EA documentation that we have developed during the past few weeks to help Kate and Jim make decisions about solutions to their IT requirements. Vince Albright, our Chief Architect, will lead the morning session and will start by describing the documentation of current and future views of the production and financial segments and how that will support the analysis and decision-making process. Then, Jim Gorman, our CFO, will lead the afternoon session, which is also the first meeting of the Capital Planning Working Group, who will work with us to develop a combined recommendation on the solution to Jim and Kate's requirements for new IT systems. Vince, what have we learned from the EA documentation activities?"

"Thanks Sam" said Vince. "The EA Working Group did a great job with Jim's and Kate's staff teams over the past two weeks in developing EA artifacts for the EA components in the production segment and the financial segment of the DMC architecture. We now have EA artifacts that describe the components in these two segments at each level of the framework. This includes the strategic goals, initiatives, and output/outcome measures related to finance and production, the flow diagrams of processes in these two lines of business, the data structure and flow diagrams for the IT systems, application/web service lists and interface diagrams, and network diagrams. Further, we were able to develop a future operating scenario together that looks three years in the future and highlights both the unique and common IT requirements in the two lines of business that these segments represent. From this scenario, several planning assumptions were revealed, which may help us determine a common solution to several IT requirements. The other aspect of the EA framework that we addressed was a set of EA components that represent IT security resources that serve these two segments, as well as an initial set of standards for voice, data, and video infrastructure resources that serve the segments. Finally, we identified the current IT workforce and training requirements related to these lines of business, but are waiting on developing the future requirements until the groups determine the recommended solution.

Vince led the two working groups in a more detailed review of the EA documentation that had been developed, and Jim then opened the afternoon working group session. "Thanks again Sam and Vince for providing the approach and oversight for the documentation of the EA segments for production and finance. Kate and I are now going to review the requirements that we have for additional IT support within our lines of business. We would like the Enterprise Architecture and Capital Planning Working Groups and our staff members to help us this afternoon to determine what the most effective way is to meet those requirements, be it separate systems or a combined solution. DMC is always interested in maximizing the return on any investment in resources we make, and it already is apparent that by looking across the entire enterprise of DMC, that our planning and decision-making will be enhanced."

Jim and Kate discussed their previous proposals for IT systems in their respective lines of business. Jim had initially identified a commercial ERP solution (WELLCO) which had the service modules that he needed. Kate had initially identified a custom-built Sales and Inventory System (SITS) as the solution for new requirements in those areas. The working groups and line of business staff members reviewed the information from the initial requests, and then used the EA documentation of these lines of business to establish what the most operationally efficient and cost effective solution would be. They were able to determine that the WELLCO commercial ERP application suite had a module available for sales and inventory functions. By contacting the vendor, they were also able to determine that this module could support the addition of some custom functionality, which would then allow it to fully meet Kate's requirements. The cost of this additional WELLCO module would be approximately $1,675,000, as opposed to the $3,000,000 that was estimated to create SITS. Further, the use of the WELLCO ERP product within both lines of business promoted additional information exchanges through the use of common data formats.

Jim addressed the group in the late afternoon after the analysis work and discussions had been completed. "Thank you all for taking the time today to help us review the creation of the first two segments of our company's architecture, and use that information to evaluate two requests for new IT support. Originally, these two requests were submitted by Kate and me separately at our annual planning conference several months ago. The estimated cost of the two separate solutions was $3,600,000. By looking at our business areas from an enterprise-wide architecture perspective, we have been able to find a combined solution that will save the company $1,325,000 and promotes higher levels of information sharing than we otherwise would have achieved. Sam, this is a win-win for Kate and me. I believe it is a win for you and Vince, because you have just shown why the EA program is needed, and how it will more than pay for itself. Sam and I will now take the combined recommendation of the EA Working Group and the Capital Planning Working Group to the Executive Committee for final approval. If approved, we will be calling on the two groups to assist in conducting the control reviews and evaluation review of the project that are part of our new capital planning and investment control process. This will lower the risk of failure and help us to mature our EA and capital planning processes. I look forward to seeing you all at those reviews."

The DMC Executive Board approved the recommendation of the working groups, and CEO Robert Danforth commended Kate, Sam, and Jim for working together to identify a more cost-efficient solution for their needs. The EA program was then approved for funding to complete the remaining segments of the DMC architecture over the following 18 months, as well as annual operations and support funding for the next two years, at which time the value of the EA program would be reviewed by the Executive Committee.

Chapter 10

The Role of Investment Planning and Project Management

Chapter Overview

This chapter introduces the concepts of the capital planning and investment control (CPIC) process and its relationship to enterprise architecture and project management. The four phases of the CPIC process are described (plan, select, control, and evaluate). The chapter concludes with a discussion of how a significant part of IT governance is implemented through the CPIC process.

> **Key Term: *Capital Planning***
> The management and decision-making process associated with the planning, selection, control, and evaluation of investments in resources, including EA components such as systems, networks, knowledge warehouses, and support services for the enterprise.

Learning Objectives

> ➢ Understand the concepts of capital planning.

> ➢ Understand the four phases of the capital planning process.

> ➢ Understand how capital planning relates to EA.

> ➢ Understand how project management relates to EA.

Introduction

The EA program is only effective if the enterprise's resources are effectively applied to gaps in operational performance. It takes people, money, facilities, software, hardware, training, and other resources to do this through the investment in an ongoing series of development and improvement projects. If there were no gaps in operational performance, there would be no requirement for new or upgraded EA components.

However, this is rarely the case, and so capital planning and project management processes are needed to manage the projects that enable the ongoing transition from the current architecture to the future architecture. These processes also help to ensure that strategic, business, and architectural alignment are maintained as the enterprise plans, selects, controls, and evaluates investments in EA components.

Home Architecture Analogy: For an architect's design to be approved, the owner's requirements must be met within the budget that is available. The architect must then work with a builder to ensure that the design is properly constructed, that the schedule is met, and that the budget is not exceeded.

Discussion

Capital Planning and Investment Control (CPIC) process supports EA by planning, selecting, controlling, and evaluating investments in new or upgraded EA components. This cyclic process promotes the attainment of the following:

- Identification of operational performance gaps in the enterprise
- Identification of new or upgraded EA components to close performance gaps
- Development of business cases that consider alternatives, alignment, and value
- Development and management of an overall portfolio of investments in the EA
- Maximizing the value of individual investments in EA components
- Encouraging a culture of learning by evaluating each completed investment

The CPIC process operates in four distinct phases that serve to (1) standardize how requirements for technology are identified within a strategic and business context; (2) associate the technology requirement with an EA component; (3) make an investment decision; and (4) implement a solution through standardized project management practices and the EA program.[22] The Project Management Plan (PMP) serves as the common documentation source for all phases of the CPIC process. Figure 10-1 shows the four phases of the CPIC process.

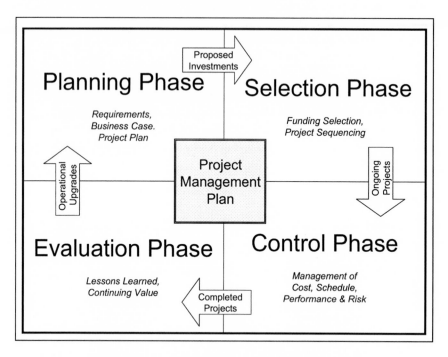

Figure 10-1: The IT Capital Planning Process

CPIC Planning Phase
The CPIC Planning Phase is where business and technology requirements that emerge throughout the enterprise are reviewed at a preliminary level for merit, need, and identification of an association with an EA component. Those requirements that are determined to have sufficient value to enterprise are then associated with an EA component and formalized in a PMP using standard templates for large and small projects. The PMP contains detailed information about the proposed investment/project

---

[22] The original concept of a CPIC process was developed by the Federal CIO Council in the late 1990's and is now codified in annual guidance from the Office of Management and Budget in Circular A-11. The OMB approach identifies three phases: select, control, and evaluate. This book adds the planning phase to recognize the importance and amount of activity that is required to properly evaluate alternative solutions and implementation strategies prior to making an investment decision in the selection for funding phase.

including the requirement, the business case, a work breakdown structure, a schedule, a budget, roles and responsibilities, measures for success, and a communications plan. The PMP is intended to be a living document that is updated throughout the lifecycle of a project from conception to completion. When the PMP is completed and all project and investment information are present, the potential investment/project moves to the CPIC Selection Phase.

CPIC Selection Phase

The CPIC Selection Phase is where a funding decision is made for a proposed investment in an EA component. The funding proposal, as documented in the PMP, is reviewed for value, alignment, strength of business case, strength of technical solution, security, risk, and return. Based on this review of the PMP, the enterprise's management determines if the investment should be made in light of available resources. Some enterprises review proposed investments as a group on a periodic basis (e.g., quarterly or annually) so as to align the selection process with budget and business cycles.

Return on Investment (ROI) can be one of the most difficult aspects of a proposed investment's business case to develop because many of the benefits of enterprise-wide technology solutions are qualitative in nature. For example, in calculating benefits attributable to the EA component that contains enterprise-wide e-mail, there will be an estimate of the dollar values for improvements in productivity, communication, record keeping, and morale; all of which are difficult to precisely measure. For that reason, enterprises should use ROI as only one of a number of factors in selecting investments in EA components.

Once a proposed investment in an EA component is selected for funding, the investment becomes an active project and the PMP is refined to reflect any updates to the implementation schedule and funding plan that may be needed for that project to be activated within the Sequencing Plan of the EA Management Plan. The project then moves to the CPIC Control Phase.

CPIC Control Phase

The CPIC Control Phase is where ongoing development and upgrade projects are evaluated for how closely cost, schedule, and EA component performance milestones are being met, and how well areas of risk are being managed.

Cost, schedule, and performance milestones are tracked by establishing baseline estimates and then managing to that baseline. This is the basis of "Earned Value Management" (EVM) which is a project management technique that looks at planned versus actual cost, schedule, and performance data throughout the life of the project. [23] One of the key concepts in EVM is that projects that significantly diverge from planned (baseline) estimates are more difficult to return to the baseline the further along that the project is. EVM emphasizes identifying significant divergence within the first third of the project's schedule in order to have the best chance to recover to baseline values, or to reset the baseline if new requirements have been added which increase cost and/or time estimates. Project planning and tracking documentation is maintained as part of the PMP and includes a Work Breakdown Structure (WBS), project task list and schedule (Gantt Chart), critical path information (PERT Chart), EVM information, and performance metrics. Performance metrics are those which measure the capability of the EA component that is being created. This could include database query speed, application refresh rate, website page refresh rate, usability, navigability, peak network bandwidth, and interoperability.

Risk is related to uncertainty and any potential obstacle to success in the project. It is important to have identified risk areas before the start of the project and implemented proactive and reactive strategies for limiting (mitigating) those risks. Sources of risk include the use of new technologies, loss of key personnel, loss of funding, adding new requirements without adding time/money (called "scope creep"), insufficient testing prior to acceptance, lack of stakeholder buy-in, and insufficient training for end-users and maintenance personnel.

CPIC Evaluation Phase
The CPIC Evaluation Phase is where (1) completed IT projects receive a Post-Implementation Review (PIR), and (2) where operational systems are periodically reviewed for continuing value. PIRs help an enterprise to review the "lessons learned" from each project and in so doing, to mature in their ability to implement similar projects in the future. For example, if an enterprise completes several website projects a year and no PIR is held, the problems, successes, approaches to risk, etc. will not be shared and an opportunity to improve in this area is lost. PIRs help to reduce cost, cycle

---

[23] The Earned Value Management System (EVMS) was developed in the 1960's by the Department of Defense to track large, complex acquisition programs.

time, and risk for IT projects, and they help to create a culture of sharing and learning in the enterprise.

Once a system is accepted into the IT operating environment, it becomes what is referred to as a "legacy" system. It is important to not only conduct PIRs just after systems are brought into the IT operating environment, but also to review these legacy systems at regular intervals (perhaps annually) to determine if each one is continuing to add sufficient value to the enterprise to merit additional spending for operations, maintenance, and upgrades. If it is found that a legacy system is not performing to the level that the enterprise needs, or is duplicating capabilities, then that system is identified for phase-out and disposal. Disposing of legacy systems (after needed data and functionality are transferred) is important to maintaining an IT operating environment that is as effective, flexible, and cost-efficient as possible.

Governance and Capital Planning

Governance processes, including CPIC, are those that provide policy and decision-making, and they should be overseen by some form of Executive Steering Committee that is comprised of the enterprise's top executives.

The CPIC process should be managed by the enterprise's Chief Financial Officer (CFO) in collaboration with the Chief Information Officer (CIO) and LOB managers. Because CPIC is primarily a financial investment decision-making process, the CFO should lead it, but it is very important in information-centric enterprises that the CIO be a partner in the process and that these two executives effectively integrate CPIC and the EA Management process. CPIC decisions in each phase of the process should be made by an executive level Capital Planning Board (CPB) that is supported by a Capital Planning Working Group (CPWG) and an Enterprise Architecture Working Group (EAWG). In this way, CPIC decision-making has senior stakeholder involvement and the documentation and analysis activities are accomplished by subordinate groups of experts in business and technology. Figure 10-2 shows theses relationships.

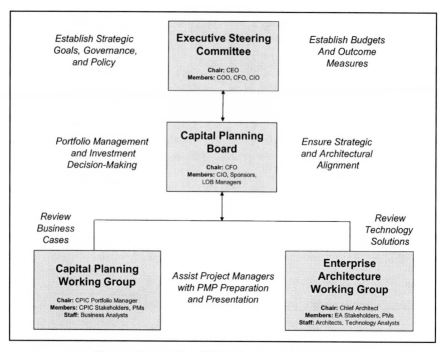

Figure 10-2: The CPIC Governance Process

The Executive Steering Committee

The ESC is a top-level policy making and decision review committee. Its purpose is to establish the enterprise's strategic goals and initiatives, governance processes, and policies to implement and integrate those processes. Enterprise-wide governance regarding the use of information technologies primarily involves six processes, which must work together to promote effective policy and decision-making: strategic planning, enterprise architecture, capital planning, project management, security, and workforce planning.

The ESC provides the CPB with policy and guidance regarding strategic goals and governance. The ESC also reviews the decisions of the CPB to ensure that they best promote the achievement of the enterprise's strategic goals.

The Capital Planning Board

The CPB is an executive-level decision-making board. The CPB decides which investments/projects are selected for funding, determines if active projects involving capital assets (including EA components) are being effectively implemented, evaluates completed projects for lessons learned, and determines if ongoing programs are continuing to add value to the enterprise.

To establish a baseline for investment decision-making, the CPB develops a portfolio to aggregate, categorize, and manage individual investments in capital assets, including EA components. This "Investment Portfolio" reveals total spending on capital assets, supports portfolio-level management, and allows for the shifting of resources away from categories with low ROI. Alternatively, general business categories can be used such as Operations, Sales and Marketing, Finance and Accounting, Human Resources, Research and Development, and Office Automation. The goal of portfolio level investment management for the CPB is to identify the right balance of capital spending between categories, and to weed out weak investments in each category.

The CPB should establish a regular schedule for reviewing investment proposals, current projects, and ongoing programs. Each investment (and investment is a new project or legacy program) in the portfolio should be reviewed at key schedule milestones or at least once a year. The CPB should be chaired by the CFO, and the members should include the CIO, program sponsors, and program managers.

The Capital Planning Working Group
The CPWG supports the CPB by (1) helping Project Managers to prepare and update PMPs, especially the business cases, (2) providing documentation and business analysis support for CPB reviews, (3) coordinating their analyses with the EAWG, and (4) maintaining an archive of CPB documents. The CPWG should be chaired by a CPIC Portfolio Manager and the members include project managers and CPIC stakeholders. Support staff for the CPWG should include experts on strategic planning, business analysis, project management, and workforce planning.

The Enterprise Architecture Working Group
The EAWG supports the CPB by (1) helping Project Managers to prepare and update PMPs, especially EA information, (2) providing documentation and technical analysis support for CPB reviews, and (3) coordinating their analyses with the CPWG. The EAWG should be chaired by the Chief Architect and the members should include project managers and EA stakeholders. Support staff for the EAWG should include the EA team and experts on information technology analysis at all levels of the EA[3] framework, security, project management, and configuration management.

The Role of Project Management

Project (and program) management is a professional discipline that focuses on developing, implementing, operating, improving, and/or retiring enterprise resources. Project and Program Managers (PMs) are responsible for meeting the goals of the project or program. Controlling successful outcomes involves the management of five primary aspects of a project/program: managing scope; controlling costs, maintaining the schedule, achieving desired levels of product performance, and mitigating risk.

Projects and Programs are terms that encompass the work that an enterprise does. Projects are different from programs in that projects create new or updated resources/capabilities. Programs include projects as well as the ongoing governance and business services that constitute most of the activities of an enterprise. Programs are oriented toward the management of existing (legacy) resources/capabilities, whereas projects build new or upgrade existing resources/capabilities. [24]

> **Key Term: *Project***
> A temporary endeavor undertaken to create a unique product, service, or result.

> **Key Term: *Program***
> A group of related projects managed in a coordinated way. Programs usually involve an element of ongoing activity,

PMs manage both projects and programs by establishing a detailed plan for accomplishing the strategic and/or tactical goals that are supported. Project Management Plan (PMP) and adjusting it to meet changes in requirements or resources. The PMP is a living document that provides information for PMs and others in all phases of the CPIC process. When the project involves the development, upgrade, or retirement of EA components, the development of the PMP also provides some of the EA artifacts needed for that component. Figure 10-3 on the next page provides an example outline of a Project Management Plan.

---

[24] Project Management Institute (PMI). The Project Management Body of Knowledge (PMBOK®) Guide: 2000 Edition.

Project Management Plan

Executive Summary

1. Project Requirements
   a. Project Description
   b. Project Sponsorship and Stakeholders
2. Strategic Alignment
   a. Alignment to Strategic Goals
   b. Value to and Impact on Strategic Initiatives
3. Architectural Alignment
   a. Alignment with the Enterprise Architecture
   b. Integration With Existing Resources
   c. Standards and Product Selection Strategy
   d. System Development Lifecycle Methodology
   e. System Performance Metrics
   f. System Standard Operating Procedures
4. Business Case
   a. Alternatives Analysis
   b. Cost-Benefit Analysis
   c. Return on Investment Analysis
5. Project Controls
   a. Cost Controls and Project Budget
   b. Schedule and Work Breakdown Structure
   c. Project Performance Goals and Metrics
   d. Risk Management
6. Project Enterprise
   a. Project Sponsor, Manager, and Team Structure
   b. Roles and Responsibilities
   c. Testing and Quality Assurance
   d. Workforce Training
7. Security and Privacy
   a. Security Plan
   b. Data Privacy Procedures
   c. Records Management Procedures

Appendix A   Business Case Worksheets
Appendix B   Reference Documents
Appendix C   Glossary of Terms

Figure 10-3: Example Outline of a Project Management Plan

PMs should develop the Project Management Plan as follows:

PMP - Executive Summary
Provide a one or two-paragraph summary of the purpose of the project, its value to mission accomplishment, the technical approach, alternatives considered, the total lifecycle cost, funding availability, the proposed schedule, and potential implementation risks.

PMP - Project Requirements: *Documentation and Analysis*
Provide a general description of the background and context of the project, as well as the EA-related requirement(s) that this project meets. Determine the outcomes that the project must achieve, and how the successful attainment of those outcomes will be measured. Describe the type of EA component(s) that this project develops, upgrades, or retires (system, application, database, website, cable plant, hardware platform, etc.). Determine if this project creates a new IT capability or upgrades an existing capability. Also determine if there is any duplication of existing capability and if so, describe why it is beneficial to create this duplication. For project sponsorship and stakeholders, identify who the funding and implementation sponsor is at the executive level; this is the person with budget approval and operational approval authority. Finally, identify who the stakeholders are in this project (i.e., users, sponsors, developers, and managers).

PMP - Strategic Alignment: *Value and Impact*
For strategic alignment, describe how this project supports the enterprise's strategic goals. Describe if this project responds to a directive or a government mandate or initiative, and how this project will meet all aspects of these requirements. For value and impact, describe the value of this project in terms of improving internal and/or external business services and optimizing the utilization of resources. Determine if re-engineering or improvement of those processes is needed before (or as part of) project implementation and operations. Describe the impact if this project is not implemented.

PMP - Architectural Alignment: *Integration, Standards, and Approach*
For EA alignment, discuss and then document the project's proposed technical approach with the enterprise's EAWG for design and operational alignment at the various levels of the EA^3 framework: strategy, business, information, applications, and technology infrastructure. Determine the costs associated with documenting the project throughout its lifecycle in the on-line EA repository, including views of EA components at all levels

of the EA³ framework in both the current and future architectures, as well as the EA Management Plan. Include these costs in the total lifecycle cost of the project. For integration, determine if there are data or telecommunication interfaces to other EA components and describe how integration, interface, and information exchange issues will be handled. For standards, determine if approved data, telecommunications, and video technical   standards at all levels of the EA³ framework are being followed. If there are new standards being introduced, explain the effect of adopting those new standards on other IT system(s), application(s), database(s), and/or website(s). Describe the approach to configuration management that will be taken in terms of using EACRs at all levels of the EA³ framework. Determine and describe the System Development Lifecycle Methodology method that will be used to organize IT system implementation efforts (e.g., waterfall, rapid application development, evolutionary, incremental/phased). For performance measures, determine the performance metrics that will be used to measure proper system design performance, to be evaluated as part of acceptance criteria, and during the operations and maintenance phase of the delivered EA component(s). Determine the Standard Operating Procedures (SOPs) that will have to be written for the operations and maintenance phase of the lifecycle, and utilize draft SOPs as part of acceptance testing.

PMP - Business Case: *Value and Results*
Perform an Alternatives Analysis to determine if there are several viable alternatives for meeting the stated EA-related requirement(s). Identify how each alternative meets or does not meet the requirement(s). Perform a Cost-Benefit Analysis for each alternative and then determine what the Return on Investment will be (using a Net Present Value discount factor) during the lifecycle. Perform a risk analysis to identify areas of risk and mitigation strategies. Select the best alternative based on (1) strategic alignment, (2) architecture alignment, (3) ROI, (4) security solution, (5) level of risk, (7) total cost of ownership, and (7) available resources. Ensure that the rest of the PMP documentation focuses only on the selected alternative. (See Appendix A for additional details on the business case).

PMP - Project Controls: Cost, Schedule, Performance, and Risk
For cost controls, describe the total lifecycle cost of this project, including planning, design, development, operations, and maintenance. Describe the source of funding for the project during the total lifecycle including operations and maintenance. Describe the method for acquiring key project resources (i.e., funding, hardware, software, operating facilities, trained personnel). Use an Earned Value Management approach to track

planned versus actual costs, as well as the baseline schedule and actual progress. For additional schedule controls, document the baseline schedule with both task (Gantt Chart) and critical path (PERT Chart) views that identify major milestones, in-progress, reviews, testing, and post-implementation events. For project performance oversight, establish what the performance metrics are for the EA components that are being created and/or upgraded in this project, especially what the acceptance criteria are prior to going operational. In the area of risk mitigation, describe what the potential obstacles to success in implementing this project are and how will this risk be mitigated (overcome the obstacle). Examples include technological risk if the enterprise is an "early adopter", cost risk imposed by budget cuts, schedule risk imposed by losses of key personnel, late shipment of hardware or software components, and implementation risk if all stakeholders were not involved in all aspects of project development.

PMP - Project Enterprise: *Structure and Responsibilities*
Identify the Project Sponsor, PM, and the project team. Determine and describe the roles and responsibilities of the Project Sponsor, PM, and other key team members. Document this in a project "Roles and Responsibilities Matrix." Determine a project Work Breakdown Structure (WBS) that identifies all of the major work areas and then decomposes each significant activity in terms of time and budget goals. Use these cost and schedule goals in the Gantt Chart and business case. For testing and quality assurance, describe the approach to testing during development and acceptance. Determine if third-party integration or verification testing is also required, and if so, describe the approach and key participants. Describe the training, user guide, operations, maintenance, and other reference materials that will have to be written for the project's delivered system(s), application(s), database(s), and website(s). Identify the technical, business process, or other training that users will be required to have in order to operate and maintain the delivered system(s), application(s), database(s), or website(s). Identify sources and cost estimates for all required training and schedule accomplishment prior to acceptance and operations. Identify back-up personnel for key positions to receive training.

PMP - Security and Privacy: *Protecting and Assuring Information*
In the area of physical security, determine and describe the facilities and other direct access protection that will be required to achieve an acceptable level of risk to prevent unauthorized access to these EA components. In the area of information security, determine how the information created/used by the EA component will be protected and authenticated. In

the area of personnel security, determine how access control will be provided for system administrators, database administrators, webmasters, security personnel, and end-users. In the area of operational security, determine and document (via a SOP) the procedures for handling end-user agreements, login and access control, incident response (i.e. virus attacks, denial of service attacks, hackers), password issuance and control, and employee termination. For testing and accreditation, determine and describe the method that will be used to test certify that the delivered EA components(s) meet the risk adjusted-goals in the areas of physical, information, personnel, and operational security. For data privacy, determine the sensitivity and classification of information on delivered EA component(s). Determine the issues related to data privacy and describe how they will be handled (e.g., access to employee's personal information). For records management, determine the issues related to records management and describe how they will be handled. Determine if information exchange and records management issues exist with other IT resources and describe how they will be handled.

PMP – Appendices.
Appendices to the PMP should provide amplifying documentation. This can include the detailed worksheets used in the business case (alternatives analysis, cost-benefit analysis, and NPV/ROI calculations), EA Artifacts, and a project glossary and list of terms.

Summary of Concepts

This chapter discussed the role of capital planning and project management processes in the EA Management Program and the implementation of EA components. The four phases of the Capital Planning and Investment Control process were described, as was an investment governance process that centers on the decision-making of the Capital Planning Board and its supporting working groups. These are the groups that perform both business case and EA alignment analyses and help PM prepare and update their Project Management Plans in all phases of the Capital Planning and Investment Control process. The role of project and program management was also discussed in the chapter and an example Project Management Plan was provided.

Chapter 10 Review Questions

1. Why is it important to integrate the EA Management Program with the enterprise's capital planning process and project management practices?

2. Describe the four basic phases of the capital planning process.

3. How can the capital planning process help support decisions on investing in future EA component upgrades or new capabilities?

4. What is a business case for investment in EA components? What are the roles of an Alternatives Analysis, Cost Benefit Analysis, and Return on Investment calculation in the business case?

5. Describe roles and responsibilities in the capital planning governance process.

6. Why is it important to have a standardized format for a Project Management Plan?

7. How are security and privacy issues described in the Project Management Plan?

8. What kinds of updates to a Project Management Plan occur in each of the four phases of the capital planning process?

9. What is meant by "architectural alignment" in developing a Project Management Plan?

10. Describe how an enterprise's Chief Information Officer, Chief Financial Officer, and Chief Operating Officer should cooperate and coordinate in developing and managing an integrated approach to enterprise architecture, capital planning, and project management.

11. Describe how cost, schedule, performance, and risk managed would be managed in a project to implement an email system in a new business location.

12. Develop a business case for the hypothetical outsourcing of an enterprise's IT Help Desk. The elements of the business case are (1) an Alternatives Analysis that compares in-house operation of the Help Desk and outsourcing to an external service provider, (2) a Cost-benefit Analysis for each of the two alternatives and (3) a Return on Investment calculation for each of the two alternatives.

Chapter 11

The Role of Information Technology Security

Chapter Overview

This chapter discusses the role of IT security as part of the EA program. IT security is one of the vertical "threads" that has an impact at all levels of the EA framework. The enterprise's IT Security Program is described in four basic parts: information security, personnel security, operational security, and physical security. The chapter also covers the elements of an IT Security Plan.

Learning Objectives

> Understand the role of information security in the EA program

> Understand the four basic elements of IT security

> Understand the parts of an IT Security Plan

Introduction

The role of IT security within the EA program is best described as an all-encompassing security solution. The desired image is that of a vertical thread that weaves through all levels of the EA³ framework. This image was chosen (as opposed to a separate dedicated level) because IT security is most effective when it is integral to the enterprise's strategic initiatives, business services, information flows, applications, and technology infrastructure.

> Home Architecture Analogy: The IT security solution is like a home's intruder detection and response service that monitors entry points, provides an alarm system, notifies occupants of a problem, and can generate a response from a security service.

Discussion

Effective IT security throughout the EA³ framework reflects an end-to-end solution for the enterprise that is implemented through an IT Security Program, which is comprised of four areas: (1) Information Security, (2) Personnel Security, (3) Operational Security, and (4) Physical Security. The IT Security Program provides coordinated, risk-adjusted solutions at each level of the EA³ framework to form the all-encompassing solution.

IT Security Threats

Threats to the security of an enterprise's business and technology operating environment come in many forms. This includes fires, floods, earthquakes, accidents, terrorism, hackers, disgruntled employees, runaway technologies, and unintentional mistakes. As the global use of IT continues to accelerate, fueled by the ubiquitous Internet, enterprises are increasingly exposed to daily threats from both the outside and the inside. How seriously the enterprise addresses these threats is often related on how aware the enterprise is of its dependency on IT to support key business services, and the probability of a threat affecting the enterprise. Without an awareness of a threat, or an appreciation of its relevance, enterprises will not invest in an IT Security Program.

One fundamental aspect of IT security is the realization that there isn't a 100% foolproof solution for any enterprise. The reason for this is that the IT Security Program is created by members of the enterprise (or contracted service providers), and even the people in the most trusted security and/or system administration positions can decide to disable, evade, or sabotage the security solutions. This type of insider threat is the "Achilles Heel" of all IT security programs, and creates what are referred to as "risk-adjusted" solutions. This means that an IT security solution is selected based on several considerations, including the cost, the level of protection needed, the effect on end-users and system administrators, and the effectiveness of available technologies.

Perhaps the best way to address IT security solutions throughout the enterprise is to create a "solution" of security within and around key business services and IT operating centers. Using a "defense in depth" approach, the IT security solution provides an integrated set of risk-adjusted security solutions in response to physical, personnel, and operational threats to the proper functioning of EA components.

Creating an Integrated IT Security Solution

An integrated IT security solution for the enterprise is best created by including IT security in the planning of all EA components and artifacts, and if possible, doing so in a top-down manner (beginning at the Strategic level of the EA³ framework) so that security is an imbedded part of strategic initiatives and business services. For information-centric enterprises, including IT security as a required design element of strategic initiatives can provide a strong and meaningful statement about the importance of protecting the business and technology operating environment.

IT security should be a consideration in business process reengineering and improvement activities, and should be a requirement for the design of information flows. IT security is also a key checklist item when making acquisition decisions for systems, hardware, software, and support services at the Systems/Services level and the Technology Infrastructure level of the EA³ framework.

The IT Security Program

The IT Security Program is intended to provide expertise, processes, and solutions for the protection of IT resources active in the business and technology operating environment. The IT Security Program supports the EA program by providing requirements for standards and procedures that are used in the planning and implementation of EA components and artifacts. Each EA component and artifact should be assessed to determine if the proper level for information security is present, and if not, that solutions are identified on a risk-adjusted basis. Risk-adjustment refers to the trade-off between how much security is desired versus the cost and effort required to implement it.

The IT Security Program looks at all possible sources of threat, including threats to the source and validity of information, control of access to the information, and threats to the physical environment where IT resources are located. The IT Security Program also provides Standard Operating Procedures (SOPs) that help to organize and improve the development and certification of new systems, the operation of legacy systems, and the response to security incidents.

The IT Security Program should be managed by a specialist in this field, and increasingly enterprises are establishing positions for an Information Systems Security Manager (ISSM). The ISSM should have business and IT operating experience in addition to training in the various elements of IT security. The ISSM should report to the CIO and work collaboratively with the Chief Architect to ensure that EA component and artifact design, implementation, and operational activities have effective security as a requirement. The ISSM should also be responsible for the development, implementation, and maintenance of the enterprise's IT Security Plan. This Plan should provide the security-related policies and procedures for the documentation, testing, certification, accreditation, operation, and disposal of EA components and artifacts at all levels of the EA framework. An example format for an IT Security Plan is provided in Table 11-1.

Information Technology Security Plan

1. Introduction
Purpose of the IT Security Program
Principles of IT Security
Critical Success Factors
Intended Outcomes
Performance Measures

2. Policy
Executive Guidance
Technical Guidance
Applicable Law and Regulations
Standards

3. Reporting Requirements
IT Security Program Roles and Responsibilities
IT Security Program Schedule and Milestones
IT Security Incident Reporting

4. Concept of Operations
IT Security Threat Summary
IT Security Risk Mitigation
Integration with Enterprise Architecture
Component/System Security Plans

5. Security Program Elements
Information Security
Personnel Security
Operational Security
Physical Security

6. Standard Operating Procedures
Test and Evaluation
Risk Assessment
Certification and Accreditation
Disaster Recovery/Continuity of Operations
Records Protection and Archiving
Data Privacy
IT Security Training and Awareness

Appendix A	Inventory of IT Components
Appendix B	Definitions of IT Security Terms
Appendix C	List of Acronyms
Appendix D	IT Security References

Table 11-1: Example IT Security Plan Format

IT Security Program Element #1: Information

In the area of information security, the IT Security Program should promote security-conscious designs, information content assurance, source authentication, and data access control. Additional information on this area is as follows:

Design: These are the physical and logical systems analysis and design activities that look at data structure, relationships, and flows. Whether traditional structured methods are used or the newer object-oriented methods are used (see Chapter 4 for additional details), IT Security should be one of the requirements that must be met for the design to be approved. IT security issues in this area mainly affect the Business Process and the Information Flow levels of the EA^3 framework.

Assurance: This is the protection of information content from being altered unintentionally or by an unauthorized source. Enterprises rely on the quality of data and information, regardless of subject matter. The quality is important, whether the data takes the form of financials, employee benefits, manufacturing, research, or government services. Controlling the access to information significantly contributes to assuring the integrity of that information. Also, configuration management activities such file naming conventions, automated document archiving (full and incremental saves), and version control of information all maximize information assurance. IT security issues in this area mainly affect the Business Process and the Information Flow levels of the EA^3 framework.

Authentication: This refers to being able to verify the source of information. It is often important to know, without a doubt, who it was that created or manipulated information. Software applications often automatically create a log entry or attach a "stamp" to information/documents created by that application. Computer machine addresses, Internet Protocol (IP) addresses, instant messaging names, and e-mail addresses that are automatically generated in on-line transactions provide a basic level of authentication, however "spoofing" of these is possible. Some enterprises are using digital signatures and a Public Key Infrastructure (PKI) to be able to authenticate someone's handling of information (e.g., banking transactions, e-commerce, and executive correspondence). IT security issues in this area affect all levels of the EA^3 framework.

Access: This focuses on who can access information within the enterprise and how that access is managed. Software applications often provide some form of access control through the use of login identifications and passwords. Some applications use what is called "user rights and permissions" to limit the extent of access that a particular user has. There are often several levels of rights and permissions, including: normal user; super user; and system administrator. The system administrator level of access often enables unrestricted use of a system, application, or database and as such, has a high level of security interest and should be monitored closely. IT security issues in this area mainly affect the Information Flow, Systems/Services, and Technology Infrastructure levels of the EA^3 framework.

IT Security Program Element #2: Personnel

In the area of personnel security, the IT Security Program should promote user authentication and IT security awareness and training as follows:

User Authentication: The verification of the identity of end-users and system administrators before they gain access to an EA component. Technologies that can help in this area include personal passwords, smart cards, identification badges, and biometrics. IT security issues in this area mainly affect the Systems/Services and Technology Infrastructure levels of the EA^3 framework.

Awareness Training: Security awareness training should be provided to all of the enterprise's end-users and system administrators. It includes having all end-users and administrators read and sign an IT Awareness Agreement before they have access to any EA component, which acknowledge that the enterprise owns these resources and hosted information. The IT Awareness Agreement should also state that access to these resources is contingent upon following the enterprise's operational and security SOPs and that monitoring of end-user and system administrator on-line activity is to be expected. IT awareness training should be repeated annually to reinforce compliance. IT security issues in this area affect all levels of the EA^3 framework.

Procedures Training: Security procedures training should be provided to end-users and system administrators to build proficiency in avoiding security breaches, recognizing threats, and reacting to IT security incidents. This training is very important because the timely response to a security incident (such as a virus attack) can mean the difference between a minor inconvenience and a total disruption of IT operations. IT security procedures training should be repeated annually or as follow-up to significant security upgrade actions or incidents. IT security issues in this area mainly affect the Systems/Services and Technology Infrastructure levels of the EA³ framework.

IT Security Program Element #3: Operations

In the area of operational security, the IT Security Program should promote the development of SOPs for EA component security, risk assessment, testing and evaluation, remediation, certification, operation, and disposal. SOPs should also be developed for extreme events such as recovery from major outages or natural disasters, and enabling the continuity of operations if all or part of the enterprise becomes disabled. Additional information on this area is as follows:

Risk Assessment: An overall evaluation of IT security risk at all levels of the EA³ framework. EA components at different levels of the EA³ framework have different security risks. Strategic risks include not promoting IT security if the enterprise is information-centric, not identifying desired IT security outcomes and enabling initiatives, and not providing sufficient resources for the IT Security Program. Business process risks include activities that expose information, applications, and/or the technology infrastructure to unauthorized access and manipulation. Information risks center on the protection of the source and integrity of data. Support application and IT infrastructure risks include corruption and/or disablement. IT security issues in this area affect all levels of the EA³ framework.

Component Security Testing and Evaluation: This is the testing of EA components or integrated groups of EA components in order to identify IT security vulnerabilities. Testing is followed by an evaluation of the nature of each vulnerability and the potential effect on the enterprise's business and operating environment if the vulnerability is left uncorrected. Testing is performed on the hardware, software, and procedures of each EA component as well as auditing security-related documentation (system and firewall logs, administrator files, reports, etc.). IT security issues in this area affect all levels of the EA³ framework.

Vulnerability Remediation: This is the act of correcting any IT security vulnerabilities found during EA component Testing and Evaluation.

Remediation actions are based on an evaluation of the effect of the vulnerability if it is left uncorrected. This involves the selection of a security solution based on the determination of an acceptable level of risk. Level of risk determinations take into consideration various alternatives for corrective action and the cost and operational affect of each alternative. Higher levels of security protection often cost more and have a more intrusive affect on business services. IT security issues in this area affect all levels of the EA³ framework.

Component Certification and Accreditation: This is the certification that all remediation actions have been properly implemented for an EA component or integrated group of EA components. Accreditation is the acceptance of component certification actions by the appropriate executive (usually the CIO or ISSM) and the issuance of a formal letter to operate that EA component in the configuration in which it was tested and evaluated. If the configuration changes, the process of risk assessment, test and evaluation, and remediation should be repeated to ensure that the IT security solution remains effective and has the identical corresponding risk level that is accepted by the enterprise. IT security issues in this area affect all levels of the EA³ framework.

Standard Operating Procedures: The documentation of IT security SOPs is important to ensuring that timely and effective action is taken by end-users and system administrators when faced with an IT security incident. SOPs also help in the training of new personnel. SOPs are normally required for items such as password management, biometrics/access control, virus incident response, denial of service attacks, hackers and other unauthorized users, spam, inappropriate material, user agreements, periodic backups, training requirements, disaster recovery, and submission of EA Change Requests. IT security issues in this area affect all levels of the EA³ framework.

Disaster Recovery: The assessment and recovery procedures for responding to a man-made or natural event that significantly disrupts or eliminates IT operations, yet does not threaten the existence of the enterprise. This includes sabotage, theft or corruption of resources, successful large scale hacker/virus attacks, building damage, fire, flood, and electrical outages. Two time-related aspects of disaster recovery need to be immediately and continually evaluated: (1) the method for recovery, and (2) the affect on mission accomplishment. Both of these may change as the amount of time increases from the moment the disaster occurred (e.g., data restore procedures and the affect on business services will probably be different for 2-minute, 2-hour, 2-day, and 2-week outages). IT security issues in this area affect all levels of the EA³ framework.

Continuity of Operations: This refers to procedures that are invoked if all or part of the enterprise are unexpectedly destroyed or forced to disband. In this scenario, the enterprise is unable to conduct any business or IT operations for a period of time. The recovery response is scripted in a Continuity of Operations Plan (COOP) that identifies where, how, and when business and IT functions would be restored. IT security issues in this area affect all levels of the EA³ framework.

IT Security Program Element #4: Physical Security

IT-related aspects of physical security that should be captured in the EA include protection for the facilities that support IT processing, control of access to IT equipment, networks, and telecommunications rooms, as well as fire protection, media storage, and disaster recovery systems.

Building Security: This focuses on the control of personnel access to the enterprise's buildings where IT resources are used. Depending on the level of building security that is desired, a perimeter around the building can be established with barriers and/or monitoring. This is augmented by limited entry points to the building, elevators, and workspaces with doors that open only with an authorized and current employee badge, appropriate lock combinations or biometric scan. IT security issues in this area mainly affect the Business Process and the Technology Infrastructure levels of the EA³ framework.

Network Operation Centers, Server Rooms, and Wiring Closets: This refers to the control of personnel access to those places where EA components are physically located. This includes network operation centers, remote server rooms, and wiring closets where voice, data, and video cables and patch panels are located. Doors to these areas should be locked and entry should be controlled by badge swipe and/or biometric devices. Access to the power and air-conditioning units that support these rooms should also be controlled and monitored. IT security issues in this area mainly affect the Business Process and the Technology Infrastructure levels of the EA³ framework.

Cable Plants: This refers to the control of personnel access to the various types of fiber and copper cable that connect the technology infrastructure together. Unauthorized tapping is possible, so some level of protection is recommended. If highly sensitive information is being carried by the cable plant, the enterprise may consider enclosing the cables in hard-to-cut metal pipes or cable run boxes along the upper wall/ceiling edges.   IT security issues in this area mainly affect the Business Process level and the Technology Infrastructure level of the EA³ framework.

Summary of Concepts

This chapter provided an overview the relationship of IT security to the EA program and the documentation of EA components. The chapter also described the four general areas that should be included in an IT Security Program and the IT Security Plan that articulates and guides program activities. IT security should be an integral part of the planning, design, implementation, testing, and operation of every EA component. In this way, an effective security solution is created that encompasses the entire architecture and that penetrates each level of the EA³ framework. Only by addressing all of the relevant aspects of IT security (information, personnel, operations, and physical) can effective IT security solutions be identified for individual EA components, or groups of EA components that function together. Finally, there should be awareness that foolproof security is not possible because EA components are designed and managed by humans, and "insider" access is the ultimate threat which cannot completely be overcome.   Therefore, effective risk-adjusted solutions throughout the EA³ framework are the goal of the IT Security Program.

Chapter 11 Questions and Exercises

1. Why is it important to include IT security in an EA program and the documentation of EA components?

2. What are the basic areas of an IT Security Program?

3. What are the Physical Security issues that should be reflected in the IT Security Plan?

4. What are the Personnel Security issues that should be reflected in the IT Security Plan?

5. What are the Information Security issues that should be reflected in the IT Security Plan?

6. What are the Operational Security issues that should be reflected in the IT Security Plan?

7. Why are there no 100 percent fool-proof IT Security solutions?

8. How can the EA Management Program help to promote effective IT security solutions?

9. What is the difference between a Disaster Recovery Plan and a Continuity of Operations Plan?

10. Describe how IT security functions at each level of the EA³ framework.

11. Find an IT Security Plan for a real-world enterprise in the public or private sector, and evaluate whether it links to an EA program. If not, suggest how the relationship could be established.

Chapter 12

The Enterprise Architecture Repository and Support Tools

Chapter Overview

This chapter describes the role of an on-line EA repository and support tools in the EA program and the documentation of EA components. The design and structure of an EA repository is discussed, and the relationship to an underlying EA documentation framework. The example of the EA³ framework and the *Living Enterprise*™ repository design is used in this discussion. Additionally, different types of EA documentation and support tools are discussed in the context of developing EA component documentation and populating the on-line EA repository.

Learning Objectives

> ➢ Understand the role of an on-line EA repository in the EA program.

> ➢ Understand how the EA repository supports documentation of EA components.

> ➢ Understand how the design of the EA repository relates to an EA framework.

> ➢ Understand the role of EA support tools in documenting EA components.

Introduction

The EA repository is intended to provide a single place for the storage and retrieval of EA artifacts that are created using EA software applications (tools). A repository works best if it is easy to access and use. For this reason, an on-line, web-based EA repository is recommended. This type of web "portal" for EA should be located on the enterprise's internal Local

Area Network to promote security of the information while still supporting access by executives, managers, and support staff.

> Home Architecture Analogy: The EA repository is like having an electronic copy of the home's current blueprints and future remodeling plans. This electronic information is stored on a home PC in a web format to allow for easy navigation with a web browser.

Discussion

Providing easy access to EA information and artifacts is essential for their use in planning, management, and decision-making. The EA repository is intended to provide this type of easy access by being a "one-stop-shop" for all of the documents that populate the various levels of the EA framework as is shown in Figure 12-1.

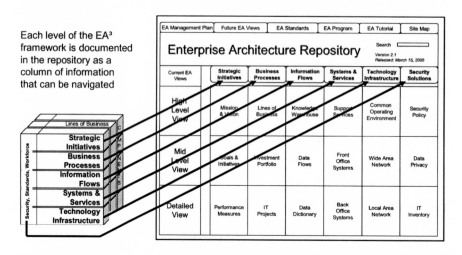

Figure 12-1: Relating the EA Framework and Repository

EA Repository

The approach to the design of the example EA repository (and the underlying EA³ framework) provided in Figure 12-1 is based on the work of John Zachman,[25] who created a very intuitive schema for visually

---

[25] Zachman, 1989.

organizing EA information. He did this by using hierarchical rows and functional columns to create cells that contain "primitive" EA artifacts which answer basic questions about information systems (who, what, why, where, when, and how). [26]

The design of the *Living Enterprise*™ EA repository is similar in that it uses hierarchical rows and functional columns. However, it is different in that (1) it is based on a separate meta-framework (the EA³ framework); (2) it uses three hierarchical levels; (3) the functional columns are not based on basic interrogative questions; (4) the cells of the matrix are changeable and are often populated with EA documentation that represents composite views of several types of primitive products; (5) it has areas for additional information on the EA program; and (6) it is designed to be implemented as a website and therefore has navigation and version control features. As is shown in Figure 12-2, this overall design for an EA repository is referred to as the *Living Enterprise*™, which is shown on the next page in Figure 12-3. This EA repository is linked to EA software tools and a database to store EA data and artifacts.

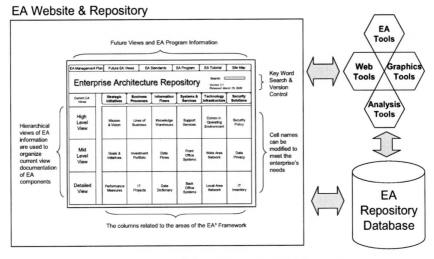

Figure 12-2: The Living Enterprise³ EA Repository

---

[26] The word "primitive" in Zachman's work refers to EA documentation that is singular in its method of development and use. For example, using traditional methods, diagramming data structure yields an Entity-Relationship Diagram and diagramming data process yields a Data Flow Diagram that are Zachman primitives in that they are fundamentally different in both symbology and use. If one were to find a way to combine them into one diagram, this would yield what Zachman calls a "composite" EA documentation product.

Enterprise Architecture Repository

Tabs: EA Management Plan | Future EA Views | EA Standards | EA Program | EA Tutorial | Site Map

Current EA Views	Goals & Initiatives	Products & Services	Data & Information	Systems & Applications	Networks & Infrastructure	Security Solutions
High Level View	Strategic Plan	Business Plan	Knowledge Warehouse	Business Systems	Wide Area Network	Security Program
Mid Level View	Goals & Initiatives	Business Processes	Information Flows	Support Systems	Local Area Network	System Certifications
Detailed View	Performance Measures	Investment Portfolio	Data Dictionary	Application Inventory	Buildings & Equipment	Data Privacy

Figure 12-3: Example EA Repository Design – *Living Enterprise* ™

In implementing the *Living Enterprise*™ approach to a web-based EA repository, it is recommended that enterprises stay with the six columns, because they directly relate to the levels of the EA³ framework, which also guides the type of EA artifacts that go in each column and cell. If another framework is needed, the number of rows and columns can be changed, along with the names of the cells. It should be noted that the amount of time, money, and effort to complete additional perspectives (rows) of EA component documentation will be significant, which is one reason that only three perspective rows were chosen for this format. Three rows provide distinct perspectives that are analogous to executive, manager, and support staff views.

One of the valuable aspects of having this approach to an EA repository is that the different levels of the enterprise can view complete perspectives of business and technology, which they otherwise might not be able to see. If limits to access are desired, then particular cells or groups of cells can be password protected.

One of the flexible features of *Living Enterprise*™ is that the purpose and names of the cells in each framework column can be changed to fit the particular needs of the enterprise. For example, the middle cell in the Business Process column can be changed from Investment Portfolio to "Customer Relationship Management" if that is more important and/or appropriate. In this way, a customized version of Living Enterprise™ can be created for each enterprise. Drawing from the descriptions of EA Components and artifacts in Chapters 4 and 5, comments on potential content for each cell is provided as follows.

Strategic Goals and Initiatives Column

Mission and Vision Cell: Here is where the enterprise's mission and vision statements are located. These are the highest level policy statements that the enterprise has, reflecting why the enterprise exists and in general what it strives to be.

Goals and Initiatives Cell: Here is where a list of the enterprise's strategic goals and initiatives is presented. For each strategic goal the desired outcome should be identified. For each strategic initiative, mapping to the goal(s) should be provided, as well as identification of the performance gaps that the initiative will correct. If there is an IT component in the initiative, that should be clearly identified. Each strategic initiative should then be hyperlinked to amplifying metrics information in the Performance

Measures Cell, as well as related investments in the Business services column.

Performance Measures Cell: Here is where the IT performance gaps are again identified for each strategic initiative. Then the outcome and output measures are provided that will measure the success of each initiative. Tracking information on the measures should also be provided, beginning with the original levels of achievement in each measurement area (called the "baseline"), and subsequent levels of achievement, which will form a trend line that tracks toward a goal level of improved level of performance.

Business Products and Services Column

Lines of Business Cell: Here is where the basic areas of activity (lines of business) for the enterprise are identified. The lines of business should support the enterprise's strategic goals and initiatives, or there is no reason to be doing those activities... they are not adding value. To better show this, the lines of business should be hyperlinked to the strategic goals and initiatives that they support in the Strategic Initiatives column.

Investment Portfolio Cell: Here is where the enterprise's investments in IT are shown. When aggregated, these investments form an "investment portfolio". This portfolio should be documented along with categories for investments in IT (e.g., IT operations, office automation, IT research and development, IT infrastructure). Information on the business case for each particular investment should be shown, to include how the investment supports a particular strategic initiative and/or LOB. Investment performance information on the overall portfolio and individual investments should also be provided in this cell.

IT Projects Cell: Here is where information on all of the active IT projects throughout the enterprise are shown. Project Management Plans and other associated documentation are the types of EA artifacts that should be archived in this area. Summaries of Earned Value Management information regarding project status are also helpful (e.g., planned vs. actual cost, schedule, and performance graphs).

Data and Information Column

Knowledge Management Cell: Here is where the enterprise's approach to Knowledge Management (KM) is provided. Items to be covered include the overall concept for sharing knowledge, information, and data, as well as whether there is an acknowledged commitment to being a learning enterprise. A learning enterprise is one which has a process for evaluating LOB processes and the management of programs and projects, and continually incorporating the lessons learned into the improvement of those processes, programs, and projects. In this way a culture of learning is created which can lead to increased levels of performance for the enterprise. Documentation of this can be effectively accomplished through a combination of diagrams and text descriptions of the EA Components that are active in aggregating data into information and then into knowledge, as well as how that knowledge is shared (e.g., knowledge warehouses, data marts, storage area networks, and databases).

Data Flows Cell: Here is where the sharing and transformation of information and data is documented for all processes in the enterprise's LOBs. Documentation should also reveal how the information and data is used within each LOB, in the form of requirements. Documentation methods should provide the structure of basic data entities/objects, the rules for relationships between these data entities/objects, and the flow of the data entities/objects through the various EA Components at the Information Level of the EA³ framework. This includes Entity-Relationship Diagrams and Data Flow Diagrams that document relational databases and are used in procedural programming languages such as COBOL, FORTRAN, and C. It also includes object-oriented documentation using the Unified Modeling Language, which documents object-based databases that are created using event-driven programming languages such as JAVA, SMALLTALK, and C++.

Data Dictionary Cell: Here is where standards and the format for the enterprise's data entities/objects are documented, and where a link is provided to a library (database repository) of those entities and objects. The library promotes the reuse of data entities and objects throughout the EA components, which increases interoperability and lowers development costs.

Systems and Applications Column

Support Services Cell: Here is where the overall view of business-related support services is presented in a format which promotes an understanding of how these resources are supporting the information sharing requirements of each LOB. There is a focus on supporting business operations in this cell. As was presented in Figure 7-7, an effective presentation format is a high level diagram that shows the applications being used within each LOB and across the enterprise, and shows this as distinct areas of support (e.g., databases, operating systems, websites, and middleware).

Front Office Systems Cell: Here is where the overall suite of front office support systems and applications are presented in a format that promotes an understanding of how they support the enterprise's information sharing requirements across all LOBs. This includes ERP solutions, supply chain management systems, customer relationship management systems, sales and marketing supports, manufacturing support, and on-line e-commerce transactions.

Back Office Systems Cell: Here is where the overall suite of back office (administrative) systems and applications are presented in a format that promotes an understanding of how they support the enterprise's administrative support requirements across all LOBs. This includes financial and accounting systems, human resource systems, a common e-mail system, telephone, video-teleconferencing, fax, print, and copying systems. Also located here are the standard desktop, laptop, and personal digital assistant applications. Enterprises increasingly are distributed across multiple geographical locations, have individuals who are telecommuting, and have individuals in the field doing remote-site work and/or meeting with customers. This creates requirements for portable computing that should be documented in this cell, along with a clear picture of how information is being shared between these computing platforms to support LOB processes.

Networks and Infrastructure Column

Common Operating Environment Cell: Here is where information about the enterprise's Common Operating Environment (COE) is presented. The COE is the integrated business and technology operating environment, wherein a seamless voice, data, and video network infrastructure hosts front office and back office services and systems.

Wide Area Network Cell: Here is where information about the enterprise's Wide Area Network (WAN) is presented. An effective way to present information about the WAN is a map with WAN symbols for hardware and communication links that are hyperlinks, that when clicked-on lead to a new level of detail about that part of the WAN (e.g., dedicated voice and data lines, wireless links, interfaces with service providers). Also appropriate for documentation in this cell is the connectivity for

Supply Chains and/or information transfer via Extranets that connect to specific external business partners and/or remote office locations. Standards for voice, data, and video WAN components should also be available in this cell.

Local Area Network Cell: Here is where information about the enterprise's Local Area Network(s) is provided. There may be several LANs (also called Intranets) in the enterprise... perhaps in particular LOBs or at headquarters and several remote offices. In this case, the relationship of these LANs and their external linkage via the WAN needs to be shown. An effective way to present information about the LAN is a map with LAN symbols for hardware and communication links that are hyperlinks, that when clicked-on lead to a new level of detail about that part of the LAN (e.g., location of segments, interface points, and hosted applications, databases, and websites).

Security Solution Column

Policy and Procedures Cell: Here is where a high level view is presented of the enterprise's policies regarding IT security. Key extracts form the enterprise's IT Security Plan are appropriate that link to specific Standard Operating Procedures (SOPs) to handle various IT security activities and the response to security incidents (e.g., password policies, access procedures, user agreements, virus protection, inappropriate material, and incident handling). The full text of the IT Security Plan and the SOPs should be available in this cell, and links to additional educational information on IT security should be available in this cell and links to additional educational information on IT security should be provided. IT Security on particular vulnerabilities should not be part of the documentation available in this cell, as it should be protected from all but those with a need-to-know. This protected information includes EA component security plans, risk analysis reports, security test and evaluation results, disaster recovery procedures, and technical diagrams of security hardware and software.

Data Privacy Cell: Here is where the enterprise's policy on information privacy is presented. How information and data are collected, archived, and disseminated should be covered for each EA component at the Business Process Level and the Information Flows Level of the EA[3] framework, with comments on how privacy requirements are being met. For example, in on-line financial transactions credit card information must be protected. For general sales and marketing databases, customer contact information must be protected.

IT Inventory Cell: Here is where an inventory of all IT resources (hardware and software) in each EA component throughout the enterprise is maintained. This inventory not only promotes effective IT security, but also enables EA planners to obtain information on the "as-is" business and technology operating environment. For example, to support a decision on purchasing an upgrade to a COTS product, it is important to know how many licenses are currently owned, and when the expiration date is. In another example, knowing how many desktop PCs of a particular type exist can help procurement decisions that accompany "technology refreshments" throughout the enterprise that need to occur every two to three years.

Tabular Information

EA Management Plan Tab: Here is where the EA Management Plan is archived.   The EA Management Plan documents the enterprise's performance gaps, resource requirements, planned solutions, and a summary of the current and future architecture.   The Plan also describes the EA management process, the implementation methodology, and the documentation framework.   It is a living document that is updated at regular intervals (e.g., annually) to provide clear version control for changes in current and future views of EA components and artifacts throughout the framework.

Future EA Summary Tab: Here is where a summary of changes to the current architecture are provided along with the EA artifacts that represent changes at each level of the EA^3 framework. It is important to show in both graphical and narrative form how the enterprise EA is changing. Also, the future scenarios can be archived in this area of the EA repository for easy access.

EA Standards Tab: Here is where information on the EA's Technical Standards Reference Model (TSRM) is presented.   As was described in Chapter 9, the technical standards for voice, data, and video products are provided in the TSRM.   This can be effectively presented in the form of a table that shows the ISO/NIST/IEEE or a local standard that is approved to meet the enterprise's requirements in each of the three categories (see Figure 9-6).   Then, approved COTS or custom-developed products are listed within each standard area, as well as those products that are approved for use on an interim (waiver) basis.

EA Program Tab: Here is where information on the EA program is archived, including schedules for the release of new version's of the EA, EA team information, budget information, contact information, or other relevant, similar information may be found.

EA Tutorial Tab: Here is where EA training information is archived to support EA awareness among stakeholders and other interested individuals. This is also where other EA reference information may be archived and/ or linked.

EA Site Map: This is a navigation map of the EA repository website.

EA Support Tools

Various types of commercial software applications (tools) are required to support EA documentation and analysis activities. At present, no one commercial tool can do all of the things that are needed in the EA program, including:

- EA repository website and content to create a visual representation of the EA³ framework;
- Dynamic views of the EA for a variety of users;
- Archived EA products, including documents, data, graphics, media, and objects;
- Management views of EA artifacts;
- Strategic planning products and performance measures;
- Business process documentation to answer key questions and solve problems;
- Physical and logical design of data entities and objects;
- Physical and logical design of voice, data, and video networks;
- Linked applications and databases;
- Portfolio of IT investments and asset inventory;
- Configuration management documentation (EACRs);
- Project planning and tracking (cost, schedule, performance, risk); and

- Security solutions for physical, information, personnel and operational needs.

Because no one EA tool can do all that is required in the EA program, a "set" of tools is required. This will include an EA modeling tool, a graphics tool, a word processing tool, a website development tool, a database, a configuration management tool, and any application development and programming tools that the enterprise needs to create or modify EA Components. Figure 12-3 provides a view of how this set of tools interrelate and how they support EA documentation product development and display via the web-based EA repository.

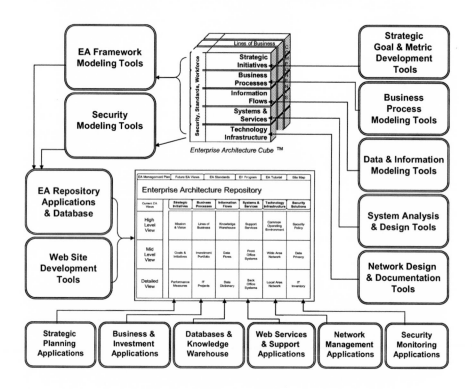

Figure 12-3: EA Tools – Product Development and Display

The following is a discussion of the contribution of the various types of software tools to EA documentation activities, the relationship of which is shown on the next page in Figure 12-4.

Web Development Tools To Create The On-Line EA Website		Graphics Tools To Create Management Views of EA Documentation Products	
EA Repository Website To Create The Web-Based EA Repository	Other Support Applications Links to Other Applications That Influence EA Program	EA Database To Create The Web-Based EA Database That Stores EA Documentation
EA Modeling Tools To Create The EA Documentation Products	Application Development Tools To Create or Modify Software Applications Used in EA Components	Database Development Tools To Create The Web-Based EA Database
Configuration Mgmt Tool To Maintain EA Documentation Quality and Version Control	Programming Tools To Create EA Components	
EA Website Host Platform / Web Server Application To Host the EA Website Repository, Database, and Associated Tools/Applications		

Figure 12-4: The Relationship and Purpose of EA Documentation Tools

EA Framework Modeling Tools
These software tools are designed to use various EA frameworks that are pre-loaded and support various methodologies to develop EA artifacts throughout the chosen framework. These tools also support the conversion of EA artifacts into HTML and XML formats for increased utilization with websites and other tools. Some EA tools come bundled with web-enabled "front-ends" and databases that allow for the creation of an EA repository to store and retrieve the EA artifacts created with the tool. Some EA tools also have configuration management capabilities that support version control for the EA artifacts.

EA Repository Web-Application
This is a web-based software application that provides (1) a user-friendly graphical front end to support easy access to, and navigation of EA Artifacts in a way that relates to the chosen EA framework, and (2) interfaces with a back-end database that stores the EA artifacts. The

database might be integral to the EA repository web application, or might be a separate database software application (e.g., when more robust storage is required).

Web Service Development Tools
These software tools provide the capability to create a web-based EA repository that links to other web services and web sites. The development of a web-based EA repository is essential to providing easy access to the entire enterprise via a protected Intranet web site. Many EA modeling tools have web-based front ends (application interfaces) and can create EA artifacts in HTML. This allows the EA modeling tool to be directly accessed through the EA repository website.

General Graphics Tools
These software tools support general graphics design requirements and the custom creation of management views of EA artifacts. The development of briefings, HMTL pages, enterprise charts, and simple flowcharts are examples of these types of products.

Strategy Modeling Tools
These software tools support the development and modeling of EA components at the Strategic Initiatives level of the EA³ framework. The resulting EA artifacts include the enterprise's strategic goals, supporting initiatives (programs and projects), and performance measures for the outputs and outcomes of each initiative. The Balanced Scorecard® methodology is a popular approach to developing these EA Artifacts and several commercial tools support this methodology, including overall EA Framework modeling tools and specific strategic planning tools.

Business Modeling Tools
These software tools support the development and modeling of EA components and the Business services level of the EA³ framework. The resulting EA artifacts include the processes and supply chains in each of the enterprise's LOBs. Business Process Reengineering (BPR) and Business Process Improvement (BPI) activities can also be documented.

Information Modeling Tools
These software tools support the development and modeling of EA components at the Information Level of the EA³ framework. The resulting EA artifacts include the logical and physical design for knowledge warehouses, data marts, databases, web sites, web portals, and data mining products. Also documented is the structure and processing of basic data

elements using traditional or object-oriented modeling tools, along with the data dictionaries and object libraries that store these products.

Application Modeling Tools
These software tools support the development and modeling of applications that support general operational and administrative processes and office automation capabilities throughout the enterprise that are not specific to a LOB. This includes financial systems, personnel and pay systems, e-mail, and applications that support collaboration, word processing, graphics, and spreadsheets. The resulting EA artifacts include the specifications for application capabilities, interfaces, standards, license inventories, and required support platforms. Documentation may also include the programming code for custom developed applications, or modified commercial applications.

Network Modeling Tools
These software tools support the development and modeling of the enterprise's internal and external voice, data and video networks, as well as associated backbone cable plants, network operations centers, server rooms, and wiring closets. The resulting EA artifacts include the logical and physical design of the networks, performance specifications, interface points, standards, and inventories.

Security Analysis and Modeling Tools
These software tools support the development and modeling of security processes, considerations, and capabilities at all levels of the EA^3 framework. The resulting EA artifacts held to develop and model physical security, operational security, personnel security, and information security requirements and solutions as they relate to business services, information flows, support applications, and network infrastructures. These tools also support the development of security planning and management documentation including Security Plans, Security Risk Assessments, Test and Evaluation Plans/Reports, Disaster Recovery Plans, Continuity of Operations Plans, and Security Certification and Accreditation Reports.

Linked Software Applications
These software applications support other IT governance processes that integrate with the EA program. This includes capital planning, program management, and workforce planning. Being able to easily assess and relate information in these other areas of governance is essential to using EA documentation to improve communication and decision-making

regarding the use of EA components in improving mission and/or Line of Business Performance.

The criteria for selecting an EA tool depends on the role it will play in the EA tool set. If it is an overall EA framework modeling tool, then a wide variety of capabilities are needed including the built-in support of various frameworks and modeling techniques, usability, scalability, development of management views, report generation, web interoperability, version control, security, training, licensing, and total cost of ownership. An example matrix for the side-by-side assessment of several EA tools in the same category is provided in Figure 12-5 on the next two pages.

Figure 12-5: Example EA Tool Evaluation Matrix

EA Tool Evaluation Matrix		Tool A		Tool B		Tool C	
Tool Requirement	Grading Weight	Grade	Score	Grade	Score	Grade	Score
Framework Support							
Multiple Built-In Frameworks							
Custom Framework Creation							
Sequencing of As-Is & To-Be Views							
Creation of Management Views of EA Products							
Incorporation of EA Management Plan							
Identification of EA Performance Gaps							
Modeling Support							
Strategic Modeling							
Business Modeling							
Data Modeling							
Application Modeling							
Infrastructure Modeling							
Custom Modeling							
Symbology							
Robustness of Provided Symbols & Icons							
Custom Creation of Symbols & Icons							
Importing of Symbols & Icons							
Performance							
Usability							
Navigability							
Built-in and Custom Queries							
Built-in and Custom Reports							
Importing of Data and Products							
Integrated Web-Based Repository							
Integrated Database and Data Dictionary							
Support of Programming Languages							
Link to Capital Planning Info.							

EA Tool Evaluation Matrix		Tool A		Tool B		Tool C	
Tool Requirement	**Grading Weight**	**Grade**	**Score**	**Grade**	**Score**	**Grade**	**Score**
Link to Project Mgmt Information							
Link to Workforce Planning Information							
Configuration Management							
Version Control							
Consistency /Completeness Checking							
Status Accounting							
Product Labeling & Dating							
Tracking Ownership of Data Entered							
Vendor							
Technical Support							
User and Administrator Training							
Product Maturity							
Proprietary Product							
Version Updating							
Vendor Stability							
Financial							
Total Cost of Ownership							
Cost Per Seat							
Licensing Flexibility							
Integration							
Supports Multiple Data Formats							
Support for Standard APIs							
Platforms Supported							
Data Interchange (XML, HTML)							
Direct Web Importing/Publishing							
Web Site Creation Capability							
Security							
User Access Controls							
Read-Only and Multi-User Controls							
Remote Access and Use							
Total Scores							

Figure 12-5: Example EA Tool Evaluation Matrix (continued)

Summary of Concepts

This chapter provided a discussion of the role of an EA repository and documentation tools in the EA program. The importance of developing a web-based EA repository was stressed in that it provides easy access to EA artifacts which can assist planning and decision-making throughout the enterprise. The various types of EA-related software tools were discussed as was the idea that a set of tools are needed to support the overall EA management program and documentation process. EA tool selection criteria were also provided.

Chapter 12 Review Questions

1. What is an EA repository and how does it support the EA implementation methodology?

2. How does the Strategic Goals column of the EA repository relate to the EA³ framework, and what EA artifacts go into the cells of this column?

3. How does the Business Process column of the EA repository relate to the EA³ framework, and what EA artifacts go into the cells of this column?

4. How does the Information Flows column of the EA repository relate to the EA³ framework, and what EA artifacts go into the cells of this column?

5. How does the Systems and applications column of the EA repository relate to the EA³ framework, and what EA artifacts go into the cells of this column?

6. How does the Technology Infrastructure column of the EA repository relate to the EA³ framework, and what EA artifacts go into the cells of this column?

7. How does the IT Security column of the EA repository relate to the EA³ framework, and what EA artifacts go into the cells of this column?

8. What considerations should be made in developing an EA Tool Evaluation Matrix?

9. Why are management views of EA artifacts important?

10. Describe how cell names and content might change between the EA repository for a government agency and the EA Repository for a business.

11. Develop an EA Tool Evaluation Matrix and evaluate two current commercial EA modeling tools.

12. Develop the management view of information flows in a business warehouse inventory stocking system.

Section IV

Enterprise Architecture as a Profession

Section IV provides commentary on the future direction of the profession and practice of EA. Section IV is organized as follows:

Chapter 13   Future Trends in Enterprise Architecture

Chapter 13 - Future Trends in Enterprise Architecture

Chapter 13 provides the author's thoughts on future trends in the profession and practice of enterprise architecture, based on readings and observations during work on EA projects. This is done to give the reader a sense of the issues that are currently of interest to enterprise architects and organizations considering EA programs. These comments are also intended to help promote discussion in each topic area as well as to encourage the adoption of a common language for EA greater collaboration among those in the profession.

Chapter 13

Future Trends in Enterprise Architecture

Chapter Overview

This chapter provides the author's thoughts on future trends and issues in the practice of enterprise architecture, based on readings and observations during work on EA projects. This is done to give the reader a sense of the issues that are currently of interest to enterprise architects and organizations considering EA programs. These comments are also intended to help promote discussion in each topic area as well as to encourage the adoption of a common language for EA greater collaboration among those in this emerging profession.

Learning Objectives

➢ Familiarize the reader with current issues in the practice of EA.

➢ Stimulate discussion of EA issues.

➢ Provide a high-level view of where the practice of EA may be going.

Introduction

EA is increasingly being used by corporations, governments, non-profit groups, and academic institutions in many nations. While there are similar benefits to be gained from EA for these large, complex, enterprises, the drivers are quite different. In the private sector, profit drives most planning and decision-making, and EA is an optional activity. In the public sector, service delivery is the primary driver, money is a use-or-lose resource, and EA may be an activity mandated by law. However, outweighing these differences is the basic similarity that public and private sector enterprises are social entities based on patterns of human interaction, which therefore must deal with issues of purpose, legitimacy, culture, goal achievement, and the sharing of information.

Discussion

It is my observation that the basic trend for EA is growth, based on the number of professional conferences on EA, articles in publications, and references to ongoing EA programs in the literature and websites of public and private sector enterprises. Systems-level approaches are too limited in that they often do not emphasize human factors or business drivers and tend to produce stovepipe views of the enterprise's processes and IT resources. Executives and government leaders now want more holistic and robust views of their enterprises, presented in ways that they can drill into the information to gain insights, see performance gaps, promote communication, and enhance decision-making. As stated at the beginning of the book, the value added proposition of EA is simply that it is the one discipline that can provide a dynamic perspective of the whole enterprise in ways that are meaningful to all levels of the enterprise.

EA is about the documentation of all types of enterprises, regardless of the nature of business, legal, and technology drivers. By developing a holistic picture of the enterprise, communication and decision-making are improved. These improvements then translate to enhanced performance as future goals are more readily identified and achieved. The difference in EA approaches center not on the applicability of frameworks, or documentation methodologies, but on access to the EA information once completed. Private sector enterprises tend to greatly restrict access to highly tailored EA approaches, as it reveals a great deal about the strengths, weaknesses, and direction of the business. Public sector enterprises often have required approaches and are more forthcoming with EA information, though it too is protected to some degree so that data privacy and security requirements are met.

As the field of EA continues to grow, the following are some of the future trends that we may see:

- Private industry models become more known
- IT resources and services become commodities, forcing new EA models
- Federal, State, and Local Government integration of EA approaches
- National, regional, and global EA standards emerge
- Military EA benefits grow, but so do vulnerabilities
- Academia grounds EA practices in social and management theory

- Universities increase EA teaching
- Professional EA certification grows
- The profession of EA matures and is recognized as a distinct career path

Private Industry Models of EA

Many if not most large size businesses have technology architectures that describe their IT systems, data flows, and network infrastructures, but they may not have enterprise architectures that incorporate strategy and business. The initial concepts of EA that were developed by John Zachman and Steven Spewak are fairly well known in the private sector, but full implementation of these ideas in businesses remains uneven. Mid-size and smaller businesses often forgo any ongoing IT systems documentation and regard EA as too expensive to undertake and maintain. The problem with all of this is that these businesses, regardless of size, cannot "see themselves" and therefore are less agile. By this I mean that they cannot make consistently informed decisions on business and technology that reflect an understanding of current capabilities and future goals. The result are meetings to pass information or make decisions wherein people are trying to describe needed change, rather than being able to show the areas needing change via the EA views. I do believe that "a picture is worth a thousand words", and businesses should realize that an updated EA repository is invaluable in terms of increasing enterprise effectiveness by decreasing the amount of time it takes to articulate a requirement or make a decision, and decreasing the amount of misinterpretation of the ideas and requirements being presented. EA also helps to mature the enterprise in terms of being able to field technology solutions that are more aligned with strategic goals, doing so in less time and with higher quality. Finally, EA helps to free a business from the proprietary solutions of vendors. By knowing its own current and future business and technology requirements, and being able to map those to open standards, the business has more leverage with commercial vendors to be able to obtain solutions that meet the enterprise's needs, not the vendor's needs.

Regarding the second trend, the private sector does not usually publish their approaches to architecture. It is understandable that businesses would not want to share the internal blueprints of their enterprises. However, that creates a dilemma for them in terms of wanting to obtain good examples of

EA from others to guide and benchmark their own efforts. One way for private sector businesses to get EA examples is to establish non-disclosure and teaming agreements with other businesses that have similar operational and technology issues. Obviously, competitors in the same market sector would not want to do this, but benchmarking partnerships can be effective between businesses in different industries if the EA issues are similar. It would be beneficial to the private sector if general descriptions of EA approaches are shared in trade publications and academic case studies. For example, case studies of EA in the banking, manufacturing, insurance, retail, transportation, and freight industries would be helpful to all businesses. Understanding how technology is leveraged to improve business performance at an enterprise level is what these EA case studies could reveal. Beyond this, comparative studies of EA practices between industry sectors would also be helpful to understand what the common areas of value are and to highlight EA management practices that work. Because of the lack of detailed private sector EA case studies, there is an opportunity for a business to gain notoriety if they were willing to share their approach to EA and specifics on how EA is adding value at the bottom line. Hopefully, some of these case studies will emerge in coming years.

IT Services and Resources Become Commodities, Forcing New EA Models

The cost of computing services and associated software and hardware, when compared to the capability it delivers, has come down consistently and dramatically during the past twenty years. The advent of client-server coincided with the general awareness of this unusual trend wherein an industry makes quantum leaps in performance on a regular basis.... and it is Moore's Law that best captured the underlying dynamic that has been fueling this performance increase. In 1965, Gordon Moore, co-founder of Intel Corporation, observed that the number of transistors per square inch on an integrated circuit had roughly doubled every year since the integrated circuit had been invented, and he predicted that this trend would continue for the foreseeable future. During the 1990's transistor density doubled about every 18-months, which is the pace that currently defines Moore's Law, and is expected to continue for another decade or two. The increases in raw computing power that resulted have made the development of new software and IT services during the past decade that would not have been able to be supported or fielded on a wide-spread basis. Large software programs a decade ago were in the 200-300 kilobyte range, and today are in the 200-300 megabyte range (or more). Data storage was also revolutionized several times over during the past twenty years as the type and capacity of internal, external, and portable hard drives have increased many fold. The largest internal hard drives of five years ago are now mid-range "thumb-drives" no bigger than a lipstick tube. The end result has been that the performance of many mid-range IT products is more than the average user needs, and the price reductions of these non-leading-edge products have made them commodities whereby it is often more cost effective to replace an IT resource (e.g., PC, printer, hard drive, monitor, hub) than to have it repaired.

What this means for EA is that IT is becoming ubiquitous and enables many more business functions than it did a decade ago. The reliability and cost effectiveness of IT resources is therefore essential to the viability of those business services, and EA methods are one of the critical success factors for ensuring that IT functions properly and in harmony with the business operating environment.

There is a debate at present over whether IT resources are strategic in nature, or are common consumables. I suggest that IT resources are both. Leading-edge IT resources such as web services and manufacturing controls can provide an enterprise with strategic competitive advantage.... in terms of helping an enterprise to be first to market with products, finding and exploiting market niches who's opportunity windows can open and close in a matter of hours/days/weeks, and in driving down costs while holding quality at acceptable levels.   More mature and common IT resources such as front and back office automation systems can help an enterprise to maintain cost-efficiency in LOB activities, and increase communication effectiveness.

How EA deals with these trends will be seen in adjustments to documentation frameworks and implementation methodologies, similar to what drove the development of the EA^3 Cube framework presented in this book.... which primarily was capability gaps in other previous EA approaches that were created as IT advancements occurred, or as issues such as security became more prominent.

Government Integration and EA

The use of EA use in the U.S. public sector is growing due to legal mandates for EA programs at the federal level, and adoption of EA as a best practice by States and Local Governments. Performance and market-based approaches to measuring government services have emerged during the past decade. Customers of government services want the Federal, State, and Local levels to increasingly integrate, so that it is easier to do things. In opposition to this general expectation is the fundamental characteristic of our form of government that protects individual and State's rights, promotes a market-based economy, and seeks to limit Federal power. As such, there will always be a desire for independence and choice that counterbalances expectations for unified approaches to government services.

Having recognized the need for a diversification of government power, it is still possible to achieve better service to citizens and industry through standardized and integrated processes that are supported by ever-improving technologies. Whether that government service involves national or homeland defense, financial assistance, healthcare, rulemaking, licensing, enforcement, or disaster response; harmonized approaches between Federal, State, and Local government agencies are needed. EA is a particularly good way to achieve integration, as the definition of "enterprise" is such that particular service areas can be focused on with different government stakeholders.

For example, homeland defense and first-responder effectiveness is largely dependent on information exchanges between all levels of government. A detailed set of current views of an EA for this government service area would be invaluable to operational effectiveness, and a detailed set of future EA views that were collaboratively developed would promote cross-agency cooperation and identify the funding and other resources that will be needed so that the changes can be planned for in forthcoming agency budgets. In a second example, integrating information on the Internet regarding government services is already occurring, but much work needs to be done so that simple searches for things like health care benefits do not yield a plethora of confusing and sometimes contradictory or outdated information. Smart searches and smart responses to on-line questions about government services are needed and EA can promote the development of information sharing strategies at all levels of government.

One of the things that will be needed to support an integrated approach to government services is an agreement on EA frameworks and implementation methodologies. This is already happening, as is evidenced by the development of a State-level approach to EA through the National Association of State Chief Information Officers (NASCIO). The development of this approach was supported through a grant from the U.S. Department of Justice.[27] Additionally, NASCIO has announced its support for the Federal EA Reference Models, which will aid in developing consistent models of services and technology between and across levels of government.

The problems with integrating government services do not stop at the national border, as they are increasingly global in scope. International trade, humanitarian relief, communications, politics, and defense treaties all rely on a robust global IT infrastructure. This infrastructure is comprised of a myriad of voice, data, and video capabilities that are carried on an equally diverse group of ground, air, and space telecommunications networks. EA on a global basis is emerging among governments and multi-national corporations as agreements are reached on IT resource connectivity and interoperability. While the diversity of communications paths will not diminish any time soon, the protocol for information exchange is increasingly becoming the Internet, which is the first apolitical, non-proprietary communications medium that has reached a global "critical mass" of participation. The growth of Internet providers and participants will continue to be significant, as will be the development of Internet-capable voice, data, and video applications. This will accelerate the need for regional and global EA programs among Internet service providers, telecommunications carriers, and commercial product developers.

Emerging EA Standards

While there are widely accepted standards for technical documentation and modeling techniques, a standard nomenclature for EA frameworks that incorporate business and technology functions continues to emerge among and between the major standards enterprises.[28] [29] [30] Many of the rapidly

---

[27] The National Association of State Chief Information Officers (NASCIO), published the NASCIO Enterprise Architecture Development Toolkit (Version 2.0) in July 2002. www.nascio.org. (See Appendix C for more details).

[28] The National Institute for Standards and Technology (NIST) does have publications on Enterprise Architecture, including a paper by James Nell entitled

developing object-oriented and component technologies are being combined with new delivery concepts based on web-services and related standards (e.g., J2EE, .NET, SOAP, UDDI, WSDL) which create new more robust common IT operating environments... topics that are at the forefront of discussions.

Perhaps the area of greatest need for standards is the lexicon of this emerging profession. There are a growing number of EA frameworks and methodologies (including the EA³ framework introduced in this book), and each one brings with it new terms or re-definitions of old terms. While this helps to mature the practice of EA, the lack of a standard base of terminology allows for the continuing proliferation of approaches and prevents meta-concepts from emerging, which serves mainly to confuse enterprises that are implementing and/or maintaining EA programs. Within the European Union, the UEML (Unified Enterprise Modeling Language) has been developed by the CIMOSA Association along with the CIMOSA Reference Architecture. In the past few years, the terms and modeling concepts of the UEML have been accepted by the European Commission. However, this standard language for modeling has not been adopted in the U.S., nor has it transcended to the level of EA. The terms and concepts introduced by John Zachman remain the de-facto standard in the U.S. for EA practices. It is the resolution of these types of differences in language and approach that will move EA forward.

The Military's Use of EA

The U.S. military is one of the largest and complex enterprises in the world. It is also an enterprise that is increasingly dependent on information to perform its warfighting and peace-keeping missions. Currently, the U.S. Department of Defense (DOD) is using the DOD Enterprise Architecture Framework (DODAF) to standardize the way that DOD agencies and military commands in the three Service Departments are modeling their IT resources. Enterprise-wide operating and support capabilities in DOD exist through the senior staffs and major military

---

"Enterprise Representation: A different paradigm for designing process-interoperability standards." http://www.mel.nist.gov/sc5wg1/paradigm.htm.

[29] ISO Standards related to EA include ISO 14258: Concepts and rules for enterprise models, and ISO 15704: Requirements for enterprise reference architectures and methodologies.

[30] European Committee for Standardization (CEN). CEN ENV 12204 (Pre-standard) Constructs for Enterprise Modeling.

commands. The increasingly integrated requirements of these top enterprises are forcing DOD to continue to develop enterprise-wide planning approaches, as exemplified by the DODAF. Military victories during the past several decades are an indicator that an increasing level of interoperability has been achieved, yet to maintain superiority more needs to be done.

One of the most pressing considerations that the military has in using EA is the vulnerabilities that a consolidation of capability and detailed documentation present. If the duplication in IT resource capabilities is completely eliminated, then there will most likely be a reliance on fewer sources of IT products and solutions. The potential to create "single points of failure" in systems and applications is increased when duplication is totally eliminated. For example, if DOD were to totally rely on a single commercial operating system, then security vulnerabilities become critical in terms of potentially enabling hackers to take down large parts of the DOD warfighting capability. For this reason, EA needs to promote a risk-adjusted level of interoperability and functional duplication, and the subsequent cost inefficiency be viewed as acceptable in order to reduce IT vulnerabilities.

Academia's Contribution to EA

As a university instructor of classes in Systems Analysis and Design for over five years, and of classes in EA for two years, it is my observation that the trend in the academic sector is one of slow growth. Universities are participating in standards bodies (e.g., IEEE, ISO, and CEN), and development groups (e.g., the Object Modeling Group - OMG). However, the real contribution that academia can and should make to EA is theory, and that is largely being ignored.

The EA frameworks and modeling approaches that are in use in the public and private sector were largely developed by commercial practitioners. While this is probably a reflection of the commercial orientation of the field at present, the lack of a tie-in of these frameworks to mature theory is hard to explain. The social sciences, management sciences, and physical sciences all have a contribution to make. In that EA is about the documentation of complex social enterprises and how they use technology to improve performance, there are many areas that academia can and should comment on. This includes the ability of particular EA frameworks to capture enterprise resources, requirements, performance gaps, and cultures. Also, determining the true qualitative and quantitative value of EA to enterprises is a question that is perhaps best answered by academics with no vested interest. Multi-disciplinary methods to evaluate the effectiveness of EA approaches are also needed.

Perhaps the most telling aspect of academia's contribution to EA is the lack of undergraduate and graduate level courses in this area of practice. Systems analysis and design (SA&D) courses remains a staple of programs in business, information studies, public administration, operations research, and computer science (there are over 20 textbooks on this subject in active use). However, there are very few courses on EA, and only a handful of practitioner books exist. Academia should recognize EA courses as the logical extension of SA&D courses, and that employers will accord higher value to graduates who understand enterprise requirements for integrated business and technology at both the systems and enterprise levels. More textbooks need to be written on EA to tie this discipline to other management and technical disciplines. Additionally, more case studies are needed of EA use in public and private sector enterprises. Finally, the *Journal of Enterprise Architecture* began publishing in August 2005, which will further the contribution of academics and practitioners.

EA Professional Certification

As a founding instructor of an EA training and certification program at Carnegie Mellon University in 2004, and co-founder of a federal EA training program in 2002, I have observed that several similar groups have been established in the U.S. and internationally during the past several years. I believe that the trend in EA certification is one of continuing growth as the number of EA programs in business and government grows. While academia needs to focus on developing EA-related theories, courses, and case studies, professional training groups need to provide EA Certification programs. The training and certification of Chief Architects to lead EA programs is essential for the advancement of the profession. Equally important is the training of other participants in the EA process including data architects, network architects, solutions architects, and IT program managers. An increasing number of EA conferences and seminars are being offered each year, and EA certification groups are emerging. More is needed in terms of initial EA training programs, advanced training programs, and continuing education programs.

Concluding Thoughts

Enterprise architecture is a growing professional discipline within the larger practice areas of business management, public administration, information management, and computer science. The reason for this growth is that public and private sector enterprises increasingly depend on information to be successful and they need to be able to see performance gaps and resource requirements on an enterprise level. To plan and operate at a systems level is to look at requirements in isolation and thereby sub-optimize the enterprise's planning and management functions.

EA is one of the two most powerful governance processes that a Chief Information Officer has to use in implementing change (the other is capital planning). When used together, EA and capital planning can improve communications about current business and technology capabilities and can provide the information that line of business managers need to make decisions about investing in future resources, including IT.

There is a need for an updated high-level EA framework, such as the one that is presented in this book (the EA^3 Cube). The need centers on a lack of recognition in other frameworks of the role of strategy and business in EA planning, as well as the incorporation of a component orientation at all levels. Seeing goals, measures, processes, information flows, applications, and networks as interchangeable components is a unique contribution that the EA^3 framework makes. Additionally, the EA^3 Cube framework can serve to connect and integrate the use of other more specialized EA frameworks and models, such as linking the Federal EA Framework, the DOD Architecture Framework, and the Federal EA (FEA) Reference Models, as well as incorporating service-oriented and/or component-driven architecture approaches in the development of views of next generation IT systems, web services, and applications.

Architecting enterprises is a challenging endeavor, especially large and/or complex enterprises. The challenge comes in many forms, including executive support, sufficient resources, choices of methodology, and stakeholder buy-in. For these reasons, many EA programs are not given priority and therefore continue to produce less value than they are capable of. Yet, as the Information Age continues to usher in and force enterprise's to re-look at their strategies for success, the role of enabling information technologies will only grow, and along with it will grow the contribution of enterprise architecture.

Appendix A

Developing a Business Case for
An Enterprise Architecture Component

The following is an example format for developing business cases for investment in EA components.[31] The purpose of the business case is to identify sufficient value in a proposed investment to merit the expenditure of resources including people's time, the enterprise's money, facilities, equipment, and other assets. The Business Case format that Federal Agencies use is a recommended additional reference.[32]

As part of the capital planning and investment control processes described in Chapter 10, the following procedure is used to identify requirements for EA components and develop a business case to justify the investment of enterprise resources to implement a solution:

1. **Requirement Identification.** A requirement for IT support is identified in an enterprise line of business (LOB), which is brought to the EA team for evaluation.

2. **Existing Solution Check.** The EA team determines that an existing EA component cannot meet the requirement.

3. **New Solution Business Case Development.** The sponsoring LOB determines that the IT requirement is of sufficient importance to merit the cost of developing a business case, and does so using the following format:

    a. **Describe the requirement** in terms of the gap in operational or administrative performance it represents to the LOB and the enterprise.

    b. Describe the **impact to the enterprise** if the performance gap created by the requirement is not resolved. Include the strategic, business, and technology impact.

---

[31] This is a business case for an individual IT investment/project, not the overall EA program. The value proposition for the EA program is covered in Chapter 3.
[32] U.S. Office of Management and Budget. OMB Circular A-11; Exhibit 300: Planning, Budgeting, Acquisition, and Management of Capital Assets; 2005.

c. **Alternatives Analysis**: identify 3 or more viable alternative solutions (if at least 3 exist).

d. Perform a **Cost-Benefit Analysis** for each alternative on a lifecycle basis to identify and financially quantify all of the direct and indirect costs and benefits, including qualitative items such as improvements in communication, morale, and competitiveness.

e. Perform a **Return on Investment** calculation for each alternative.

f. Perform a **Net Present Value** adjustment for each ROI calculation to account for anticipated cost increases over the investment's lifecycle due to inflation.

4. <u>**New Solution Business Case Evaluation**</u>. The business case's alternatives are evaluated by the Architecture Working Group (AWG) for the correctness of the analysis, and alignment with the EA at each level of the framework. The Capital Planning Working Group (CPWG) then reviews the business case for the correctness of the financial analysis. A coordinated recommendation is made to the executive-level Capital Planning Board (CPB) as to whether the business case should be approved or disapproved for funding and implementation.

5. <u>**New Solution Business Case Approval**</u>. The CPB reviews the business case in the context of the enterprise's overall investment portfolio using criteria that identify value from a strategic, business, and technology perspective:

a. <u>Strategic Value</u>: Does the investment in the proposed new solution align with and contribute to the enterprise's strategic goals and initiatives? Are the outcome measures of success clearly identified?

b. <u>Business Value</u>: Does the solution effectively close the operational or administrative gap in LOB performance? Does the proposed investment generate a sufficient level of return compared to other competing investment requests? If this is a mandatory requirement (e.g., meets a regulatory requirement), has the most cost efficient and operationally effective approach been identified?

c. <u>Technology Value</u>: Does the solution provide an effective technical solution? Is the solution aligned with EA standards, and if not, has a waiver been recommended by the AWG?

Can the solution also support other LOB requirements in the common operating environment?

6. **New Solution Implementation.** If the business case is "selected" (approved) for funding by the CPB, the proposed solution becomes an implementation project that is managed by the sponsoring LOB. The project is reviewed by the CPB at key milestones and/or periodically as part of the capital planning process' "Control Phase" oversight of all projects. These CPB Control Reviews focus on the proper management of cost, schedule, and performance within the project (e.g., within ten percent of baseline estimates). When the project is completed, the CPB, AWG, and CPWG participate in a post-implementation review to identify lessons-learned that can help in the operations and maintenance of the EA component, and in maturing and improving overall project management practices in the enterprise. On a periodic basis throughout the EA component's lifecycle, the CPB reviews the value of providing ongoing funding for the operation and maintenance of that EA component. In this way, the entire business and technology operating environment is evaluated for continuing value.

Appendix B

Example Approach to Enterprise Architecture: The U.S. Federal Government

Overview

While there are many examples of EA programs in the public, private, non-profit, and academic sectors, perhaps the best known wide-scale implementation of EA can be found in the U.S. Federal Government. More information is available on EA in this sector because each Federal Agency is required by law to develop and maintain an EA program. Nearly a decade has passed since EA programs became mandatory and a great deal of guidance and best practice information has been written for Federal Agencies to use. There are dozens of agencies in the Executive Branch of the Federal Government, with a wide variety of missions, cultures, and resources. This diversity of mission, the standardized guidance on EA that they follow, and differences in the several types of frameworks in use make for a rich source of examples on EA implementation. For the purposes of this chapter, the discussion will be limited to how EA policy and implementation guidance originated, the frameworks being used, and how integrated governance across the Executive Branch of the Federal Government might be achieved.

EA Policy Background

In early 1996 the U.S. Congress passed a law that required U.S. Federal Agencies to develop and maintain an IT architecture for their agency. Known as the Clinger-Cohen Act,[33] this law was a reaction to the failure of a number of large IT projects in various agencies, and the Act's mandates reflected the government's observations of best practices in the private sector.[34] The Act required federal agencies to improve IT leadership and

---

[33] The Clinger Cohen Act (Public Law 104-106) was originally called the Information Technology Management Reform Act of 1996 (ITMRA). In 1997, the law was renamed to honor its primary sponsors, Senator William Cohen of Maine, and Congressman William Clinger of Pennsylvania.

[34] One of the catalysts for IT reform and the development of the Clinger-Cohen Act, was a 1994 report by the staff of Senator William Cohen entitled "Computer Chaos: Billions Wasted." This report detailed the failure of a number of large

governance by placing the responsibility for IT resource governance on the Agency Head; reformed IT procurement practices; and established CIO positions in each Agency to develop and main and an integrated set of IT management processes that would cumulatively result in effective IT governance. Among these processes are performance-based management, capital planning, IT architecture, strategic planning, security planning, workforce planning, and agency-level IT contracting. In later Federal guidance, IT architecture was referred to as enterprise architecture, in recognition of the importance of having an agency's architecture be driven by strategic and business requirements, and having IT be viewed as a resource to meet those requirements.[35] Figure B-1 provides a policy view of the interrelationships of federal guidance and agency governance processes and programs that implement that guidance in an integrated manner. The "Policy Cycle" that is depicted begins in the upper left quadrant with law and guidance; moves to the upper right quadrant where high-level agency policy is represented; moves down to the lower right and left quadrants where CIO-level implementation programs are reflected at the Agency and sub-Agency levels; and finishes in the center where program execution and governance occur, and feedback to high-level Agency originates.... completing the cycle.

---

scale IT programs in several Federal Agencies to be completed and/or deliver expected levels of service.

[35] This additional guidance on federal Enterprise Architecture practices includes the Office of Management and Budget Circulars A-11 and A-130, and the E-Government Act of 2002 (Public Law 107-347).

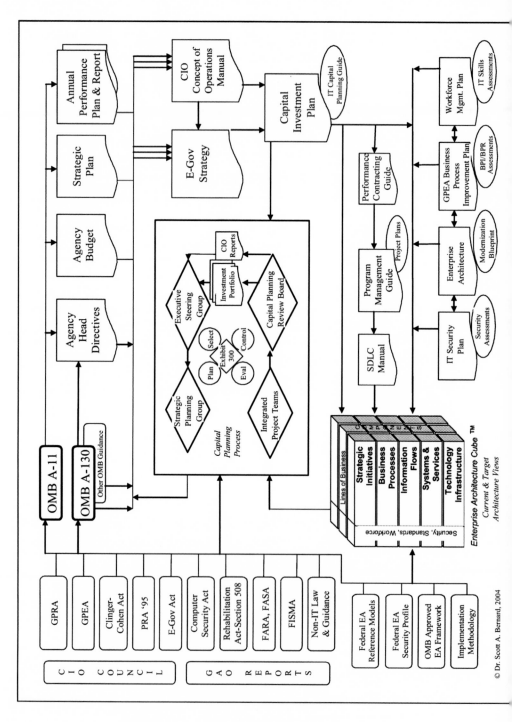

Figure B-1. Federal IT Policy and Governance

The First Federal EA Model – The FEAF

A few months after the Clinger-Cohen Act was passed in early 1996, the formation of a Federal CIO Council was authorized by an Executive Order from President William J. Clinton.[36] Following this, there were several years of limited activity in Federal Agencies and the CIO Council due to a lack of additional funding from Congress for the implementation of Clinger-Cohen Act mandates. Congress' expectation was that agencies would re-direct IT-related spending to create better governance, which did not occur for two to three years. In 1998, the Federal CIO Council pursued the development of guidelines and approaches to implementing EA and capital planning processes in federal agencies. The result was the publication of the *Federal Enterprise Architecture Framework* [37] in late 1999 that introduced the FEAF approach, which was collaboratively developed by government officials and EA experts including Rob Thomas, Mike Tiemann, George Brundage, John Zachman, and Steven Spewak.

There are four levels, four sub-architectures, and eight components in the FEAF. The four levels are: Level I where the components of the EA are introduced; Level II where the business and design pieces of the FEAF are introduced; Level III where the three design models are shown (data, application, and technology); and Level IV that identifies the kinds of models that describe the business architecture and three design architectures. The eight components of FEAF implementation are: (1) Architecture Drivers, (2) Strategic Direction, (3) Current Architecture, (4) Target Architecture, (5) Transitional Processes, (6) Architectural Segments, (7) Architectural Models, and (8) Standards, as is shown in Figure B-2.

---

[36] Executive Order 13011 was signed by President Clinton in July 1996 to reinforce and further explain the mandates of the Clinger-Cohen Act.
[37] Federal CIO Council. Federal Enterprise Architecture Framework, Version 1.1. U.S. Government Printing Office, Washington DC. September 1999.

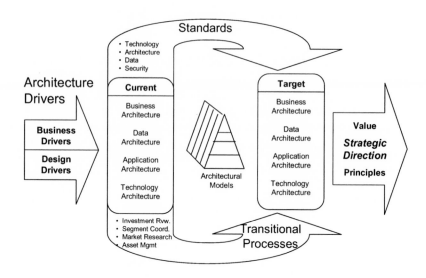

Figure B-2. The Federal Enterprise Architecture Framework [38]

As is stated in the *Federal Enterprise Architecture Framework*, the FEAF is intended to:

- Organize Federal information on a Federal-wide scale;
- Promote information sharing among Federal agencies;
- Help Federal enterprises develop their architectures;
- Help Federal enterprises quickly develop their IT investment processes; and
- Serve customer needs better, faster, and more cost effectively.

The Federal CIO Council specifically endorsed the use of the Zachman Framework for organizing the models of the design architectures at Level IV. The Spewak EAP modeling approach is also endorsed in the FEAF as a way to support initial EA program implementation in a way that also allows for artifact development using the Zachman Framework (see Chapter 5 for details on the relationship of these two foundational EA approaches).

---

[38] Ibid

Implementing the FEAF

To further explain how to implement the FEAF framework, *A Practical Guide to Federal Enterprise Architecture* (Practical Guide) was published by the Federal CIO Council in early 2001.[39] While this guidance is considered by Federal experts to fall short of a detailed EA implementation methodology, it does provide a comprehensive description of why EA is important to mission accomplishment, and how a Federal Agency EA program should be established. Figure B-3 shows the eight activities that constitute an EA process for agencies to use in implementing their EA programs and the FEAF framework.

Figure B-3: The Federal EA Implementation Process [40]

The following are excerpts from the Practical Guide that describe the eight elements of EA process implementation.[41]

---

[39] Federal CIO Council. A Practical Guide to Federal Enterprise Architecture, Version 1.0. U.S. Government Printing Office, Washington, DC. February 2001.
[40] Ibid

Element 1: Obtain Executive Buy-In and Support

"Gaining executive commitment to any new initiative requires the development of a strong business case and a communications approach to effectively convey that business case. Since the concept of an EA is not intuitively understood outside the CIO enterprise, the CIO should create a marketing strategy to communicate the strategic and tactical value for EA development to the Agency Head, other senior agency executives, and business units."

Element 2: Establish Management Structure and Control

"EA roles should be evaluated based on the size of the enterprise, the complexity of the business and architecture, and other factors to effectively determine the correlation of roles assigned to personnel. In a large enterprise with complex business services, an individual may be responsible for one specific role. In smaller agencies or enterprises, an individual may be assigned several roles and responsibilities."

Element 3: Define an Architecture Process and Approach

"The EA will be used as a tool to facilitate and manage change within the agency enterprise. The scope and nature of the agency and the changes to be made will dictate the scope and nature of the architecture to be developed. While the EA is an excellent tool to manage large and complex environments, the depth and detail of the EA needs to be tailored to the individual enterprise." The depth and detail in the EA varies not only with the size and complexity of the enterprise, but also the many types of risks associated with change. Regardless, the scope of the enterprise architecture for the strategic planner and business owner views (as defined by the architecture framework selected) needs to encompass the entire enterprise. The agency will understand the relationships and dependencies among its lines-of-business and thus position itself to make informed decisions on how to approach defining EA depth and detail for these lines-of-business. The first activity in this process is to determine the intended use of the architecture. It drives the rest of the EA development process. The subsequent activities describe how to scope, characterize, select EA products, build, and use the EA. The selected approach should include (1) a data collection phase, (2) preliminary product generation, (3) review and revision stages, and (4) publication and delivery of the architecture products to an appropriate repository. Each of these activities is described in more detail in the following subsections."

---

[41] Ibid

Element 4: Develop a Baseline Enterprise Architecture

"The next step is to build the architecture products based on the purpose of the architecture and the chosen framework. This consists of the essential products, supporting products (if needed), and individually defined products (e.g., briefing charts, interview notes) driven by architecture-specific needs and processes. To facilitate integration with other architectures, it is crucial to include all depictions of relationships with applicable external components, that is, entities outside the Agency. It may be useful, resources permitting, to conduct some proof-of-principle analyses at various stages of architecture development. For example, one could conduct trial runs of the EA development process using carefully selected subsets of the areas to be analyzed. The architecture core team should ensure that the products are consistent and properly interrelated. If the products are not applied and populated uniformly, the Chief Architect and architecture core team will be unable to compare or contrast the products or perform thorough analyses. Regardless of the scope and complexity of the views to be developed, the architecture core team should apply a consistent approach to developing the baseline and target architectures."

Element 5: Develop a Target Enterprise Architecture

"The target architecture should define a vision of future business operations and supporting technology. A long-term blueprint is absolutely necessary. A key consideration is the determination of the date of the target, how far into the future is the projected target. Realization of an enterprise's mission and vision statements needs:

- A focus on business areas or information needs with the greatest potential payoff for the enterprise.
- Development of conceptual models and tools to enable decision makers and staff to better recognize, understand, and discuss information requirements.
- An enterprise-wide understanding of the big picture and the need for shared information.
- A recognition of information as a strategic resource that should be managed using architectures as tools.
- Periodic assessments of the enterprise's progress towards its target environment.
- Alignment with the enterprise's strategic plan.

The target architecture describes the desired capability and structure of the enterprise business services, information needs, and IT infrastructure at some point in the future. Therefore, the target architecture is often referred to as the "To-Be" or "As-Planned" architecture. The target architecture may include alternatives, options, and unknowns - this is acceptable. The EA process is iterative - unknowns are filled in over time."

Element 6: Develop the Sequencing Plan

"The changes needed to transition from the current state of the enterprise to the goals and conditions expressed by the target architecture cannot be achieved in a single quantum step. Evolving the enterprise from its baseline to the target architecture needs multiple concurrent interdependent activities and incremental builds. The best way to understand and control this complex evolutionary process is by developing and maintaining a systems migration roadmap or sequencing plan. The sequencing plan should provide a step-by-step process for moving from the baseline architecture to the target architecture. The sequencing plan may be supported by a set of architecture products, similar to the baseline and target architecture products - generated for several intermediate points in time between the baseline and target environments. The succession from one point in time to the next, and on to the target timeframe, establishes a migration sequence. Because the sequencing plan represents the current environment, as well as the development programs that are both planned and under way, it becomes a primary tool for program management and investment decisions. To remain current and to support continued coordinated improvements across the enterprise, the sequencing plan should be maintained and updated as time and circumstances dictate."

Element 7: Use the Enterprise Architecture

"Using the EA to implement new projects provides a positive impact on the enterprise. If the EA is not successfully used, the entire development effort to this point is for naught. In this section, the emphasis shifts to integrating use of the EA across multiple activities and organizational groups. Success depends on active management, proactive architects, and receptive project personnel. It also depends on integrating the EA process with other enterprise life cycle processes, particularly the CPIC process. Establishing the EA captures the state of the enterprise and the plan for its future - literally a snapshot of the enterprise and its plans for improvement. For the EA to provide the strategic information asset base as intended, it should become a crucial tool for decision support and communication in the mainstream of daily business operations. Accepting and applying this asset in the Agency's operational paradigm is a technical and cultural challenge."

Element 8: Maintain the Enterprise Architecture

"The EA is, by definition, a set of models that collectively describe the enterprise and its future. Its value to the business operations is more than just IT investment decision management. The EA is the primary tool to reduce the response time for impact assessment, tradeoff analysis, strategic plan redirection, and tactical reaction. Consequently, the EA must remain current and reflect the reality of the enterprise's enterprise. In turn, the EA needs regular upkeep and maintenance, which is a process as important as its original development. Maintaining the EA should be accomplished within the enforcement structure and configuration control mechanisms of the enterprise. EA maintenance is the responsibility of the CIO, Chief Architect, and the EAPMO. Using a system of oversight processes and independent verification, the architecture core team periodically assesses and aligns the EA to the ever-changing business practices, funding profiles, and technology insertion. The EA should remain aligned to the enterprise's modernization projects and vice versa. The management controls to accomplish EA maintenance are the same ones established to initiate the program and to develop the EA."

EA programs grew in civilian-oriented (non-military) Federal Agencies between 1998-2002, largely following the FEAF model and the EA process described in the *Practical Guide*. Other models being followed at the time included the Treasury Enterprise Architecture Framework (TEAF) and the C4ISR EA Framework, which later was renamed the Department of Defense Architecture Framework (DODAF). A late 2001 update to Federal guidance contained in OMB Circular A-130 went so far as to limit the approved EA approaches to the FEAF, TEAF, and DODAF, and in 2002-2003 annual guidance contained in OMB Circular A-11 added the Federal EA (FEA) Reference Models as the mandatory EA reporting method for all Federal Agencies. Therefore, it is not only the law that Federal Agencies must have an EA program that helps to improve mission performance, but the types of EA frameworks that can be used, and the methods for reporting EA information are dictated as well. Where there is flexibility is in the way that agencies implement the EA management program and documentation process. As such, the *Practical Guide's* approach to the implementation of these frameworks has some flexibility to accommodate the different missions and cultures of the various Federal Agencies.

The EA activities that characterized efforts in 1999-2001 largely focused on Y2K activities and EA's that documented intra-agency business services, data and information flows, IT systems, and supporting networks.

In the civilian-oriented Federal Agencies, there was little focus on multi-agency processes or collaborative solutions in future EA views due to a lack of emphasis on collaboration and the fact that Federal Agencies were still struggling to understand what EA was and how to implement it, which caused them to mainly focus on documenting their own environment. Similarly, during 1999-2001, the focus within the Department of Defense was on Y2K, understanding the C4ISR approach to EA and on producing documentation within each Defense Agency and major military unit.

The Second Federal EA Model – FEA Reference Models and Security Profile

Reflecting a change in Presidential Administrations, in mid-2001 The Office of Management and Budget (OMB) published the President's Management Agenda (PMA) to clearly articulate President George W. Bush's views on how to achieve a more citizen-focused and market-based approach to providing Federal Government services. Five PMA strategy areas were identified, one of which was "Expanding Electronic Government." The fact that e-Government solutions made the "top-5" list reflects the growing importance that IT has in enabling Federal Agencies to accomplish their missions. What was also unique about the PMA's e-Government strategy area was its emphasis on developing collaborative, multi-agency solutions for providing on-line Federal Government services. The emphasis prior to the PMA was on the development of early e-Government capabilities *within* each agency.... and while multi-agency collaboration was encouraged, it was not emphasized. As a result, the Executive Branch of Government had continued to be characterized by duplicative IT systems and applications including dozens for financial management, human resources, grants administration, law enforcement, rulemaking, statistics, health care, and defense.

To achieve the PMA's goal of Expanding e-Government, OMB officials sought ideas from all of the Federal Agencies in early 2002 for collaborative initiatives to improve on-line service delivery.... and they received hundreds of suggestions. From these suggestions, twenty three Executive Branch-wide e-Government initiatives were selected for implementation. This group of initiatives were called the "Quicksilver e-Government Initiatives" and they covered many types of services that could be categorized as: government-to-citizen (G2C); government-to-business (G2B); and government-to-government (G2G) electronic services.

The process of reviewing and selecting the Quicksilver e-Government Initiative group also led OMB to realize that a new approach to EA was needed in order to reflect a shift in focus to multi-agency collaboration and the reduction of duplicative services. To enable this shift in focus, OMB announced the establishment of the Federal Enterprise Architecture (FEA) program in mid-2002, with the goal of being "a business and performance-based framework to support cross-agency collaboration, transformation, and government-wide improvement.... it provides OMB and the Federal Agencies with a new way of describing, analyzing, and improving the Federal Government and its ability to serve the citizen." [42] The Quicksilver e-Government Initiatives are now referred to as Federal Line of Business Initiatives.

The FEA consists of five "Reference Models" that are intended to promote "cross-agency analysis and the identification of duplicative investments, gaps, and opportunities for collaboration within and across Federal Agencies." [43] These five Reference Models are intended to work together to assist Federal Agencies in developing EA approaches that are strategy and performance driven, and also to provide the first standardized formats for reporting EA information to OMB from each Agency. This standardized EA information is submitted annually to OMB as part of the Federal Budget submission process that is described in OMB Circular A-11. The Fiscal Year (FY) in the Federal Government runs from October 1st to the next September 30th.

The Federal Budget development process is how Agency EA and IT Programs get reviewed and funded, and the process works generally as follows. In order for the President to be able to submit a proposed Fiscal Year (FY) Federal Budget to Congress each January for the next Fiscal Year that begins in October, OMB must begin working on that FY Budget two years in advance, due to the complexity and amount of information needed from Agencies and the Administration. In an ideal-world example, inputs for the FY 2007 Federal Budget would be developed by Agencies in April-August 2005, submitted to OMB in September 2005, reviewed by OMB in October-November 2005, presented to Congress by the President in January 2006, debated in Congress in February-June 2006, and approved (as amended by various House and Senate Committees) by

---

[42] Federal Enterprise Architecture Program Management Office (FEAPMO) website. www.feapmo.gov.
[43] Ibid

Congress in the form of thirteen Authorization and Appropriation Bills in July-August 2006, to enable Federal Agencies to know their forthcoming budgets and implement approved and funded EA and IT Programs October 1, 2006 through September 30, 2007.

As previously described, specific EA and IT Program funding requests are submitted from each Agency in September to OMB to be considered for inclusion in the Federal FY Budget that actually begins to be executed a year later. The format for submitting these requests is contained in an "Exhibit 300 Funding Request" document which is provided in updated OMB Circular A-11 guidance that is sent to all of the Federal Agencies each June-July (see Figure B-1). The Exhibit 300 format requires agencies to submit a business case and technical information on each IT Program to show how that program efficiently and effectively helps the Agency to accomplish its mission. Part of this information is derived from the five FEA Reference Models, which are shown in Figure B-4.

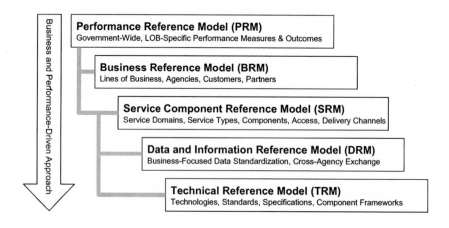

Figure B-4. Federal Enterprise Architecture (FEA) Reference Models

Each of the Reference Models of the FEA is intended to provide Federal Agencies with a standardized way to develop the EA artifacts and data that help Agencies to categorize, and report on their major and/or mission critical IT Programs. This FEA Reference Model information is submitted as part of the Exhibit 300 Budget Request that is submitted to OMB each September (which requires linkage between the EA and capital planning processes in each Agency). The FEA Reference Models are in some ways an "EA data mining tool" that examines other EA artifacts to extend or categorize those artifacts and the EA resources, systems, components, and programs that they document. Examples of other EA artifacts that the FEA Reference Models are designed to examine and enhance are: business process models, system or process performance measures, data models, web service models, project tracking information, system documentation, application standards information, and network infrastructure standards and documentation. The following are more detailed descriptions of the purpose and utilization of each of the FEA Reference Models.

FEA Performance Reference Model (PRM)

The Performance Reference Model (PRM) provides Federal Agencies with a standardized way to develop and use outcome and output performance measures. This helps agencies link strategic goals to the performance of specific IT programs. Figure B-5 from OMB's FEA website (www.feapmo.gov) shows the PRM model and its three distinct measurement areas; inputs, outputs, and outcomes.

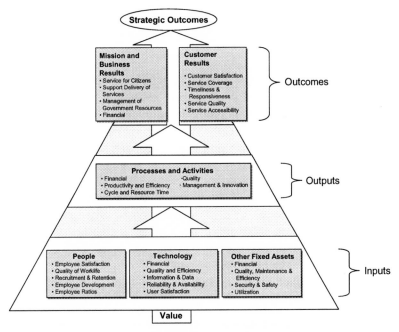

Figure B-5. The FEA Performance Reference Model

One of the main tenants of the PRM is to promote the identification and linkage of process inputs to outputs, and then to desired agency outcomes. The PRM is meant to be completed before the other FEA Reference Models so that the agency has a clear idea of the purpose of their strategic initiatives and where there are gaps in agency performance that IT programs can help overcome. The following is the reporting table for

PRM information that is currently used for Exhibit 300 submission on each major and/or mission critical IT program that an Agency has. Hypothetical PRM data from FEAPMO is provided below for a Trade Program.

Exhibit 300 - PRM Reporting Table (Example Data)						
Fiscal Year	Measurement Area*	Measurement Category**	Measurement Indicator	Baseline	Planned Improvements to the Baseline	Actual Results
2007	Mission & Business Results	International Affairs & Commerce	# of exporters entering new market	5,853 exporters	2% increase	283 new (4.8%)
2007	Customer Results	Customer Benefit	# of trade leads from e-Trade.gov website	1,358 leads	10% increase	185 leads (13.6%)
2007	Processes and Activities	Management and Innovation	# of businesses registered on e-Trade.gov website	10,465 businesses	6% increase	593 new busines ses (5.7%)
2007	Technology	Efficiency	Query response time	10.5 seconds	20% decrease	3.1 sec. (29.5%)

FEA Business Reference Model (BRM)

Version 2.0 of the FEA's Business Reference Model helps Federal Agencies to categorize their government business activities (internal and external processes) at three levels: Business Area; Line of Business/Internal Functions; and Sub-Functions. In version 2.0 of the BRM, there were 4 general government Business Areas (Services for Citizens, Mode of Delivery, Support Delivery of Services, and Management of Government Resources); 39 Business/Internal Functions; and 153 Sub-Functions. The BRM also helps OMB to determine which Federal Agencies are involved in similar activities. This promotes participation in related e-Government Initiatives, as well as multi-agency collaboration on infrastructure support requirements and the development of solutions to other mission-specific requirements. Figure B-6 from the FEA Program Management Office shows version 2.0 of the BRM.

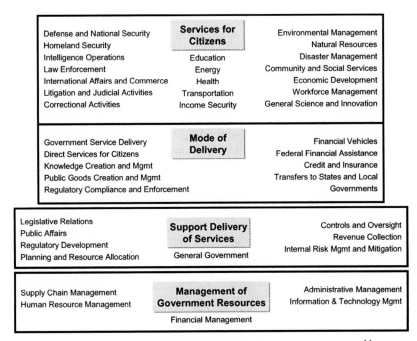

Defense and National Security Homeland Security Intelligence Operations Law Enforcement International Affairs and Commerce Litigation and Judicial Activities Correctional Activities	**Services for Citizens** Education Energy Health Transportation Income Security	Environmental Management Natural Resources Disaster Management Community and Social Services Economic Development Workforce Management General Science and Innovation
Government Service Delivery Direct Services for Citizens Knowledge Creation and Mgmt Public Goods Creation and Mgmt Regulatory Compliance and Enforcement	**Mode of Delivery**	Financial Vehicles Federal Financial Assistance Credit and Insurance Transfers to States and Local Governments
Legislative Relations Public Affairs Regulatory Development Planning and Resource Allocation	**Support Delivery of Services** General Government	Controls and Oversight Revenue Collection Internal Risk Mgmt and Mitigation
Supply Chain Management Human Resource Management	**Management of Government Resources** Financial Management	Administrative Management Information & Technology Mgmt

Figure B-6. The FEA Business Reference Model [44]

The reporting of BRM information is also done annually through an Exhibit 300 submission for each of the Agency's major and/or mission critical IT programs. The following is the current format of the Exhibit 300 BRM reporting table, with hypothetical data for an Air Traffic Control Program. Information on how to select BRM categories is provided in annual OMB Circular A-11 guidance.

Business Area	**Line of Business**	**Sub-Function**
Services for Citizens	Transportation	Air Transportation
Mode of Delivery	Knowledge Creation and Management	Knowledge Dissemination

FEA Service Component Reference Model (SRM)

The Service Component Reference Model (SRM) is a business and performance-driven EA categorization model that assists Federal Agencies

---

[44] Ibid

in identifying and classifying "Service Components," which support the achievement of business and/or performance objectives. According to the FEA Program Management Office,[45] "the SRM is structured across horizontal and vertical service domains that, independent of the business functions, can provide a leverage-able foundation to support the reuse of applications, application capabilities, components, and business services." The SRM has three levels of classification: Service Domain, Service Type, and Component. The identification of classification areas is primarily accomplished by answering "what functionality does the program/system provide?" and "what logical module or area of the program/system supports that functionality?" Figure B-7 shows the SRM.[46]

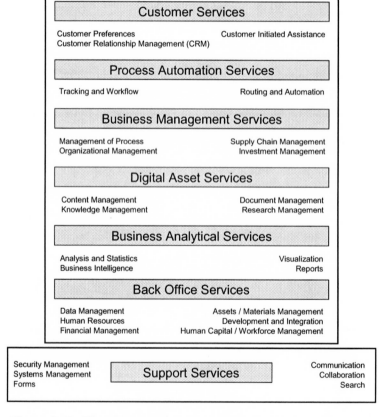

Figure B-7. The FEA Service Component Reference Model

---

[45] Ibid
[46] Ibid

Along with all FEA information, the reporting of SRM data is done annually through an Exhibit 300 submission for each of the Agency's major and/or mission critical IT programs. The following is the current format of the Exhibit 300 SRM reporting table, with hypothetical data for a Labor Statistics Program. Information on how to select SRM categories is provided in annual OMB Circular A-11 guidance. At the component level, Agencies can add new descriptions that are not in the guidance.

Service Domain	Service Type	Component
Customer Services	Customer Initiated Assistance	Labor Statistics Archive
Business Analytical Services	Analysis and Statistics	Labor Statistics Publication

FEA Data Reference Model (DRM)

The Data and Information Reference Model (DRM) version 1.0 provides a standardized method for categorizing and describing the data and information that support government line of business operations. The DRM also helps Federal Agencies to develop standard data formats that will increase the sharing of information across the entire Federal Government. Figure B-8 shows the DRM.

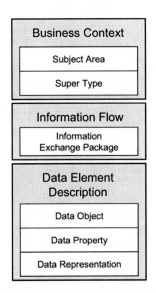

Figure B-8. The FEA Data and Information Reference Model (DRM)

According the FEA Program Management Office, the Business Context level "identifies a major topic of concern to the government such that various lines of business perform activities that create and use closely related information to achieve significant outcomes. It also identifies a conceptual category of data entities with the intent of accommodating mappings to similar data groupings currently defined by government agencies." The Information Flow level documents "information that is generated or required by a Unit of Work and is subsequently passed to another Unit of Work." The Data Element Description level documents Data Objects which the FEA Program Management Office defines as "a set of ideas, abstractions or things in the real world that can be identified with explicit boundaries and meaning, and whose properties and behavior follow the same rules." Data Properties are defined as "a peculiarity common to all members of and Object Class" and Data Representation is defined as "the combination of a value domain, data type, and if necessary, a unit of measure of a character set." [47]

The DRM is still in draft form at this time, and discussions regarding implementation between OMB and Federal Agencies may change this Reference Model. One theme for implementation being discussed is for a particular Federal Agency to take a "lead" role in establishing DRM standards and definitions for areas of information exchange that they are involved with, and be supported by other Agencies with similar interests. In this way, the workload of establishing DRM standards and definitions is distributed among many Agencies, which will speed up the implementation process and increase Agency buy-in.

FEA Technical Reference Model (TRM)

The Technical Reference Model (TRM) is a component-driven, classification model that is used to identify the standards, specifications, and technologies that support the development, implementation, and exchange of business and application components (Service Components) that may be used and leveraged in a Component-Based or Service-Orientated Architecture. There are four levels of TRM categorization: Service Area, Category, Standard, and Specification. Figure B-10 from the FEAPMO website shows version 1.0 of the TRM.

---

[47] Ibid

Service Access and Delivery

Access Channels	**Delivery Channels**	**Service Requirements**	**Service Transport**
Web Browsers	Internet, Intranet	Legislative / Compliance	Network Services
Wireless / PDA Device	Extranet	Authentication / Single Sign-On	Transport
Collaboration / Communication	Peer to Peer (P2P)	Hosting	
Other Electronic Channels	Virtual Private Network (VPN)		

Service Platform and Infrastructure

Support Platforms
Wireless / Mobile
Platform Independent (J2EE)
Platform Dependent (.NET)

Database / Storage
Database
Storage Devices

Delivery Services
Web, Media
Application
Portal

Software Engineering
Integrated Development Environment (IDE)
Software Configuration Management (SCM)
Testing Management, Modeling

Hardware/ Infrastructure
Servers / Computers
Embedded Technology Devices
Peripherals
WAN / LAN
Network Devices / Standards
Video Conferencing

Component Framework

Security
Certification / Digital Signature
Supporting Security Services

Data Interchange
Data Exchange

Presentation / Interface
Static Display
Dynamic Server-Side Display
Content Rendering
Wireless / Mobile / Voice

Business Logic
Platform Independent
Platform Dependent

Data Management
Database Connectivity
Reporting and Analysis

Service Interface and Integration

Integration
Middleware
Database Access
Transaction Processing
Object Request Broker

Interoperability
Data Format / Classification
Data Types / Validation
Data Transformation

Interface
Service Discovery
Service Description / Interface

Figure B-10. The FEA Technical Reference Model [48]

The reporting of TRM data is also done annually through an Exhibit 300 submission for each of the Agency's major and/or mission critical IT programs. The following is the current format of the Exhibit 300 TRM reporting table, with hypothetical data for a wireless network. Information on how to select TRM categories is provided in annual OMB Circular A-11 guidance. At the Specification level, Agencies can add new descriptions that are not in the TRM guidance.

Service Area	Service Category	Service Standard	Service Specification
Service Access and Delivery	Access Channel	Web Browser	Product A
Service Access and Delivery	Service Transport	Transport	HTTP, WAP

---

[48] Ibid

Using the FEA Reference Models with Existing EA Frameworks

One of the challenges that federal agencies currently face is the co-utilization of the EA frameworks that they chose in the 1998-2001 timeframe (FEAF, TEAF, or DODAF), and the new the FEA Reference Models. While the early public sector EA frameworks did not exclude cross-organizational EA documentation, these frameworks were not often used in that manner. Rather, Federal Agencies used these frameworks to document the intra-Agency business and technology operating environment, and external interfaces to other enterprises. The orientation of the FEA Reference Models forces agencies to look beyond their own organizational boundaries and understand their processes and resources through the lens of collaboration. Unfortunately, as of this writing, the FEA is not yet complete or well understood in Agencies in terms of how to implement it and how to relate it to the other implemented frameworks. Further, it is not yet clear whether OMB intends for the FEA to become an EA framework that replaces the others. Until that is clarified, perhaps the best way for agencies to co-utilize the FEA and the FEAF/TEAF/DODAF is to use the FEA to guide the development of future views of the EA, and use the FEAF, TEAF, or DODAF to document those views. The problem that remains then is how to map the EA Artifacts in the FEAF/TEAF/DODAF to the products required by the FEA Reference Models. This is both a question of methodology and subsequent utilization. Figure B-11 shows potential mappings and relationships between the FEA Reference Models and various existing EA frameworks.

FEA Reference Models	EA3 Cube Framework Levels	FEAF Framework Levels	DODAF Framework Areas	Zachman EA Framework	Spewak EAP Planning
Performance Reference Model	Strategic Goals &Initiatives	Business	Operations	Time, Motivation	----
Business Reference Model	Business Products & Services			Function	Business
Data and Information Reference Model	Data & Information	Data	Systems	Data	Data
Service Component Reference Model	Systems & Applications	Application		Organization	Application
Technical Reference Model	Networks & Infrastructure	Technology	Technical	Network	Technology
Security & Privacy Profile	Security Thread	----	----	Network	----

Figure B-11. FEA and EA Framework Relationships

The FEA Security and Privacy Profile

As was covered in Chapter 11, IT Security is a major concern for all IT operating environments and is an issue that spans all levels of EA. The FEA's "Security and Privacy Profile" can be thought of as an overlay that encompasses and influences all of the Reference Models, yet can be maintained separately due to the sensitivity on some of the information on security vulnerabilities and capabilities. The Security and Privacy Profile also provides a methodology for making risk-adjusted security decisions regarding IT resources, and using best practices such as the Security checklists developed by the National Institute of Science and Technology (NIST), which cover the development of system security plans, test and evaluation methods, and recurring system certification and accreditation. Data Privacy is a related area of concern that the Security Profile addresses by providing guidance on how to build Data Privacy into Federal Agency business services so they become part of the supporting IT system/web service lifecycle.

Draft Repeatable Methodology – FEA Security and Privacy Profile

A repeatable methodology for implementing the FEA Security Profile in federal agencies might involve various stakeholders in the agency's enterprise architecture and security programs/processes who work together to complete the following 10-step *Security and Privacy Profile Methodology* that addresses two levels of agency activity: (1) Lines of Business, Sub Functions, Services, Processes; and (2) Programs / Systems:

Level I: Lines of Business / Sub Functions / Services / Processes:
1. Establish the Agency Enterprise Architecture Approach.
2. Identify Line of Business Services/Processes.
3. Relate Business and Security Objectives.
4. Develop Security Context and Condition Data.
5. Validate and Measure Context/Condition Data.

Level II: Programs / Systems:
6. FIPS-199 System Security Categorization.
7. NIST SP-800/53a Security Controls.
8. Perform Tradeoff Analysis.
9. Implement Security Controls.
10. Monitor LOB and System Level Security Effectiveness.

OMB and FEAPMO are working to formalize this type of guidance for the FEA Security and Privacy Profile in the fiscal year 2006 timeframe.

Federal Agency EA Program Assessment

In 2004, the Office of Management and Budget (OMB) developed an EA Assessment Framework (EAAF) that is based on an evaluation "scorecard" to assist Federal Agencies in assessing their EA Programs. The scorecard contains four primary assessment areas (Change, Integration, Convergence, and Business Alignment) and thirteen sub-areas. Each sub-area is scored 0 to 5, indicating the degree to which the EA Program has been formalized and how much impact on business operations the EA Program has in the Agency. Agencies should be striving to meet the Level 5 criteria in each EA Program assessment sub-area.

Evaluating Federal Agency EA Management Maturity

In 2001, the U.S. Government Accountability Office (GAO) developed an approach to evaluating the maturity of Federal Agency EA Programs, which was updated in 2003.. Called the EA Management Maturity Framework (EAMMF), this EA evaluation approach establishes five stages of maturity and core elements at each stage to measure the management of Agency EA Programs, as shown in Figure B-12.[49] The concepts of the EAMMF are grounded in the eight elements of establishing and managing an EA Program that are articulated in the Federal CIO Council's *Practical Guide to Federal Enterprise Architecture*. GAO has used the EAMMF in 2001, 2003, and 2005 to evaluate EA program management in over 1001 federal agencies. GAO has also used the EAMMF as part of Congressionally-requested audits of particular federal programs or agencies.

---

[49] U.S. Government Accountability Office. Information Technology: A Framework for Assessing and Improving Enterprise Architecture Management (Version 1.1). Randolph C. Hite. GAO-03-584G. April 2003. U.S. Government Printing Office, Washington DC.

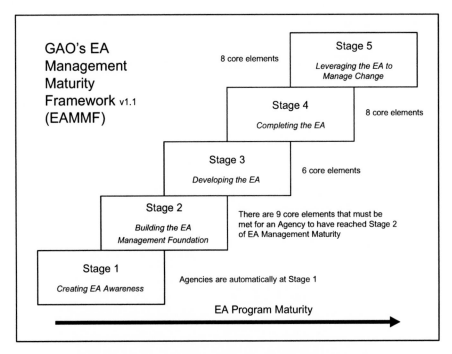

Figure B-12. The EA Maturity Model Framework

The five stages of EA program maturity in version 1.1 of the EAMMF are described as follows: [50]

EAMMF Stage 1: Creating EA Awareness
"At Stage 1, either an enterprise does not have plans to develop and use an architecture, or it has plans that do not demonstrate an awareness of the value of having and using an architecture. While Stage 1 agencies may have initiated some EA activity, these agencies' efforts are ad hoc and unstructured, lack institutional leadership and direction, and do not provide the management foundation necessary for successful EA development as defined in Stage 2."

EAMMF Stage 2: Building the EA Management Foundation
"An enterprise at Stage 2 recognizes that the EA is a corporate asset by vesting accountability for it in an executive body that represents the entire enterprise. At this stage, an enterprise assigns EA management roles and responsibilities and establishes plans for developing EA products and for measuring program progress and product quality; it also commits the

---

[50] Ibid

resources necessary for developing an architecture—people, processes, and tools. Specifically, a Stage 2 enterprise has designated a Chief Architect and established and staffed a program office responsible for EA development and maintenance. Further, it has established a committee or group that has responsibility for EA governance (i.e., directing, overseeing, and approving architecture development and maintenance). This committee or group is often called a steering committee, and its membership includes both business and IT representatives (i.e., the committee has enterprise-wide representation). At Stage 2, the enterprise either has plans for developing or has started developing at least some EA products, and it has developed an enterprise-wide awareness of the value of EA and its intended use in managing its IT investments. The enterprise has also selected a framework and a methodology that will be the basis for developing the EA products and has selected a tool for automating these activities."

EAMMF Stage 3: Developing the EA

"An enterprise at Stage 3 focuses on developing architecture products according to the selected framework, methodology, tool, and established management plans. Roles and responsibilities assigned in the previous stage are in place, and resources are being applied to develop actual EA products. Here, the scope of the architecture has been defined to encompass the entire enterprise, whether enterprise-based or function-based. Although the products may not be complete, they are intended to describe the enterprise in business, performance, information/data, service/application, and technology terms (including security explicitly in each), as provided for in the framework, methodology, tool, and management plans. Further, the products are to describe the current ("as-is") and future ("to-be") states and the plan for transitioning from the current to the future state (the sequencing plan). As the products are developed and evolve, they are subject to configuration management. Further, through the established EA management foundation, the enterprise is tracking and measuring its progress against plans, identifying and addressing variances, as appropriate, and then reporting on its progress."

EAMMF Stage 4: Completing the EA

"An enterprise at Stage 4 has completed its EA products, meaning that the products have been approved by the EA steering committee (established in Stage 2) or an investment review board, and by the CIO. The completed products collectively describe the enterprise in terms of business, performance, information/data, service/application, and technology for both its current and future operating states, and the products include a transition plan for sequencing from the current to the future state. Further, an independent agent has assessed the quality (i.e., completeness and accuracy) of the EA products. Additionally, evolution of the approved products is governed by a written EA maintenance policy approved by the head of the enterprise."

EAMMF Stage 5: Leveraging the EA to Manage Change
"An enterprise at Stage 5 has secured senior leadership approval of the EA products and a written institutional policy stating that IT investments must comply with the architecture, unless granted an explicit compliance waiver. Further, decision-makers are using the architecture to identify and address ongoing and proposed IT investments that are conflicting, overlapping, not strategically linked, or redundant. Thus, Stage 5 entities are able to avoid unwarranted overlap across investments and ensure maximum systems interoperability, which in turn ensures the selection and funding of IT investments with manageable risks and returns. Also at Stage 5, the enterprise tracks and measures EA benefits or return on investment, and adjustments are continuously made to both the EA management process and the EA products."

According to the GAO Report that promulgated the EAMMF, all of the core criteria at a particular Stage must be met, along with all of the criteria of lower stages before an Agency can claim that level of EA management maturity.

Using the EA³ Cube Framework in the Federal Sector

The EA³ "Cube" framework described in this book was developed independent of and before the publication of the FEA Reference Models. Further, the EA³ framework is intended for use in the public, private, non-profit, and academic sectors because it is based on general characteristics of any social enterprise, as well as the work of John Zachman and Steven Spewak. That being said, the EA³ framework may be of use in the federal sector as an EA framework that can be used in place of the FEAF/TEAF/DODAF to document the business and technology operating environment in a way that the EA artifacts called for in the FEA Reference Models. One of the limitations of the FEAF/TEAF/DODAF approaches is that strategy, refined information, and technology components are not well addressed. The EA³ framework does address these areas, as do the FEA Reference Models. Therefore, the EA³ framework may be well suited to help federal agencies organize and implement the process of documenting

EA components in the current and future views. The development of the EA Management Plan (called a "Modernization Blueprint" in more recent federal guidance) can also follow the recommendations in this book, though specific additional information may be required per federal guidance. The following is a summary of how the EA³ framework can be used to "bridge" between existing FEAF/TEAF/DODAF documentation and the FEA Reference Models, or as the preferred EA framework and methodology.

- Existing agency EA programs that use the FEAF/TEAF/DOADF are enhanced and expanded in scope using the EA³ Cube framework and methodology that is described in this book. Existing current (as-is) and future (to-be) EA documentation is mapped to the EA³ Cube once LOBs and components at each level of the EA³ Cube are identified.

- Future views are organized and new/upgraded EA components are identified through the development of future operating scenarios. Additional documentation for strategy, security, workforce, or other EA areas not previously covered are also completed.

- The agency's Capital Planning (CPIC) process is used to develop an updated IT investment portfolio that will fund the future EA components that were identified in the previous step. The four phases of CPIC activities (Plan, Select, Control, Evaluate) and standardized Program/Project Management process are used to ensure the successful implementation of future EA components.

- EA³ Cube information from current and future views are used for agency planning and decision-making, as well as annual reporting using the FEA Reference Models.

- EA3 Cube information is stored in an access-controlled, web-based on-line repository within the agency (such as the *Living Enterprise*™) for easy access by all stakeholders.

- The "Finish" line at the bottom of the diagram highlights the value-added outcomes that the use of EA information can provide the agency, including:

  - Strategic Alignment of IT Resources
  - Improved Service Delivery
  - Reduced IT Operating Costs
  - Improved Decision-Making and Communication

Appendix C

Example Approach to Enterprise Architecture: State-Level EA Concepts

The National Association of State Chief Information Offices (NASCIO) has developed a general approach to EA for States and other government agencies to use in developing their own EA frameworks, programs, and documentation. The NASCIO approach promotes the integration of EA planning and governance across all levels of government (Federal, State, and Local). The NASCIO EA Framework has four basic components: (1) the Architecture Blueprint; (2) the Business Architecture; (3) the Technology Architecture; and (4) the Architecture Governance Framework, as is shown in Figure C-1.

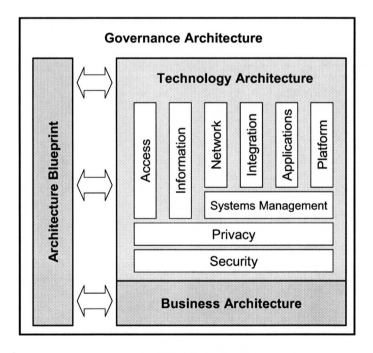

Figure C-1: The NASCIO EA Framework

NASCIO also developed an "EA Development Toolkit" that provides a customizable implementation methodology for use by government enterprises at all levels. NASCIO intends for the Toolkit to be used by State and Local Governments to develop their own customized EA frameworks as follows.

"An EA framework is a methodology for developing an enterprise's IT support functions. Ideally, when governments establish their infrastructures using common enterprise architecture, making systems work together will be simpler because each would have addressed the items that are crucial to interoperability of systems developed for specific business needs. Enterprise architecture is critical because it provides the blueprint for the integration of information and services at the design level across agency boundaries. Enterprise architecture is the blueprint for allowing data to flow from agency to agency, just as water flows through the pipes and electricity flows through the wiring of a well-planned home." [51]

---

[51] NASCIO Enterprise Architecture Framework Toolkit, Version 2.0. July 2002. NACIO Offices: 167 W. Main Street, Suite 600 Lexington, Kentucky 40507-1324 www.nascio.org

Appendix D

Example Approach to Enterprise Architecture: Department of Defense Architecture Framework

The Department of Defense (DOD) first engaged in organization-wide IT resource management when it promulgated the Corporate Information Management (CIM) initiative in the late 1980's. Cancelled in 1997, CIM did begin the process of reviewing DOD's approach to IT resource alignment and consolidation. The follow-on program in DOD called for the development of a Command, Control, Communications, Computer, Intelligence, Surveillance, and Reconnaissance (C4ISR) Architecture.

This approach was renamed in 2002 to be the DOD Architecture Framework (DODAF) and is the only currently authorized method for DOD agencies and military units to model their technical, systems and operating environment. The DODAF is intended to maintain a focus on the warfighting mission while reducing IT functional duplication across DOD and improving the interoperability of IT resources within DOD's overall "Global Information Grid."

The DODAF is based on the development of a hierarchical set of views in each of three modeling areas (operations, systems, technology) as well as a hierarchical set of composite views (called "all views"). The DODAF approach allows for a variety of documentation techniques in developing the models. Figure D-1 on the next page shows the DODAF and its relationship to the EA^3 framework, as well as examples of the core EA artifacts in each of the four areas of the DODAF approach.

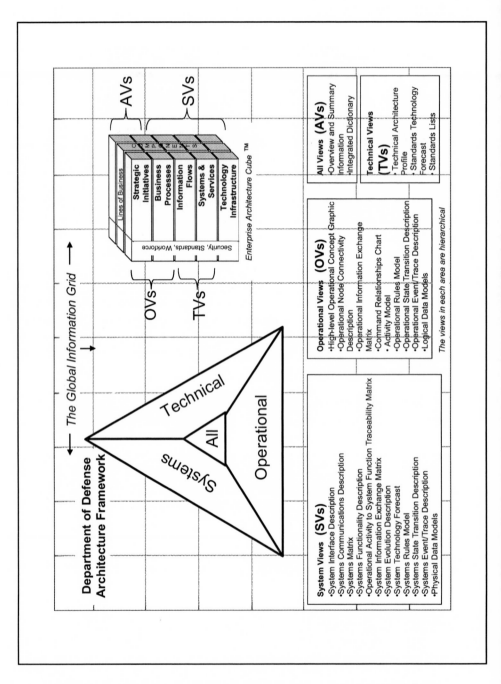

Figure D-1: Relating the DOD Architecture Framework and EA³ Cube

Appendix E

Enterprise Architecture Artifacts

The following is a list of the EA artifacts that are recommended for use when documenting an enterprise using the EA^3 Cube framework, with cross-references to Zachman and DODAF. Examples of each follow.

EA^3 Cube Level/Thread	Artifact ID #	Artifact Name (* Composite Artifact)	Zachman Mapping	DODAF Mapping
Strategic Goals & Initiatives (I)	S-1	Strategic Plan*	C6/R1	AV-1
	S-2	SWOT Analysis	C5/R1	
	S-3	Concept of Operations Scenario		AV-1
	S-4	Concept of Operations Diagram	C2/R1	OV-1
	S-5	Balanced Scorecard™ *	C6/R4, C6/R5	
Business Products & Services (B)	B-1	Business Plan*	C2/R2, C5R1	
	B-2	Node Connectivity Diagram	C3/R1	OV-2
	B-3	Swim Lane Process Diagram *	C4/R2	OV-5
	B-4	Business Process/Service Model	C2/R2	OV-5
	B-5	Business Process/ Product Matrix *	C4/R2	
	B-6	Use Case Narrative & Diagram	C6/R3, C6/R4	OV-6a, SV-10a
	B-7	Investment Business Case*		
Data & Information (D)	D-1	Knowledge Management Plan	C1/R1, C1/R2	
	D-2	Information Exchange Matrix*	C3/R2, C4/R2	OV-3
	D-3	Object State-Transition Diagram	C1/R3	OV-6b, SV-10b
	D-4	Object Event Sequence Diagram	C2/R2, C5/R3	OV-6c, SV-10c
	D-5	Logical Data Model	C1/R3	OV-7, SV-11
	D-6	Physical Data Model	C1/R4	
	D-7	Activity/Entity (CRUD) Matrix *	C1/R3, C4/R2	SV-9
	D-8	Data Dictionary / Object Library	C1/R5	AV-2
Systems & Applications (SA)	SA-1	System Interface Diagram	C3/R4, C3R2	SV-1
	SA-2	System Communication Description	C2/R4, C3/R2	SV-2
	SA-3	System Interface Matrix *	C2/R4	SV-3
	SA-4	System Data Flow Diagram	C2/R3	SV-4
	SA-5	System/Operations Matrix *	C2/R4	SV-5
	SA-6	Systems Data Exchange Matrix *	C2/R3	SV-6
	SA-7	System Performance Matrix *	C2/R3	SV-7
	SA-8	System Evolution Diagram	C2/R4	SV-8
	SA-9	Web Application Diagram	C2/R3	
Networks & Infrastructure (NI)	NI-1	Network Connectivity Diagram	C3/R5	
	NI-2	Network Inventory	C3/R5	
	NI-3	Capital Equipment Inventory	C3/R5	
	NI-4	Building Blueprints *	C3/R5	
	NI-5	Network Center Diagram	C3/R5	
	NI-6	Cable Plant Diagram	C3/R5	
	NI-7	Rack Elevation Diagram	C3/R5	
Security (SP)	SP-1	Security and Privacy Plan*	C4/R5	
	SP-2	Security Solutions Description	C4/R5	
	SP-3	System Accreditation Document*	C4/R5	
	SP-4	Continuity Of Operations Plan*	C4/R5	
	SP-5	Disaster Recovery Procedures *	C4/R5	
Standards (ST)	ST-1	Technical Standards Profile	C3/R4	TV-1
	ST-2	Technology Forecast	C3/R4	TV-2, SV-9
Workforce (W)	W-1	Workforce Plan*	C4/R1	
	W-2	Organization Chart	C4/R2	OV-4
	W-3	Knowledge and Skills Profile	C4/R3	OV-4

EA³ Framework Area	Artifact # and Name

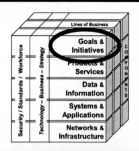

S-1: Strategic Plan

A Strategic Plan is a high-level policy and planning document that an enterprise uses to document its direction, competitive strategy, most important goals, and the enabling programs and projects (strategic initiatives). The Strategic Plan covers a future period, usually 3-5 years.

Description

A Strategic Plan is a composite EA artifact that should guide the enterprise's direction over a 3-5 year period in the future by providing the following items, each of which are primitive (basic) EA artifacts. Full versions of abbreviated primitive artifacts are separate artifacts.

- Provide a Mission Statement and a Vision Statement that succinctly captures the purpose and direction of the enterprise.

- Develop a Statement of Strategic Direction that fits the enterprise's purpose, ensures survivability, allows for flexibility, and promotes competitive success. This statement is a detailed description of where the enterprise intends to go.

- Summarize the results of a SWOT Analysis that is based on the statement of strategic direction and which identifies the enterprise's strengths, weaknesses, opportunities, and threats. The full SWOT analysis is artifact S-2.

- Summarize the situation and planning assumptions for several 'Concept of Operations' CONOPS Scenarios that support the enterprise's strategic direction. This summary should include *one current scenario* that describes at a high-level the coordination of ongoing activities in each line of business, as well as *several future scenarios* that account for different combinations of internal and external drivers identified through the SWOT Analysis. The complete scenarios are artifact S-3.

- Develop a CONOPS Diagram that in a single picture captures the essence of and participants in the current operating scenario. This graphic is artifact S-4.

- Develop a General Competitive Strategy for the enterprise that incorporates the current and future CONOPS scenarios and moves the enterprise in the intended strategic direction in a way that and address internal/external drivers such as culture, line of business requirements, market conditions, competitor strategies, and risk.

- Identify Strategic Goals that will accomplish the competitive strategy, and specify the executive sponsors who are responsible for achieving each goal.

- Identify Strategic Initiatives and resource sponsors for the initiatives, which are the ongoing programs or development projects that will accomplish each Strategic Goal.

- Summarize Outcome Measures for each Strategic Goal and Initiative, using the Balanced Scorecard™ or similar approach. The full scorecard is artifact S-5.

Relationship to Other EA Frameworks

FEAF: Business Level	FEA: PRM	Zachman: C6/R1	DODAF: AV-1

EA³ Framework Area	Artifact # and Name
	**S-2: SWOT Analysis** The Strength, Weakness, Opportunity, and Threat (SWOT) Analysis takes a holistic look at the enterprise by identifying internal and external factors which when mapped can reveal areas for improvement and focus.

Example

One of the earliest activities the enterprise performs in developing a strategic plan is a 'Strength, Weakness, Opportunity, Threat' (SWOT) Analysis. This analysis looks at internal and external factors to determine areas that the enterprise should focus on to increase its survivability and success, as well as areas that the enterprise should avoid, or decrease its exposure to. The results of the SWOT Analysis should be summarized in the Strategic Plan along with the matrix table illustrated below, and the full SWOT Analysis is archived in the EA Repository as a separate primitive artifact (S-2). The following is an example of a way to summarize a SWOT Analysis.

External Factors **Internal Factors** ➡️ ⬇️	Internal Strengths (S) **S1.** User Community **S2.** Relationships **S3.** Involved Leadership **S4.** In-house Technology **S5.** Legacy Architecture **S6.** Training Budget **S7.** Culture	Internal Weaknesses (W) **W1.** Policy / Regulations **W2.** Governance Value **W3.** IT Skills – Systems **W4.** Enterprise Architecture **W5.** IT Skills – Process **W6.** Low Usability/Implementation
External Opportunities (O) **O1.** Contracting **O2.** Government **O3.** New Technology **O4.** Partnerships	**SO** **S5/O3:** Legacy Web Portals **S1/O3:** Security	**WO** **W4/O4:** EA Sharing
External Threats (T) **T1.** Funding **T2.** Market Drivers **T3.** Merger **T4.** Advanced Technology **T5.** IT Adoption Rate	**ST** **S1/T2:** FED Requirements **S6/T5:** IT Training **S1/T5:** IT Awareness	**WT** **W4/T1:** Funding Data

From the identification of Internal Strengths (S), Internal Weaknesses (W), External Opportunities (O), and External Threats (T) for the enterprise, a matrix arrangement like the example above can help to reveal internal and external areas to focus on. This SWOT Analysis is also used to help enterprise architects and strategic planners to develop Concept of Operations (CONOPS) scenarios that detail current and future operating environments.

Relationship to Other EA Frameworks

FEAF: Business Level	**FEA:** PRM, BRM	**Zachman:** C5/R1	**DODAF:** None

EA³ Framework Area	Artifact # and Name

S-3: CONOPS Scenario

A Concept of Operations Scenario is a narrative document that describes how the enterprise operates currently or will operate several years in the future given certain stated internal and external factors identified in the SWOT Analysis. The scenario is footnoted with planning assumptions.

Example

Planning Assumptions

1. New Video Teleconferencing capability.

2. Product roll-outs at National conferences.

3. Need to hold detailed product discussions on short notice, globally.

4. 24x7 work availability.

5. Increased suburban commuting and telecommuting.

6. Tracking of Govt. reports to anticipate product needs.

7. Changing population demographics, driving new product development.

8. Increased cost benefit of solar powered lighting.

9. Additional product features to attract customers

10. Global use of PDAs for employee communication.

11. Integration of sales, marketing, and production information.

12. Accurate customer quotes on the fly.

Jeff Linder, Vice President of Industrial Sales for Danforth Manufacturing Company (DMC) had just finished a presentation at the 2008 National Highway Safety Conference along with Richard Danforth, DMC's CEO, who had teleconferenced in on the big display screen behind the podium.[1] As Jeff was leaving the main conference room, Andrea Newman, Director of Safety and Transportation for the State of Tennessee, asked Jeff if they could talk about the new line of solar-powered highway lights he had just given a presentation on. [2, 3]

"Thanks for taking a minute to talk Jeff. I want to tell you about a situation we have in Tennessee and see if your new product line can help" said Andrea as they found a table in the refreshment area.[4] "No problem, thanks for asking" Jeff said. Andrea pulled up a document on her tablet computer and said "Jeff, here is a report that shows an increasing number of serious accidents in rural areas of Tennessee involving passenger cars and agricultural equipment or commercial trucks. We've attributed it to the growth of suburban communities further out in the countryside that then depend on two-lane country roads for commuting into the city.[5] When you put slow tractors and trucks together with cars that are in a hurry at all hours to get somewhere, you have a recipe for disaster." "Isn't this problem being seen in other places around the country?" asked Jeff. "Yes, and one of the contributing factors that is consistently coming out of investigations of the night-time accidents is the lack of good lighting on these country roads.[6] I am thinking that your highway grade solar lighting can help us provide more night visibility on high-risk rural roads without needing electrical infrastructure." [7, 8]

Jeff thought for a minute before responding. "You know, the new line of highway lights has options to incorporate 911 emergency call boxes and Global Positioning System (GPS) equipment that can connect to both State and local level first responders.[9] This might be useful in also improving response times should an accident occur in spite of the improved lighting." Andrea nodded and said, "Yes, I doubt that better lighting will solve the entire problem, but it will help people see each other better, and these other options can improve accident response times. What is the pricing on these units?"

Jeff pulled his Personal Digital Assistant (PDA)[10] out of his pocket and connected to DMC's marketing and sales database at headquarters via a satellite Internet link.[11] "Andrea, these units are $11,300 each, including the GPS and 911 features." Andrea took notes and responded, "If I can get permission to conduct a pilot test in a couple of months can you provide the lights?" Jeff asked "How many miles of road?" "About four miles in the particular area I'm thinking of" said Andrea. "Ok, the suggested density for the new unit is 18 per mile, so that would be 72 units total. I can give you our 10 percent early-adopter discount, so the total would be $732,240. Let me check what the shipping time would be."

Jeff sent a high priority email to Bob Green, Vice President of Manufacturing. Bob was in the factory when he received Jeff's email on his PDA, and after checking the DMC Production Scheduling System, responded two minutes later that a special order for 72 units could be completed and shipped 35 days from when the order is received. Jim relayed this information to Andrea, who said, "Wow, that's fast. I have all the information I need to propose the project, I'll get back to you next week" [12]

Relationship to Other EA Frameworks

FEAF: Business Level	FEA: None	Zachman: None	DODAF: None

EA³ Framework Area	Artifact # and Name

S-4: Concept of Operations Diagram

A Concept of Operations (CONOPS) diagram is a high-level graphical depiction of the how the enterprise functions, either overall, or in a particular area of interest.

Example Diagram

This CONOPS Diagram shows at a high level how a fictitious system called the 'Hurricane Warning System' would conduct its primary mission of providing a coordinated weather surveillance and reporting capability using land-based, sea-based, airborne, and space-based resources.

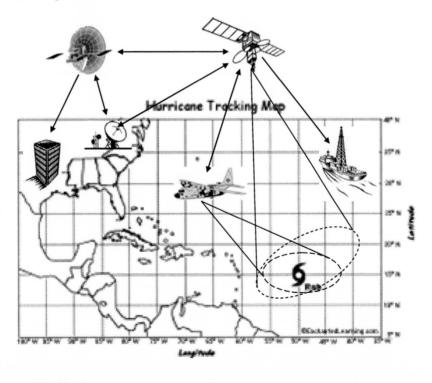

Relationship to Other EA Frameworks

FEAF: Business Level	**FEA:** None	**Zachman:** C2/R1	**DODAF:** OV-1

S-5: Balanced Scorecard™

The Balanced Scorecard™ goes beyond financial measures of success for an enterprise and establishes goals and measures in four key business views: *Customer;, Financial; Internal Business Processes; and Learning and Growth.*

Description

"The Balanced Scorecard™ suggests that people should view the enterprise from <u>four</u> perspectives, (not just a money perspective) and should develop metrics, collect data, and analyze the enterprise relative to each of these perspectives, as is shown in the figure to the right."

"The Balanced Scorecard™ is a management and measurement system that enables enterprises to clarify their vision and strategy and translate them into action. The scorecard provides feedback around both the internal business processes and external outcomes in order to continuously improve strategic performance and results. When fully deployed, the balanced scorecard transforms strategic planning from an academic exercise into the nerve center of an enterprise."[1]

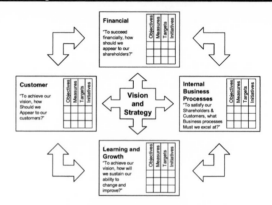

[1] Balanced Scorecard Institute

Balanced Scorecard™	Strategic Initiative 1	Strategic Initiative 2	Strategic Initiative 3	Strategic Initiative 4	Strategic Initiative 5
Financial Perspective					
Strategic Objective					
Outcome Measure 1					
Outcome Measure 2					
Output Measure A					
Output Measure B					
Output Measure C					
Internal Business Process Perspective					
Strategic Objective					
Outcome Measure 1					
Outcome Measure 2					
Output Measure A					
Output Measure B					
Output Measure C					
Customer Perspective					
Strategic Objective					
Outcome Measure 1					
Outcome Measure 2					
Output Measure A					
Output Measure B					
Output Measure C					
Learning and Growth Perspective					
Strategic Objective					
Outcome Measure 1					
Outcome Measure 2					
Output Measure A					
Output Measure B					
Output Measure C					

Relationship to Other EA Frameworks

FEAF: Business Level	**FEA:** PRM	**Zachman:** C6/R4 & R5	**DODAF:** None

EA³ Framework Area	Artifact # and Name

B-1: Business Plan

The Business Plan provides a high-level description of the key line of business functions, and financial strategy that will accomplish the strategic goals and initiatives.

Description

The following items are often found in a Business Plan:

1. Business Overview
2. Executive Team Profile
3. Relationship of Business Activities to Strategic Goals
4. Organizational Structure
5. Market Outlook and Competitive Strategy
6. Business Cycles
7. Capitalization Summary
8. Financial Strategy
9. Current Financial Status Summary
10. Business Partnerships and Alliances

Relationship to Other EA Frameworks

FEAF: Business Level	FEA: None	Zachman: C2/R2, C5/R1	DODAF: None

EA³ Framework Area	Artifact # and Name

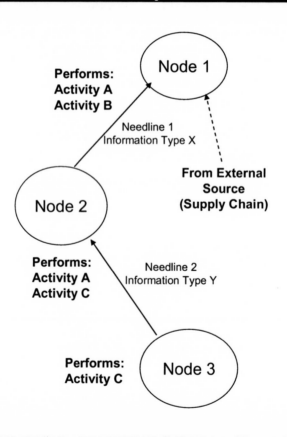

B-2: Node Connectivity Diagram

The Node Connectivity Diagram shows the operational nodes, activities performed at each node, node-to-node relationships, and information exchanges. The purpose of this diagram is to show, at a high level, who are the operating groups in the enterprise (lines of business) and how they share information.

Example

Node 1

Performs:
Activity A
Activity B

Needline 1
Information Type X

From External
Source
(Supply Chain)

Node 2

Performs:
Activity A
Activity C

Needline 2
Information Type Y

Performs:
Activity C

Node 3

Relationship to Other EA Frameworks

FEAF: Business Level	FEA: BRM	Zachman: C3/R1	DODAF: OV-2

EA³ Framework Area	Artifact # and Name

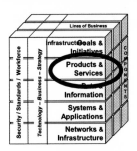

B-3: Swim Lane Process Diagram

A Stakeholder Activity Diagram shows which stakeholders (those with a vested interest in the enterprise) are involved with line of business processes, and the timing of that interaction. The diagram uses the format of 'swim lanes' to arrange stakeholders by row, and timeframes by column, then overlaying activities with flowchart symbology.

Example

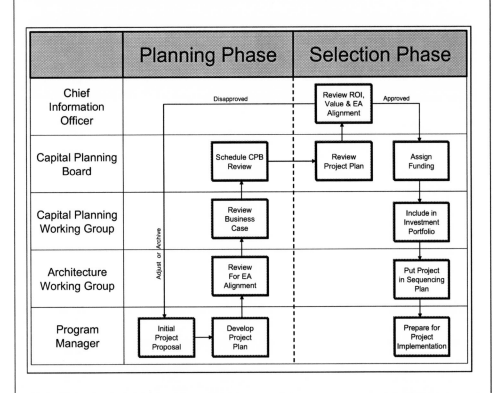

Relationship to Other EA Frameworks

FEAF: Business Level	**FEA:** BRM	**Zachman:** C4/R2	**DODAF:** OV-5

EA³ Framework Area	Artifact # and Name

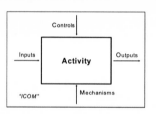

B-4: Business Process Diagram

A Business Process Diagram shows a detailed breakdown of an activity, including how each step in the activity relates to the others. The B-4 diagram follows the IDEF-0 modeling technique to show what the inputs, controls, outputs, and mechanisms are for each step in the process.

Description and Example

Inputs: Items that initiate/trigger the activity and are transformed, consumed, or become part.
Controls: Guide or regulate the activity; usually indicate when/ how a process will be performed.
Outputs: The results produced by the activity; the reason for which the process was performed.
Mechanisms: Systems, people, and equipment used to perform the activity.

IDEF-0 activity modeling is suitable for business process documentation in that it provides both high level context views, and more detailed views of each step in the activity in a format that can be further decomposed and interrelated with other processes to show linkages. This type of diagram is useful in showing linkages between steps and internal/external influences, but may not indicate a time sequence.

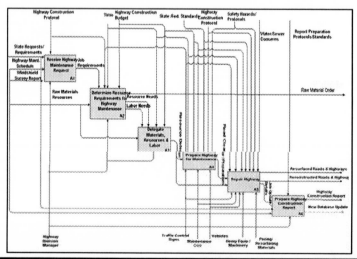

Relationship to Other EA Frameworks

FEAF: Business Level	FEA: BRM	Zachman: C2/R2	DODAF: OV-5

EA³ Framework Area	Artifact # and Name

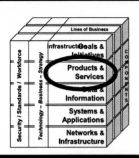

B-5: Activity/Product Matrix

The Business Activity & Product Matrix maps the lifecycle of revenue-producing products to various lines of business throughout the enterprise. This matrix highlights who owns business processes and products, as well as the extent of supply chains.

Example

The Activity/Product Matrix maps the lifecycle of each revenue-producing product that the enterprise produces to the line(s) of business that support one or more phases of the product lifecycle. This matrix allows the enterprise to see where the vertical and horizontal (cross-cutting) business product activities are located, as well as to help define ownership of those processes. The B-5 Activity/Product Matrix can then be used with various Data & Information level artifacts (e.g. D-7 Activity/Entity Matrix) to further map the product lifecycle to requirements for data across the enterprise.

	Line of Business A	Line of Business B	Line of Business C	Line of Business D	Line of Business E	Line of Business F	Line of Business G	Remarks
Business Product								
Product 1	R					F	L	
Product 2		M	W	D	S	F	L	
Product 3		M	W	D	S	F	L	
Product 4	R					F	L	
Product 5		M				F	L	
Product 6		M	W	D	S	F		

R = Research & Develop   W = Warehouse   S = Service   L = Legal
M = Manufacture   D = Distribute   F = Financials

The product lifecycle illustrated in this example has five sequential stages (research and development, manufacturing, warehouse storage, sales/distribution, and servicing) and two parallel administrative functions (financials and legal). Product lifecycles are different within most enterprises, and adjustments to the B-5 matrix should be made accordingly.

Relationship to Other EA Frameworks

FEAF: Business Level	**FEA:** BRM	**Zachman:** C4/R2	**DODAF:** None

EA³ Framework Area	Artifact # and Name

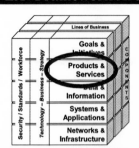

B-6: Use Case Narrative & Diagram

A Use Case narrative follows the Unified Modeling Language (UML) format for identifying business requirements, their context, stakeholders (actors), and business rules for their interaction with systems, services, and applications that are identified as technology solutions requiring development.

Example

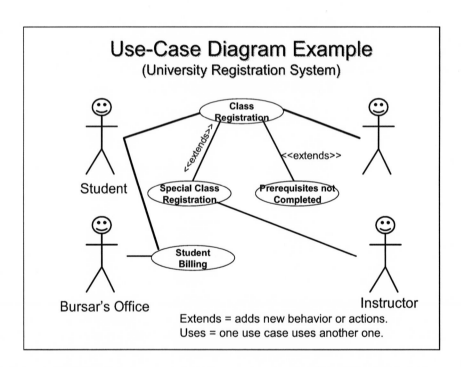

Use-Case Diagram Example
(University Registration System)

Student

Class Registration

<<extends>>

<<extends>>

Special Class Registration

Prerequisites not Completed

Student Billing

Bursar's Office

Instructor

Extends = adds new behavior or actions.
Uses = one use case uses another one.

Relationship to Other EA Frameworks

FEAF: Business Level	**FEA:** BRM	**Zachman:** C6/R3, C6/R4	**DODAF:** OV-6a, SV-10a

B-7: Investment Business Case

An Investment Business Case uses a standard format to describe the value, risk, and return on investments made in technology and other resources. The Business Case also contains an alternatives analysis, program performance tracking metrics, architecture information, and security status information.

Example

1. **New Requirement.** A new requirement for resource(s) or support is identified in a line of business (LOB), which is brought to the EA and capital planning teams for evaluation.

2. **Existing Solution Check.** The EA and capital planning teams determine that an existing EA component cannot meet the requirement.

3. **New Solution Business Case.** The sponsoring LOB determines that the requirement is of sufficient importance to merit the cost of developing a business case:

   - Business Need. Describe the requirement in terms of the gap in operational or administrative performance it represents to the LOB and the enterprise.
   - Impact if Not Resolved. Describe the impact to the enterprise if the performance gap is not resolved, including strategic, business, and technology impact.
   - Alternatives Analysis. Identify 3 or more viable alternative solutions (if 3 exist).
   - Cost-Benefit Analysis. Quantify the direct and indirect costs and benefits for each alternative on a lifecycle basis, including qualitative items.
   - Return on Investment. Do a ROI calculation for each alternative.
   - Net Present Value Adjustment. Do a NPV adjustment for each ROI calculation to account for anticipated cost increases over the investment's lifecycle.

4. **Business Case Evaluation.** The business case's alternatives are evaluated by the Architecture Working Group (AWG) for the correctness of the analysis, and alignment with the EA at each level of the framework. The Capital Planning Working Group (CPWG) then reviews the business case for the correctness of the financial analysis. A coordinated recommendation is made to the executive-level Capital Planning Board (CPB) as to whether the business case should be approved or disapproved.

5. **Business Case Approval.** The CPB reviews and approves/disapproves the business case in the context of the enterprise's overall investment portfolio using criteria that identify value from a strategic, business, and technology perspective:

6. **Implementation.** If the business case is "selected" (approved) for funding by the CPB, the proposed solution becomes an implementation project that is managed by the sponsoring LOB. The project is reviewed by the CPB at key milestones and/or periodically as part of the capital planning process' oversight of all projects.

Relationship to Other EA Frameworks

FEAF: None	FEA: Exhibit 300	Zachman: None	DODAF: None

EA³ Framework Area	Artifact # and Name

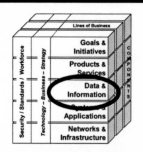

D-1: Knowledge Management Plan

The Knowledge Management (KM) Plan provides a detailed description of how knowledge, information, and data are shared across the enterprise. The KM Plan includes descriptions and diagrams of information sharing between systems, applications, knowledge warehouses, and databases

Description and Example

KM Plan Contents

- The approach to managing data, information, and knowledge across the enterprise
- How data and information-sharing support the Business Plan
- Data and information-sharing strategies and diagrams for each line of business
- Data and information sharing strategies with external partners and customers
- Which types of data in the enterprise require extra protection
- The lifecycle for data and information that is key to the success of the enterprise (data creation, sharing, updating, storage, retrieval, and deletion)

Example of a High Level KM Diagram

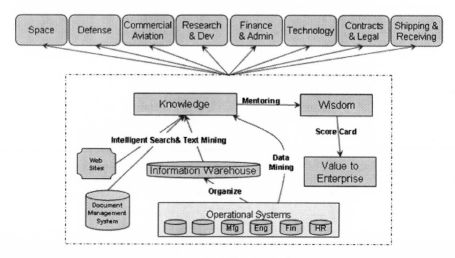

Relationship to Other EA Frameworks

FEAF: Data Level	FEA: DRM	Zachman: C1/R1, C1/R2	DODAF: None

EA³ Framework Area	Artifact # and Name

D-2: Information Exchange Matrix

The Information Exchange Matrix describes relevant attributes of data exchanges between systems. These attributes include size, logical specification of the information i.e., media, timeliness required, and the security classification and properties of the information.

Example

Information exchanges express the relationships across four important aspects of the architecture (information, activities, locations, and times) with a focus on the specific aspects of the information flow. Information exchanges identify which business nodes exchange what information during the performance of what activities and in response to which events. Additional information on who is performing the activity can be added, if needed for security analysis. The detailed information in the Information Exchange Matrix may be hard to collect but it is necessary to fully understand the information flow in the enterprise and its security aspects.

The matrix also identifies the event that triggers the information exchange (e.g., set schedule or citizen request). The matrix keys the exchange to the producing and using activities and nodes and to the needline (from the Node Connectivity Diagram) the exchange satisfies. The Information Exchange Matrix partitions each high-level needline into its component parts, i.e., into distinct information exchanges between business nodes. An example format for this artifact is provided below. Additional characteristics may be added to the D-1 matrix based on the purpose or goals of the enterprise.[1]

INFORMATION DESCRIPTION					SOURCE		DESTIN-ATION		INFORMATION EXCHANGE ATTRIBUTES			
NEEDLINE IDENTIFIER	INFORMATION EXCHANGE NAME/ID	CONTENT	MEDIA	SIZE	SENDING NODE	SENDING ACTIVITY	RECEIVING NODE	RECEIVING ACTIVITY	TRIGGERING EVENT	FREQUENCY TIMELINESS THROUGHTPUT	SECURITY	INTEROPER-ABILITY REQUIREMENTS
			DIGITAL, VOICE, TEXT, IMAGE, ETC.	RANGE LIMITS								

[1]K. Sowell and A. Reedy

Relationship to Other EA Frameworks

FEAF: Data Level	FEA: DRM	Zachman: C3/R2, C4/R2	DODAF: OV-3

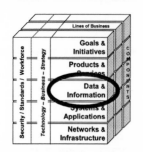

D-3: Object State Transition Diagram

A State Transition Diagram uses the notation from the Unified Modeling Language to show how the lifecycle of a specific data object. This diagram shows changes to attributes, links, and/or behavior(s) of the "On-Line Order" object that are a result of internal or external system events which trigger changes in state.

Example

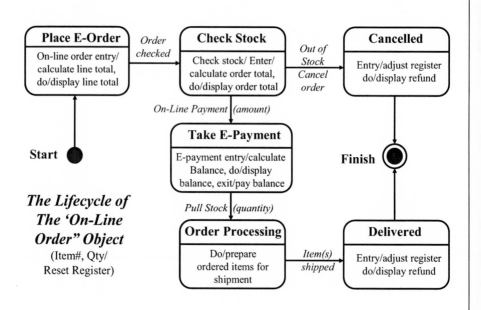

| **Place E-Order** | | **Check Stock** | | **Cancelled** |
| On-line order entry/ calculate line total, do/display line total | *Order checked* | Check stock/ Enter/ calculate order total, do/display order total | *Out of Stock Cancel order* | Entry/adjust register do/display refund |

On-Line Payment (amount)

Take E-Payment

E-payment entry/calculate Balance, do/display balance, exit/pay balance

Start

Finish

The Lifecycle of The 'On-Line Order" Object
(Item#, Qty/ Reset Register)

Pull Stock (quantity)

| **Order Processing** | | **Delivered** |
| Do/prepare ordered items for shipment | *Item(s) shipped* | Entry/adjust register do/display refund |

Relationship to Other EA Frameworks

| **FEAF:** Data Level | **FEA:** DRM | **Zachman:** C1/R3 | **DODAF:** OV-6b, SV-10b |

EA³ Framework Area	Artifact # and Name

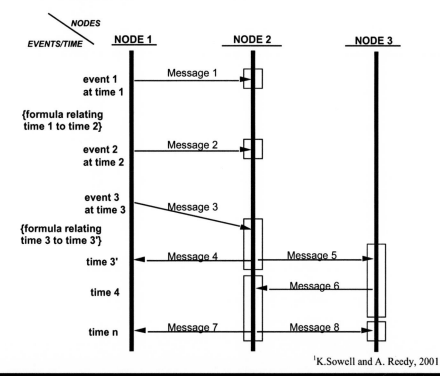

D-4: Object Event Trace Diagram

Also called an Object 'Sequence' Diagram, the D-5 diagram allows the tracing of actions in a set of scenarios or operational threads. Each model should focus on a critical sequence of events and a description of this scenario should accompany the model.

Example

With time proceeding from the top of the diagram to the bottom, a specific diagram lays out the sequence of information exchanges that occur between business nodes for a given scenario. These information exchanges are associated with events and actions (see Information Exchange Matrix). The direction of the event arrows shows flow of control, in terms of the business process, from node to node.[1]

[1]K.Sowell and A. Reedy, 2001

Relationship to Other EA Frameworks

FEAF: Data Level	FEA: DRM	Zachman: C2/R2, C5/R3	DODAF: OV-6c, SV-10c

EA³ Framework Area	Artifact # and Name

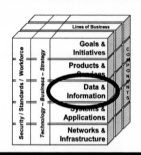

D-5: Logical Data Model

A semantic data model can be developed using traditional structured methods and symbology (Entity Relationship Diagram), or one can use the object-oriented method and symbology of the Unified Modeling Language (UML), which produces a Class Diagram and/or Object Diagram.

Example

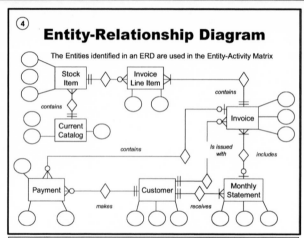

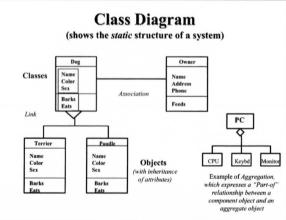

Relationship to Other EA Frameworks

FEAF: Data Level	FEA: DRM	Zachman: C1/R3	DODAF: OV-7, SV-11

D-6: Physical Data Model

The Physical Data Model is used to describe how the information represented in the Logical Data Model is actually implemented in automated information systems.

Example

There should be a mapping from a given Logical Data Model to the Physical Data Model (PDM). The PDM is a composite model whose components can vary greatly, as shown in the template below. For some purposes, an entity-relationship style diagram of the physical database design will suffice. Data Definition Language may also be used in the cases where shared databases are used to integrate systems. References to message format standards (which identify message types and options to be used) may suffice for message-oriented command and control subsystems. Descriptions of file formats may be used when file passing is the mode used to exchange information. Interoperating systems may use a variety of techniques to exchange data, and thus have several distinct partitions in their PDM with each partition using a different form.[1]

Physical Data Model Provides

Message Format:
- Standards Reference
- Message Type(s)
- Message Fields with Representation
- Map From the Logical Data Model to the Message Fields

File Structure:
-Standards Reference
-Record and File Descriptions
-Map from Logical Interface Model to Record Fields

Physical Schema:
-DDL or ERA Notation with sufficient detail to generate the schema
-Map from the Logical Data Model to the Physical Data Model with Rationale

[1] K. Sowell and A. Reedy, 2001

Relationship to Other EA Frameworks

FEAF: Data Level	FEA: DRM	Zachman: C1/R4	DODAF: OV-7, SV-11

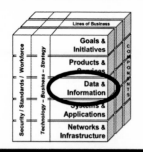

D-7: Activity/Entity Matrix

An Activity/Entity Matrix is developed by mapping which data entities are affected by related line of business activities. Often called a 'CRUD' Matrix because it identifies the basic types of transformations that are performed on data (Create, Read, Update, Delete) through a business process.

Example

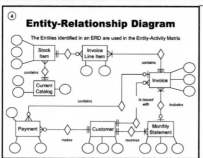

④ **Entity-Relationship Diagram**

The Entities identified in an ERD are used in the Entity-Activity Matrix

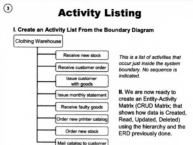

③ **Activity Listing**

I. Create an Activity List From the Boundary Diagram

Clothing Warehouse

- Receive new stock
- Receive customer order
- Issue customer with goods
- Issue monthly statement
- Receive faulty goods
- Order new printer catalog
- Order new stock
- Mail catalog to customer

This is a list of activities that occur just inside the system boundary. No sequence is indicated.

II. We are now ready to create an Entity-Activity Matrix (CRUD Matrix; that shows how data is Created, Read, Updated, Deleted) using the hierarchy and the ERD previously done.

⑤ # Entity-Activity Matrix

Entity-Activity (CRUD) Matrix:

		Entity Type						
		Stock Item	Invoice	Invoice Line Item	Customer	Monthly Statement	Warehouse	Catalog
1	Receive new stock	U						
2	Receive customer order	R			R			
3	Issue customer with goods	U	C	C	U			
4	Issue monthly statement		R		R	C		
5	Receive faulty goods			R	R			
6	Order new printed catalog							C
7	Order new stock	R						
8	Mail catalog to customer				R			

Entity-Activity Matrix (CRUD): C=Create, R=Read, U=Update, D=Delete

Check matrix that:
- Is every entity affected by at least one activity, if not, it's "singular" and should be dropped?
- Is there *just one* "Create" activity for each entity?
- Note that "Create" may be a boundary activity, that may have happened through internal processes.

Matrix may be used to:
- Define the scope of the problem
- Describe a "system map"
- Partition the system (Cluster Analysis)
- Determine "who owns the data and/or processes (activities)

Relationship to Other EA Frameworks

FEAF: Data Level	FEA: DRM	Zachman: C1/R3, C4/R2	DODAF: SV-9

EA³ Framework Area	Artifact # and Name

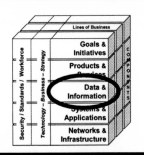

D-8: Data Dictionary

The Data Dictionary provides a comprehensive listing of the data entities that are collected and maintained by the enterprise, including standards for the attribute fields, keys, and relationships. The Data Dictionary may also include a 'library' of re-useable Data Objects that use UML methods.

Example

FIELD NAME	DATA TYPE	FIELD LENGTH	KEY	CAPTION	DESCRIPTION	SAMPLE
PRT_ID	NUMBER	5	PK	PROTOTYPE ID	A sequential number that uniquely identifies each record in tblPrototype	66352
PROP_ID	NUMBER	5	FK	PROPOSAL ID	A sequential number that uniquely identifies each record in tblProposal	37642
PRT_PRDLINE	TEXT	20		PROTOTYPE PRODCUT LINE	The target Solar Cell product line	Consumer
PRT_VOLTAGE	NUMBER	5		PROTOTYPE VOLTAGE	Electrical output, in volts	3.5
PRT_DESCRIPTION	TEXT	100		PROTOTYPE DESCRIPTION	A brief description of the prototype	...
PRT_WIDTH	NUMBER	20		PROTOTYPE WIDTH	Width, in inches, of the prototype	2
PRT_LENGTH	NUMBER	20		PROTOTYPE LENGTH	Length, in inches, of the prototype	4.25
PRT_THICKNESS	NUMBER	20		PROTOTYPE THICKNESS	Thickness, in inches, of the prototype	.375
PRT_WEIGHT	NUMBER	20		PROTOTYPE WEIGHT	Weight, in ounces, of the prototype	10
PRT_START	DATE			PROTOTYPE START DATE	Date development of the prototype began	11/29/2000
PRT_END	DATE			PROTOTYPE END DATE	Date development of the prototype was completed	5/17/2001

Relationship to Other EA Frameworks

FEAF: Data Level	FEA: DRM	Zachman: C1/R5	DODAF: AV-2

EA³ Framework Area	Artifact # and Name

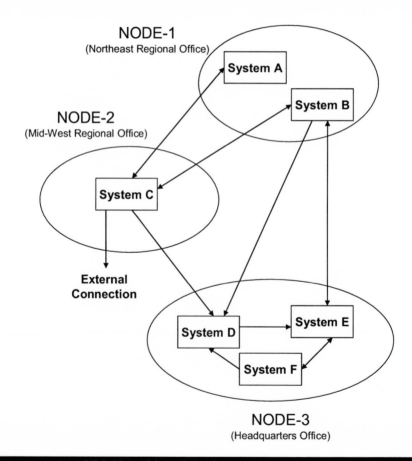

SA-1: System Interface Diagram

The System Interface Diagram shows the logical and/or physical interfaces between the enterprise's systems for information, production, etc. where information and/or other resources are exchanged.

Examples

NODE-1
(Northeast Regional Office)

System A

System B

NODE-2
(Mid-West Regional Office)

System C

External
Connection

System D → System E

System F

NODE-3
(Headquarters Office)

Relationship to Other EA Frameworks

FEAF: Application Level	FEA: SRM	Zachman: C3/R4, C3/R2	DODAF: SV-1

EA³ Framework Area	Artifact # and Name

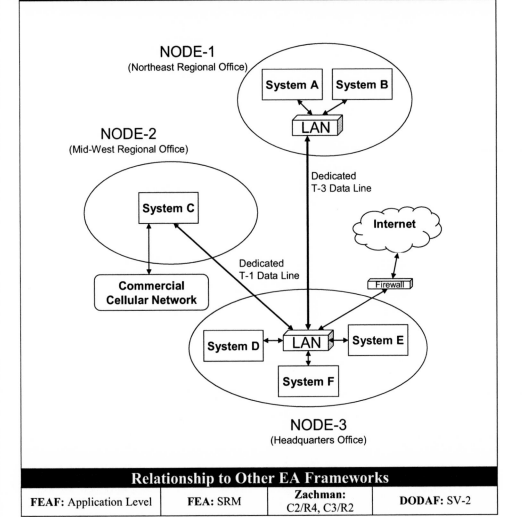

SA-2: System Communication Description

The S-2 artifact compliments the S-1 System Interface Diagram by providing a description of how data is communicated between systems throughout the enterprise, and includes specifics about links, paths, networks, and media.

Example

NODE-1
(Northeast Regional Office)

System A   System B

LAN

NODE-2
(Mid-West Regional Office)

System C

Dedicated
T-3 Data Line

Internet

Commercial
Cellular Network

Dedicated
T-1 Data Line

Firewall

System D   LAN   System E

System F

NODE-3
(Headquarters Office)

Relationship to Other EA Frameworks

FEAF: Application Level	**FEA:** SRM	**Zachman:** C2/R4, C3/R2	**DODAF:** SV-2

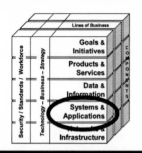

SA-3: System Interface Matrix

The System Interface Matrix shows the nature and status of physical and logical interfaces between information systems throughout the enterprise.

Example

1. Provides detail on the interface characteristics of the SA-1 artifact.
   - Allows quick overview
   - Enables rapid assessment of potential re-use or redundancies
2. Useful tool for managing the evolution of systems, infrastructures, technology insertion, functional upgrades.
3. Interface characteristics that could be captured include:

   Status (existing, planned, potential, deactivated), purpose, classification level, key interface(s)

System Interface Matrix

	System 1	System 2	System 3	System 4	System 5	System 6	System 7	System 8	System 9
System 1	*								
System 2	X	*							
System 3		X	*						
System 4		X		*					
System 5			X		*				
System 6	X	X	X	P	P	*			
System 7			X		P		*		
System 8					R	R		*	
System 9	X								*

X = Existing Interface   P = Planned Interface   R = Retire Interface

Relationship to Other EA Frameworks

FEAF: Application Level	**FEA:** SRM, TRM	**Zachman:** C2/R4	**DODAF:** SV-3

EA³ Framework Area	Artifact # and Name

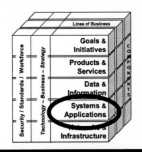

SA-4: System Data Flow Diagram

The System Data Flow Diagram is better known as a 'Data Flow Diagram' and is intended to show the processes within a system that exchange data, and how those exchanges occur. The SA-4 artifact compliments the B-4 Business Process Diagram, and can be decomposed to show additional detail.

Example

1. Captures and describes system functions and the data flows between them.

2. Documents system functional hierarchies.

3. Primary purpose is to:

    • Develop a clear description of the necessary system data flows that are input (consumed) and output (produced) by each system

    • Ensure functional connectivity is complete

    • Support appropriate level of functional decomposition for additional detail

4. Is the systems counterpart to the B-4 Business Process Model (IDEF-0 diagram).

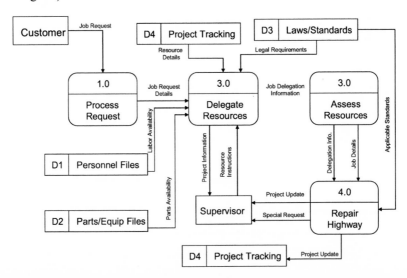

Relationship to Other EA Frameworks

FEAF: Application Level	FEA: SRM, DRM	Zachman: C2/R3	DODAF: SV-4

EA³ Framework Area	Artifact # and Name

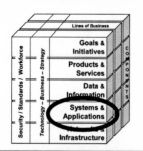

SA-5: System/Operations Matrix

The System/Operations Matrix relates operational activities to system functions within and between lines of business throughout the enterprise.

Example

1. Relates operational activities to system functions
2. Identifies the transformation of an operational need into a purposeful action performed by a system
3. Supports decision making as follows:
   - Identify 'stovepipe' systems and opportunities for automation
   - Identify redundant systems and functions
   - Analyze gaps in performance
   - Target investment opportunities

System / Operations Matrix					
Operational Activity	Call for Sales Data	Input Sales Data	Update Sales Data	Distribute Sales Data	Use Sales Data
System Function					
Load Sales Data Input Template	X				
Display Sales Data Input Template	X				
Load New Sales Database	X				
Receive New Sales Data		X			
Load Historical Sales Database			X		
Update New Sales Data Sub-Table			X		
Update Historical Sales Database			X		
Receive Sales Data Corrections		X			
Update Historical Sales Database			X		
Send New Sales Data				X	
Send Updated Historical Sales Data				X	
Receive New Sales Data Querry					X
Send New Sales Data				X	X
Receive Historical Sales Data Query					X
Send Updated Historical Sales Data				X	X

Relationship to Other EA Frameworks

FEAF: Application Level	**FEA:** BRM, SRM	**Zachman:** C2/R4	**DODAF:** SV-5

EA³ Framework Area	Artifact # and Name

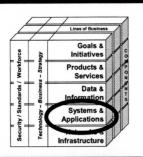

SA-6: System Data Exchange Matrix

The System Data Exchange Matrix uses a table format to show which systems exchange particular types of data within and between lines of business throughout the enterprise.

Description and Example

The System Data Exchange Matrix describes, in tabular format, data exchanges between systems within a systems node and across systems nodes. The focus of the System Data Exchange Matrix is on how the data exchanges actually are (or will be) implemented, in system-specific details covering such characteristics as specific protocols and data or media formats. These aspects of exchanges, while difficult to document, are critical to understanding the potential for overhead and security constraints introduced by the physical aspects of the implementation. The System Data Exchange Matrix relates to, and grows out of, the Information Exchange Matrix. That is, the automated portion(s) of each information exchange in the Information Exchange Matrix is associated with the system interface that carries the corresponding system data in the System Interface Description. The business characteristics for the information exchange are replaced with the corresponding system data exchange characteristics. For example, performance attributes for the business information exchanges are replaced by the actual system performance attributes for the automated portion(s) of the information exchange. Automation may introduce characteristics that are not intrinsic to the business information exchange.[1]

Identification & Traceability				Nature of Transaction				Source & Destination				Performance			Security		
								Source		Destination							
Needline	System Interface	Information Exchange	Data Exchange	Data Element Name	Size	Format/Standard	Triggering Event	System	System Function	System	System Function	Frequency	Timeliness	Throughput	Classification	Priority	Services

[1] K. Sowell and A. Reedy, 2001

Relationship to Other EA Frameworks

FEAF: Application Level	FEA: SRM, TRM	Zachman: C2/R3	DODAF: SV-6

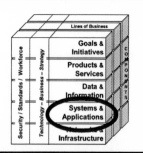

SA-7: System Performance Matrix

The System Performance Matrix lists the metrics that are important with regard to reliability, availability, and maintainability.

Example

1. Specifies the quantitative characteristics of system:
   - Hardware/software
   - Interfaces
   - Communication components
2. Identifies both current and future parameters.
3. Includes all relevant technical performance characteristics, for instance:
   - Mean Time Between Failure
   - Restart Rate
   - System Initialization Time
   - Data Transfer Rate

System Performance Measures

Measure Area	Type of Measure	Original Baseline	Current Status	Target
System Maintainability	Percentage	0.45	0.52	0.6
System Availability	Percentage	0.86	0.93	0.95
System Start-up (Initialization) Time	Seconds	32	23	15
System Restart (Re-boot) Time	Seconds	35	26	18
Hosted Application Start-up Time (>100 MB)	Seconds	28	26	25
Hosted Application Start-up Time (<100 MB)	Seconds	19	17	15
Data Throughput Capacity (# of input types)	Megabytes	100	250	500
Mean Time Between Hardware Failures	Days	68	69	90
Mean Time Between Software Failures	Days	12	14	20
System Settings Back-up Time	Minutes	22	21	18
System Data Back-up Time	Minutes	146	137	120
Email Outbox Transfer Rate (<1MB)	Seconds	12	11	10
Email Outbox Transfer Rate (<300KB)	Seconds	5	4	2

Relationship to Other EA Frameworks

FEAF: Application Level	FEA: SRM, TRM	Zachman: C2/R3	DODAF: SV-7

EA³ Framework Area	Artifact # and Name

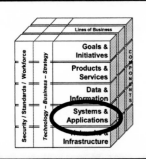

SA-8: System Evolution Diagram

The System Evolution Diagram shows the evolution of a system including the relationship and timing of consolidations installations, upgrades, and retirements, sometimes shown in the context of changes to other systems, applications, websites, and databases.

Example

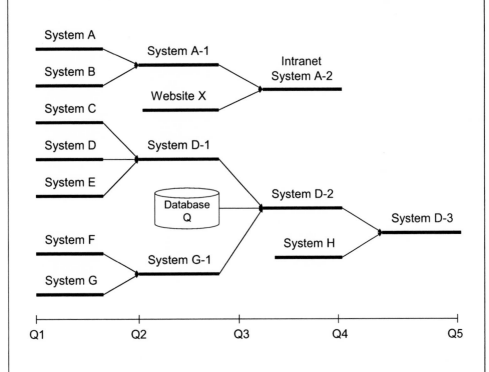

Relationship to Other EA Frameworks

FEAF: Application Level	**FEA:** SRM, TRM	**Zachman:** C2/R4	**DODAF:** SV-8

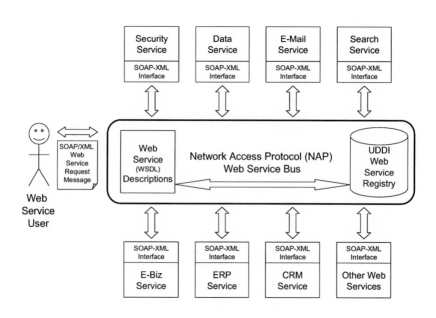

SA-9: Web Application Diagram

The web application diagram shows the logical relationships between web-based information services, in this case showing a detailed diagram of services that interact via standard protocols and interfaces that promote platform-independent data interchanges.

Example

Relationship to Other EA Frameworks			
FEAF: Application Level	**FEA:** SRM, TRM	**Zachman:** C2/R3	**DODAF:** SV-2

EA³ Framework Area	Artifact # and Name

NI-1: Network Connectivity Diagram

The Network Connectivity Diagram shows the physical connections between the enterprise's voice, data, and video network… including external Wide Area Networks (WANs) and Local Area Networks (LANs)… also called 'extranets' and 'intranets.'

Example

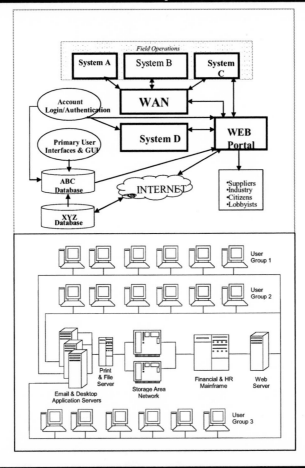

Relationship to Other EA Frameworks

FEAF: Technology Level	**FEA:** TRM	**Zachman:** C3/R5	**DODAF:** None

EA³ Framework Area	Artifact # and Name

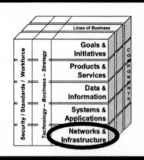

NI-2: Network Inventory

The Network Inventory lists all of the hardware and software on the enterprise's voice, data, and video networks throughout the enterprise. The list may include bar code numbers or other unique identifiers.

Example

DMC, Inc. Network Equipment Inventory

Description	Bar Code	Location	Vendor	Model #
Data Network				
100-Port Stackable Switch #1	DMC-620	Bldg 1	SMV	73G20
100-Port Stackable Switch #1	DMC-621	Bldg 1	SMV	73G20
100-Port Stackable Switch #1	DMC-622	Bldg2	SMV	73G20
100-Port Stackable Switch #1	DMC-623	Bldg3	SMV	73G20
100-Port Stackable Switch #1	DMC-624	Bldg 3	SMV	73G20
100-Port Stackable Switch #1	DMC-625	Bldg 4	SMV	73G20
100-Port Stackable Switch #1	DMC-626	Bldg 4	SMV	73G20
50-Port ATM/Gigabyte Router	DMC-611	Bldg 1	Hamre	H7500
50-Port ATM/Gigabyte Router	DMC-612	Bldg 2	Hamre	H7500
50-Port ATM/Gigabyte Router	DMC-613	Bldg 3	Hamre	H7500
50-Port ATM/Gigabyte Router	DMC-614	Bldg 4	Hamre	H7500
Application Server #1	DMC-616	Bldg 1	Kayprime	K455
Application Server #2	DMC-617	Bldg 1	Kayprime	K455
Application Server #3	DMC-618	Bldg 1	Kayprime	K455
Print Server #1	DMC-603	Bldg 1	Kayprime	K430
Print Server #2	DMC-604	Bldg 3	Kayprime	K430
Web Server #1	DMC-605	Bldg 1	Kayprime	K502
Web Server #2	DMC-606	Bldg 3	Kayprime	K502
Internet Firewall	DMC-610	Bldg 1	Gladiator	3000
Color Network Printer	DMC-370	Bldg 1	HG	755
B/W Network Printer #1	DMC-375	Bldg 2	HG	380G
B/W Network Printer #2	DMC-375	Bldg 3	HG	380G
B/W Network Printer #3	DMC-375	Bldg 4	HG	380G
B/W Network Printer #4	DMC-375	Bldg 5	HG	380G
Telecommunications Network				
Master PBX Switch	DMC-801	Bldg 1	Westcom	W9000
PBX 100-Line Node Controller	DMC-802	Bldg 1	Westcom	W9002
PBX 100-Line Node Controller	DMC-803	Bldg 2	Westcom	W9002
PBX 100-Line Node Controller	DMC-804	Bldg 3	Westcom	W9002
PBX 100-Line Node Controller	DMC-805	Bldg 4	Westcom	W9002
VOIP Interface Unit	DMC-807	Bldg 1	Westcom	W1380
GreenBerry Cell Phone Unit	DMC-808	Bldg 1	Greenberry	KJ1700
Video Network				
VTC Roll-Around Unit #1	DMC-960	Bldg 1	ClearTel	CT1800
VTC Network Interface Box	DMC-961	Bldg 1	ClearTel	CT739

Relationship to Other EA Frameworks

FEAF: Technology Level	FEA: TRM	Zachman: C3/R5	DODAF: None

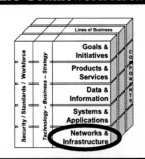

NI-3: Capital Equipment Inventory

The Capital Equipment Inventory lists all of the non-information technology capital (depreciable) equipment in each line of business throughout the enterprise. The list may include bar code numbers or other unique identifiers.

Example

DMC, Inc. Capital Equipment Inventory

Description	Bar Code	Location	Vendor	Model #
Manufacturing Equipment				
Robotic Welder #1	DMC-1501	Bldg 4	Daiwoo	4R35
Robotic Welder #2	DMC-1502	Bldg 4	Daiwoo	4R35
Robotic Welder #3	DMC-1503	Bldg 4	Daiwoo	4R35
Die Cast Extractor #1	DMC-1546	Bldg 4	Avex	500G
Die Cast Extractor #2	DMC-1547	Bldg 4	Avex	500G
Metal Press-Stamper	DMC-1560	Bldg 4	Avex	360 Series
Final Assembly Unit	DMC-1565	Bldg 4	Avex	200 Series
Quality Control Checker	DMC-1607	Bldg 4	Humbart	H201G
Boxing Unit #1	DMC-1615	Bldg 3	Janro	J-700
Boxing Unit #1	DMC-1616	Bldg 3	Janro	J-700
Storage Shelving Unit #1	DMC-901	Bldg 2	SMG	J3000
Storage Shelving Unit #2	DMC-902	Bldg 2	SMG	J3000
Building Equipment				
40-Ton Air Conditioner #1	DMC-465	Bldg 1	Liebert	400L
40-Ton Air Conditioner #1	DMC-466	Bldg 2	Liebert	400L
40-Ton Air Conditioner #1	DMC-467	Bldg3	Liebert	400L
40-Ton Air Conditioner #1	DMC-468	Bldg 4	Liebert	400L
Fire Sensing Control Box #1	DMC-763	Bldg 1	GE	1600
Fire Sensing Control Box #2	DMC-764	Bldg 2	GE	1600
Fire Sensing Control Box #3	DMC-765	Bldg 3	GE	1600
Fire Sensing Control Box #4	DMC-766	Bldg 4	GE	1600
Diesel Back-up Generator #1	DMC-248	Bldg 3	Honda	36H-750
Diesel Back-up Generator #2	DMC-249	Bldg 4	Honda	36H-750

Relationship to Other EA Frameworks

FEAF: None	FEA: None	Zachman: None	DODAF: None

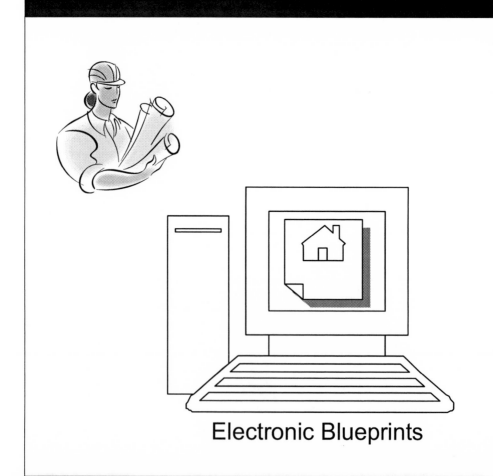

NI-4: Building Blueprints

The NI-4 artifact is a full set of electronic blueprints for all of the physical buildings and rooms throughout the enterprise. The blueprints aid in planning and decision-making regarding the placement of workspaces, production facilities, warehouses, networks and other business functions.

Electronic Blueprints

Relationship to Other EA Frameworks

FEAF: None	FEA: None	Zachman: None	DODAF: None

EA³ Framework Area	Artifact # and Name

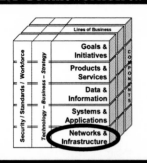

NI-5: Network Center Diagram

The NI-5 artifact is an overhead diagram of the information technology network center. This diagram can be part of the NI-4 set of blueprints, and is maintained electronically to support the numerous changes to network center(s) and server rooms that can be expected over a number of years.

Example

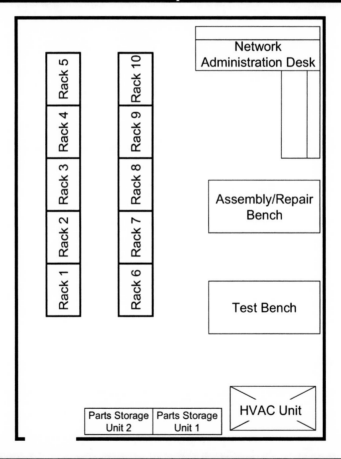

Relationship to Other EA Frameworks

FEAF: None	FEA: None	Zachman: None	DODAF: None

EA³ Framework Area	Artifact # and Name

NI-6: Cable Plant Diagram

The Cable Plant Diagram shows physical connectivity between voice/data/video networks throughout the enterprise and to global suppliers. The diagram should show the types of cable (fiber, CAT-6, etc.) and the bandwidth (T-1, OC-3, etc.) of each cable run between network centers, server rooms, wiring closets, and external connections.

Example

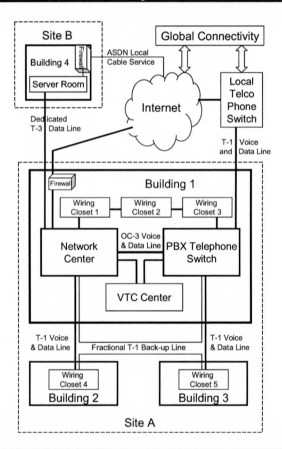

Relationship to Other EA Frameworks

FEAF: None	FEA: None	Zachman: C3/R5	DODAF: None

EA³ Framework Area	Artifact # and Name

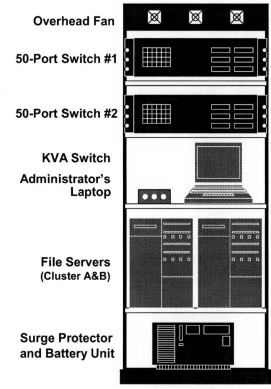

NI-7: Rack Elevation Diagram

This diagram provides a front and rear view of each of the information technology equipment racks that go into a network center, server room, and/or wiring closet. This diagram supports the NI-5 and NI-6 diagrams and is maintained electronically to support the numerous changes that can be expected over a number of years.

Example

Overhead Fan

50-Port Switch #1

50-Port Switch #2

KVA Switch

Administrator's Laptop

File Servers
(Cluster A&B)

Surge Protector and Battery Unit

Rack 1 - Front   Rack 1 - BACK

Relationship to Other EA Frameworks

FEAF: None	FEA: None	Zachman: None	DODAF: None

EA³ Framework Area	Artifact # and Name

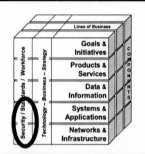

SP-1: Security Plan

The Security Plan provides both high-level and detailed descriptions of the security program that is in effect throughout the enterprise. This includes physical, data, personnel, and operational security elements and procedures. Chapter 11 provides additional detail on Security Plans.

Example Outline

1. Introduction
Purpose of the IT Security Program
Principles of IT Security
Critical Success Factors
Intended Outcomes
Performance Measures

2. Policy
Executive Guidance
Technical Guidance
Applicable Law and Regulations
Standards

3. Reporting Requirements
IT Security Program Roles and Responsibilities
IT Security Program Schedule and Milestones
IT Security Incident Reporting

4. Concept of Operations
IT Security Threat Summary
IT Security Risk Mitigation
Integration with Enterprise Architecture
Component/System Security Plans

5. Security Program Elements
Information Security
Personnel Security
Operational Security
Physical Security

6. Standard Operating Procedures
Test and Evaluation
Risk Assessment
Certification and Accreditation
Disaster Recovery/Continuity of Operations
Records Protection and Archiving
Data Privacy

Relationship to Other EA Frameworks

FEAF: None	FEA: SPP	Zachman: C4/R5	DODAF: None

EA³ Framework Area	Artifact # and Name

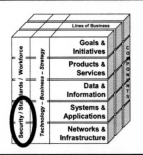

SP-2: Security Solutions Descriptions

The Security Solutions Description provides a high-level view of how security is provided for selected resources throughout the enterprise. The solutions cover four dimensions of security: physical, data, personnel, and operations and may include diagrams or matrices.

Example Outline

Operational Security

In the area of operational security, the Security Program should promote the development of standard operating procedures (SOPs) for all EA components that support line of business operations. SOPs should also be developed for recovery from major outages or natural disasters, and for enabling the continuity of operations if all or part of the enterprise becomes disabled.

Data Security

In the area of information security, the Security Program should promote security-conscious designs, information content assurance, source authentication, and data access control. The assessment of types of data being handled for privacy protection concerns should also be done (e.g. customer credit data or employee SSNs

Personnel Security

In the area of personnel security, the Security Program should promote user authentication and IT security awareness, and new user/recurring training. badges, biometrics, card swipe units, cipher locks, and other methods of combining personnel and physical security solutions should be implemented.

Physical Security

The elements of physical security that should be captured in the EA include protection for the facilities that support IT processing, control of access to IT equipment, networks, and telecommunications rooms, as well as fire protection, media storage, and disaster recovery systems.

Relationship to Other EA Frameworks

FEAF: None	FEA: SPP	Zachman: C4/R5	DODAF: None

EA³ Framework Area	Artifact # and Name

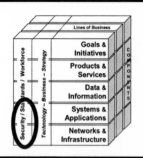

SP-3: System Accreditation Document

The System Accreditation Document uses a standard format for evaluating the security status of information systems throughout the enterprise. There are a number of parts to a system security accreditation as are illustrated in the example.

Example Outline

1. <u>System Security Plan</u>. This opening section of the System Accreditation Document provides an overview of the business context that the information system operates in, states the current security status of the system (last accreditation), and summarizes the contents and finding of the other accreditation documents.

2. <u>System Risk Assessment</u>. This section of the document uses a standardized format for showing areas of risk to the information system in the four primary areas security threat areas that are covered in artifact SP-2; physical, data, operational, and personnel. Assigns a level of risk based on the business context for system operations and the type of system data to be protected. Provides security risk remediation strategies (how to avoid a security risk, or deal with it if a problem occurs) for each area of risk that is identified.

3. <u>System Test and Evaluation</u>. Also called a system 'penetration test.' The System Test and Evaluation (ST&E) section of the document provides the results of a live test that attempts to enter the system through other-than-normal log-in procedures, as well as attempts to overwhelm the system (denial of service attack), or infect the system with an active virus, worm, or other type of problematic element that reduces or eliminates information system functionality.

4. <u>Remediation Plan</u>. This section of the document provides the status of corrective actions taken to fix all of the security risks found during the risk assessment/ST&E.

5. <u>Approval to Operate</u>. This section of the document is the formal (signed) approval to operate the information system that is provided by the designated person in the enterprise (usually the Chief Information Officer or the IT Security Manager).

Relationship to Other EA Frameworks

FEAF: None	FEA: SPP	Zachman: C4/R5	DODAF: None

EA³ Framework Area	Artifact # and Name

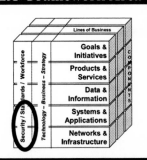

SP-4: Continuity of Operations Plan

The Continuity of Operations Plan (COOP) uses a standard format for describing where all or part of the enterprise will relocate to if the normal operating location cannot be occupied for an extended period (more than a few days) due to a natural or man-made event.

Example Contents

The activation of the COOP relocation site may have to be accomplished in the midst of a local or national disaster that makes clarity, brevity, completeness, and flexibility (backups) key to success. The following are some of the recommended elements in a COOP document:

1. COOP Activation. Conditions for Activating the COOP.

2. COOP Roles and Responsibilities. A matrix of the roles and responsibilities (by position) of all personnel throughout the enterprise who are involved in activating the COOP. Alternates are provided for each position.

3. COOP Checklist. A step-by-step checklist of actions for each person participating in the COOP.

4. COOP Relocation Site Map and Directions. How to get to the COOP site from various probable routes.

5. COOP Relocation Site Activation. The process for activating the COOP site, establishing internal/external communications, and reconstituting key enterprise functions at the COOP site.

6. COOP Relocation Site Inventory. An inventory of systems, equipment, and supplies at the COOP relocation site, along with the person(s) responsible for ensuring that the systems are operational and the equipment is present when needed.

7. COOP Relocation Site De-Activation. Procedures for de-activating the COOP site and restoring it to a 'ready status' after a real relocation event or training exercise.

Enterprise Functions Have to Relocate

Relationship to Other EA Frameworks

FEAF: None	FEA: SPP	Zachman: C4/R5	DODAF: None

EA³ Framework Area	Artifact # and Name

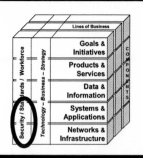

SP-5: Disaster Recovery Plan

The Disaster Recovery Plan is an assessment matrix and set of procedures to handle outages in various business and/or technology capabilities that do not require the enterprise to relocate its operations. Outages can be caused by natural or man-made events (e.g. fire, flood, power outage).

Example Contents

The activation of the Disaster Recovery Plan may have to be accomplished in the midst of a natural or man-made disaster that makes clarity, brevity, completeness, and flexibility (backups) key to success. The following are some of the recommended elements in a Disaster Recovery Plan:

1. Disaster Recovery Activation. Conditions for Activating the COOP.

2. Recovery Roles and Responsibilities. A matrix of the roles and responsibilities (by position) of all personnel throughout the enterprise who are involved in activating the COOP. Alternates are provided for each position.

3. Disaster Impact and Recovery Assessment. A standard matrix for assessing the type and duration of the outage, as well as the systems and functions throughout the enterprise that are affected. Depending on the type of outage and the projected period of outage (minutes, hours, days), the recovery procedure may differ.

4. Recovery Procedures. The procedures that are used to restore the business and/or system functions that have been disrupted. Examples include:

- Electrical Outage
- Air Conditioning/Heating Outage
- Building Damage (Fire, Flood, Earthquake)
- Room Damage (Fire, Flood, Earthquake)
- Virus Infection of Information System(s)
- Loss of Internal or External Data Communications
- Loss of Internal or External Telephone Communications

Enterprise Functions <u>Do Not</u> Relocate

Relationship to Other EA Frameworks

FEAF: None	FEA: SPP	Zachman: C4/R5	DODAF: None

EA³ Framework Area		Artifact # and Name

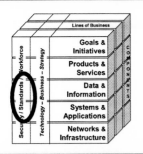

ST-1: Technology Standards Profile

The Technology Standards Profile is a listing of business services and associated technologies that are accepted by the enterprise as being a primary or secondary standard. Further detail can be added regarding particular types of standards (e.g. data, telecommunications) and vendor products.

Example

Technical Standards Profile						
Item Description	International Standard 1	International Standard 2	National Standard	Local Standard	Standard Product	Alternative Product
Information Systems Hardware						
Network Router	ISO 802.1	CEN 7102	NIST 400-1		Sasco 7300	IronBox 300H
Network Server	ISO 802.1	CEN 7102	NIST 400-1		Gell 2000	CowBox 710
Network Printer	ISO 802.1	CEN 7102	NIST 400-1		Micop 85	HV 550
Desktop PC	ISO 802.1	CEN 7102	NIST 400-1		Gell 1650	CowBox 200
Information Systems Software						
Server Operating System	ISO 802.1	CEN 7102	NIST 400-1		MacroSwift OS	BlueCap Linux
Desktop Operating System	ISO 802.1	CEN 7102	NIST 400-1		MacroSwift OS	Linux Desktop
Desktop Office Automation Suite	ISO 802.1	CEN 7102	NIST 400-1		MacroSwift SuitePro	Kona Big Suite
Computer Aided Design	ISO 802.1	CEN 7102	NIST 400-1		Grafex CAD	MacroCAD
Telecommunications System Hardware						
PBX Central Switch	ISO 877.1F	CEN 7306	IEEE T735	Verizo 679	Westel 7200	BlamoTel 80X
PBX Central Switch	ISO 877.1F	CEN 7306	IEEE T735	Verizo 679	Westel 7202	BlamoTel 83B
Desk Telephone	ISO 877.1F	CEN 7306	IEEE T735	Verizo 679	Westel 58J	BlamoTel 10J
Telecommunications System Software						
PBX Switching Controller	ISO 877.1F	CEN 7306	IEEE T735	Verizo 679	Westel PBX Max	Blamo PBX
VOIP Interface	ISO 877.1F	CEN 7306	IEEE.T735	Verizo 679	Westel VOIP Max	Blamo VOIP
Video Conferencing System Hardware						
Roll-Around VTC Unit	ISO 478.3		IEEE A845		PhotoVox 1300	Humbel 850
Desktop VTC Unit	ISO 478.3		IEEE A845		PhotoVox 350	PictureHi 75G
VTC Multiplexer & Control Box	ISO 478.3		IEEE A845		PhotoVox M46	
Video Conferencing System Software						
Desktop Video Conferencing	ISO 478.3		IEEE A845		MacroSwift Meet	

Relationship to Other EA Frameworks

FEAF: Technology	FEA: TRM	Zachman: C3/R4	DODAF: TV-1

EA³ Framework Area	Artifact # and Name

ST-2: Technology Forecast

The Technology Forecast supports and relates to the ST-1 Technology Standards Profile. The Technology Forecast documents expected changes in any of the standards listed in the ST-1 artifact, where future changes appear to be happening or about to happen.

Example

- Captures expected changes in technology related standards and conventions
- Identifies critical technology standards, their fragility, and impact of changes to the architecture
- Contains specific predictions about the availability of emerging standards, and relates to specific System/Application (SA) framework elements

Technology Forecast			
Forecast Area	**Short Term** (Next) 12 Months)	**Mid-Term** (12-24 Months)	**Long Term** (2-3 Years Away)
Operating Systems	Macrovox GT basic Operating System will be supported until late 2007	Macrovox GT-2 will be launched in early 2006	Linux is gaining in capability and reliability, should consider migration to Linux in mid 2006 as an alternative to Macrovox GT upgrade.
Office Automation Suite	Kona Big Suite upgrade finished in early 2005	Kona Big Suite II is due out in late 2006, will provide xml data exchange between applications and a bundled graphics and photo editor.	Kona Project X is going to incorporate a database application
Desktop PCs	Gell 2000 became standard in 2004, is installed on 70% of desktops; will be 100% in mid-2005.	Gell 2000 units will remain	Conduct vendor fly off in early 2006 based on updated application and performance requirements
Desktop Monitors	15" Color CRTs being replaced by 21" Color LCDs as Desktops are replaced; 100% in mid 2005	LCD units will remain	Conduct vendor fly off in early 2006 based on desktop PC compatability and user requirements
Persistent Storage	5 Gigabyte PCMCIA type 2 card available	10GB card expected	40+GB cards
Personal Digital Assistants	Executive level only - Greenberry X400	Office Directors also get Greenberry X400s	Conduct vendor fly off in early 2006 based on updated application and performance requirements

Relationship to Other EA Frameworks

FEAF: Technology	FEA: TRM	Zachman: C3/R4	DODAF: TV-2, SV-9

An Introduction to Enterprise Architecture – 2ⁿᵈ Edition 334

EA³ Framework Area	Artifact # and Name

W-1: Workforce Plan

The Workforce Plan provides a high-level description of how human capital is managed throughout the enterprise. The Workforce Plan includes strategies for hiring, retention, and professional development at the executive, management, and staff levels of the enterprise. .

Example

Workforce Plan Outline

- Summary of Human Capital Management Strategy

- Line of Business Requirements

- Executive Level Competencies and Professional Development Plans

- Management Level Competencies and Professional Development Plans

  o Line of Business A
  o Line of Business B
  o Line of Business C
  o Line of Business D

- Staff Level Competencies and Professional Development Plans

  o Line of Business A
  o Line of Business B
  o Line of Business C
  o Line of Business D

- Performance Review Process

- Benefits Program

- Training and Tuition Assistance Program

Relationship to Other EA Frameworks

FEAF: None	FEA: None	Zachman: C4/R1	DODAF: None

EA³ Framework Area	Artifact # and Name

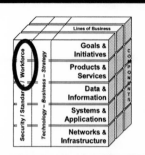

W-2: Organization Chart

The Organization Chart shows how positions and personnel are organized in hierarchical diagrams or matrix formats. Organization Charts help to show lines of authority, working relationships, as well as ownership of resources, products, and processes.

Example

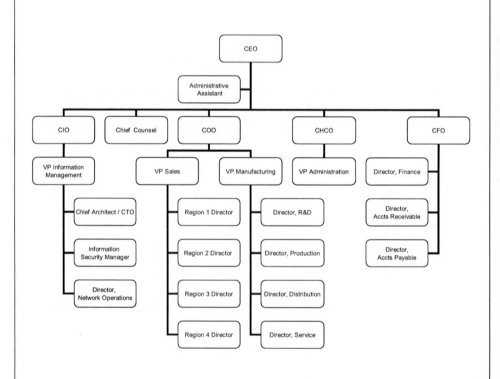

Relationship to Other EA Frameworks

FEAF: None	**FEA:** None	**Zachman:** C4/R2	**DODAF:** OV-4

EA³ Framework Area	Artifact # and Name

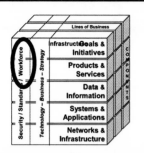

W-3: Knowledge & Skills Profile

The Knowledge and Skills Profile provides a detailed inventory of what a person should know and be able to do in a particular position within the enterprise. The example provided is a "Knowledge, Skills, and Abilities" List for Enterprise Architects developed by Carnegie Mellon University in 2004.

Example

Carnegie Mellon University

Institute for Software Research International
Enterprise Architecture Education Standards - Copyright CMU/ISRI - 2004   Developed by Dr. Scott A. Bernard

Enterprise Architecture Education Standards ©		Junior Architect	Mid-Level Architect	Senior Architect	Notes
Knowledge and Skill Areas (KSAs)		EA Apprentice (0-2 Years)	EA Journeyman (3-5 Years)	EA Master (5+ Years)	
1.0	EA Practice and Theory				
1.1	Governance: Planning and Decsion-Making			x	
1.2	Organizational Theory: Culture and Communication		x	x	
1.3	The Information Age: Driver of Architectures	x	x	x	
1.4	Enterprise Architecture Frameworks	x	x	x	
1.5	Architectue Implementation Methodologies	x	x	x	
1.6	Enterprise Architecture Critical Success Factors	x	x	x	
1.7	Architecture Use in Planning/Decision-Making	x	x	x	
1.8	Architecture Maturity Evaluation			x	
2.0	EA Documentation				
2.1	Strategic Goals, Initiatives, and Plans	x	x	x	
2.2	Business Sub-Architecture	x	x	x	
2.3	Information and Data Sub-Architecture	x	x	x	
2.4	Service Sub-Architecture	x	x	x	
2.5	Systems Sub-Architecture	x	x	x	
2.6	Techology Sub-Architecture	x	x	x	
2.7	Security Sub-Architecture	x	x	x	
2.8	Architecture Standards and Artifact Types	x	x	x	
3.0	EA Implementation				
3.1	EA Program and Project Establishment		x	x	
3.2	EA Requirements and Scope		x	x	
3.3	EA Framework and Methodology Selection		x	x	
3.4	EA Tool and Repository Selection		x	x	
3.5	Documenting the Current Architecture		x	x	
3.6	Documenting the Future Architecture		x	x	
3.7	Architecture Transition Management		x	x	
3.8	Architecture Configuration Management		x	x	
4.0	EA Project & Program Management				
4.1	EA Project and Program Management Basics			x	
4.2	Requirements Determination			x	
4.3	Project and Program Schedules			x	
4.4	Project and Program Budgets			x	
4.5	Alternatives Analysis			x	
4.6	Managing Risk			x	
4.7	Earned Value Management			x	
4.8	EA Team Development			x	

Relationship to Other EA Frameworks

FEAF: None	FEA: None	Zachman: C4/R3	DODAF: OV-4

Glossary of Terms and Abbreviations

Enterprise Architecture Terms

Actionable. EA documentation and data that is useful to executives, managers, and support staff for resource planning and decision-making.

Alignment. Conformance to a policy, standard, and/or goal.

Architecture. A systematic approach that organizes and guides design, analysis, planning, and documentation activities.

Architecture Segment. A part of the overall EA that documents one or more lines of business, including all levels and threads.

Artifact. An EA artifact is a documentation product, such as a text document, diagram, spreadsheet, briefing slides, or video clip. EA artifacts document EA components.

Business Case. A collection of descriptive and analytic information about an investment in resource(s) and/or capabilities.

Capital Planning. The management and decision-making process associated with the planning, selection, control, and evaluation of investments in resources, including EA components such as systems, networks, knowledge warehouses, and support services for the enterprise.

Change Management. The process of setting expectations and involving stakeholders in how a process or activity will be changed, so that the stakeholders have some control over the change and therefore may be more accepting of the change.

Component. EA components are those plug-and-play resources that provide capabilities at each level of the framework. Examples include strategic goals and measures; business services; information flows and data objects; information systems, web services, and software applications; voice/data/video networks, and associated cable plants.

Composite. An EA artifact that uses several documentation modeling techniques and/or represents several types of EA components.

Configuration Management. The process of managing updates to EA components and artifacts, ensuring that standards are being followed.

Crosscutting Component. An EA component that serves several lines of business. Examples include email systems that serve the whole enterprise, and financial systems that serve several lines of business.

Culture. The beliefs, customs, values, structure, normative rules, and material traits of a social organization. Culture is evident in many aspects of how an organization functions.

Current View. An EA artifact that represents an EA component or process that currently exists in the enterprise.

Data. Data items refer to an elementary description of things, events, activities, and transactions that are recorded, classified, and stored, but not organized to convey any specific meaning. Data items can be numeric, alphabetic, figures, sounds, or images. A database consists of stored data items organized for retrieval.

Enterprise. An area of common activity and goals within an organization or between several organizations, where information and other resources are exchanged.

Enterprise Architecture. The analysis and documentation of an enterprise in its current and future states from an integrated strategy, business, and technology perspective.

Executive Sponsor. The executive who has decision-making authority over the EA program and who provides resources and senior leadership for the program.

Framework. A structure for organizing information that defines the scope of the architecture (what the EA program will document) and how the areas of the architecture relate to each other.

Future View. An EA artifact that represents an EA component or process that does not yet exist in the enterprise.

Governance. A group of policies, decision-making procedures, and management processes that work together to enable the effective planning and oversight of activities and resources.

Horizontal Component. A horizontal (or crosscutting) component is a changeable goal, process, program, or resource that serves several lines of business. Examples include email and administrative support systems that serve the whole enterprise.

Information. Information is data that have been organized so that they have meaning and value to the recipient. The recipient interprets the meaning and draws conclusions and implications.

Information Technology. A type of resource that supports the creation, analysis, sharing, archiving, and/or deletion of data and information throughout an enterprise.

Knowledge. Knowledge consists of data or information that have been organized and processed to convey understanding, experience, accumulated learning, and expertise as they apply to a current problem or activity. Data that are processed to extract critical implications and to reflect past experience and expertise provide the recipient with organizational knowledge, which has a very high potential value.

Knowledge Warehouse. A knowledge warehouse is the component of an enterprise's knowledge management system where knowledge is developed, stored, organized, processed, and disseminated.

Line of Business. A distinct area of activity within the enterprise. It may involve the manufacture of certain products, the provision of services, or internal administrative functions.

Methodology. The EA methodology defines how EA documentation will be developed, archived, and used; including the selection of a framework, modeling tools, and on-line repository.

Mission Statement: A succinct description of why the enterprise exists.

Performance Gap. An identified activity or capability that is lacking within the enterprise, which causes the enterprise to perform below desired levels or not achieve strategic or tactical goals.

Program. A group of related projects managed in a coordinated way. Programs usually involve an element of ongoing activity.

Project. A temporary endeavor undertaken to create a unique product, service, or result.

Primitive. An EA artifact that uses one modeling technique to describe one type of EA component.

Stakeholder. Everyone who is or will be affected by a program, activity, or resource. Stakeholders for the EA program include sponsors, architects, program managers, users, and support staff.

System. A type of EA component that is comprised of hardware, and software, and activities that has inputs and outputs.

Vertical Component. An EA component that is contained within one line of business. Examples include a system, application, database, network, or website that serves one line of business.

Vision Statement. Succinctly describes the competitive strategy of the enterprise

Enterprise Architecture Abbreviations [52]

3NF	Third Normal Form
AA	Alternatives Analysis
ABC	Activity-Based Costing
ABM	Activity-Based Management
ACL	Access Control List
ADD	Architectural Design Document
ADP	Automated Data Processing
AES	Advanced Encryption Standard
AFCEA	Armed Forces Communications and Electronics Association
AI	Artificial Intelligence
AMPS	Advanced Mobile Phone Service
ANSI	American National Standards Institute
API	Application Program Interface
ARNET	Acquisition Reform Network
ARPA	Advanced Research Projects Agency
ASCII	American Standard Code for Information Interchange
ATM	Asynchronous Transfer Mode
B2B	Business to Business
B2G	Business to Government
BAA	Business Area Analysis
BLOB	Binary Large Object
BLSM	Base-Level System Modernization
BOD	Board of Directors
BOM	Bill of Materials
BPO	Blanket Purchase Order
BPR	Business Process Reengineering
BRM	Business Reference Model
BSD	Business Systems Design
CEA	Certified Enterprise Architect
C&A	Certification and Accreditation
C/S	Client Server
C3I	Command, Control, Communications, and Intelligence
C4ISR	Command, Control, Communications, Computer, Intelligence, Surveillance and Reconnaissance
CAD	Computer Aided Design
CADM	C4ISR Architecture Data Model
CAI	Computer-Assisted Instruction
CASE	Computer Aided Systems (or Software) Engineering
CBA	Cost-Benefit Analysis
CBSE	Component-Based Software Engineering
CBT	Computer-Based Training
CCA	Clinger-Cohen Act
CCB	Change Control Board; Configuration Control Board
CCIA	Computer & Communications Industry Association
CCITT	Comite Consultatif International Telegraphique et Telephonique
CCR	Configuration Change Request
CDR	Critical Design Review

---

[52] Some abbreviations have generously been provided by the Federal Enterprise Architecture Certification Institute (www.feacinstitute.org).

CDRL	Contract Data Requirements List
CDSA	Intel's Common Data Security Architecture
CFO	Chief Financial Officer
CFR	Code of Federal Regulation
CGI	Common Gateway Interface
CGM	Computer Graphics Metafile
CHCO	Chief Human Capital Officer
CICG	Critical Infrastructure Coordination Group
CIF	Capital Investment Fund
CIM	Corporate Information Management
CIMOSA	CIM Open Systems Architecture
CIO	Chief Information Officer
CIP	Capital Investment Plan
CIP	Critical Information Protection
CKO	Chief Knowledge Officer
CLIN	Contract Line Item Number
CM	Configuration Management; Change Management
CMA	Certificate Management Authority
CMIP	Configuration Management Integration Plan
CMM®	SEI's Capability Maturity Model® for software development
CMMI	SEI's Capability Maturity Model Integration
CMP	Configuration Management Plan
CMSS	Configuration Management Support System
CMWG	Configuration Management Working Group
COE	Common Operating Environment
COM	Component Object Model
COM+	Extended Component Object Model
CONOPS	Concept of Operations
COTR	Contracting Officer's Technical Representative
CORBAâ	Common Object Request Broker Architecture
CORBAMedä	Common Object Request Broker Architecture/Medical
CORBASecä	Common Object Request Broker Security
COSNaming	Common Object Service Naming
COTS	Commercial Off-the-Shelf
CP	Certificate Policy
CPB	Capital Planning Board
CPI	Continuous Process Improvement
CPIC	Capital Planning and Investment Control
CPM	Critical Path Method
CRUD	Create, Read, Update, Delete
CSF	Critical Success Factor
CSO	Chief Security Officer
CSOR	Computer Security Objects Registry
CSS	Cascading Style Sheet
CSU/DSU	Channel Service Unit/Data [or Digital] Service Unit
CTO	Chief Technology Officer
CURE	COTS Usage Risk Evaluation
CWBS	Contractor Work Breakdown Structure
CWM	Common Warehouse Metamodel (OMG)
DB	Database
DBA	DB Administrator
DBDD	Database Design Document
DBMS	Database Management System
DCAA	Defense Contract Audit Agency
DCAM	Distributed Component Architecture Model
DCE	Distributed Computing Environment
DCMA	Defense Contract Management Agency

DCOM	Distributed Component Object Model
DD/DS	Defense Data Dictionary System
DDL	Data Definition Language
DEIS	Defense Enterprise Integration Service
DES	Triple Data Encryption Standard
DFARS	Defense Federal Acquisition Regulation Supplement
DHCP	Dynamic Host Configuration Protocol
DIA	Defense Intelligence Agency
DID	Data Item Description
DII	Defense Information Infrastructure
DII COE	Defense Information Infrastructure Common Operating Environment
DISA	Data Interchange Standards Association
DISA	Defense Information Systems Agency
DISN	Defense Information Systems Network
DITSCAP	DOD IT Security Certification & Accreditation Process
DLA	Defense Logistics Agency
DLL	Dynamic Link Library
DM	Data Management
DMS	Diminished Manufacturing Source
DNP	Distributed Network Protocol
DNS	Domain Name Service; Distributed Network Supervisor
DOD	Department of Defense
DODAF	DOD Architecture Framework
DOM	Document Object Model
DoS, DOS	Department of State; Disk Operating System
DRM	Data Reference Model
DTC	Design-To-Cost
DTF	Domain Task Force
DVD-ROM	Originally Digital Video Disk; Digital Versatile Disk
DW	Data Warehouse
EA	Enterprise Architecture
EAI	Enterprise Application Integration
EAMV	Enterprise Architecture Management View
EBCDIC	Extended Binary Coded Decimal Interchange Code
e-Biz	Electronic Business
EC	Electronic Commerce; European Community
EDI	Electronic Commerce/Electronic Data Interchange
ECP	Engineering Change Proposal
EDI	Electronic Data Interchange
EDR	Environmental Data Registry
EDW	Enterprise Data Warehouse
e-Gov	Electronic Government
EIEITC	Enterprise Interoperability and Emerging IT Initiatives Committee
EIS	Executive Information System
ERD	Entity Relationship Diagram
ERP	Enterprise Resource Planning
ESP	Evolutionary Spiral Process; Enterprise Solution Provider
ESP	Encapsulating Security Payload
EVMS	Earned Value Management System
FAIR	Federal Activities Inventory Reform Act
FAM-A	Functional Area Model – Activity
FAM-D	Functional Area Model – Data
FAM-O	Functional Area Model – Object
FAR	Federal Acquisition Regulation
FARA	Federal Acquisition Reform Act
FASA	Federal Acquisition Streamlining Act

FAWG	Federal Architecture Working Group
FB	Functional Baseline
FBCA	Federal Bridge Certification Authority
FDR	Functional Requirements Document
FEA	Federal Enterprise Architecture
FEA PMO	Federal Enterprise Architecture Program Management Office
FEAC	Federal Enterprise Architecture Certification
FEAC	Federal Enterprise Architecture Certification (Institute)
FEAF	Federal Enterprise Architecture Framework
FFRDC	Federally Funded Research and Development Center
FGDC	Federal Geographic Data Committee
FIPS	Federal Information Processing Standard
FISMA	Federal Information Security Management Act
FPI	Functional Process Improvement
FPKI	Federal Public Key Infrastructure
FPKIPA	Federal Public Key Infrastructure Policy Authority
FRS	Functional Requirements Specification
FTP	File Transfer Protocol
FURN	Framework User Role Name
FY	Fiscal Year—Federal is October 1 through September 30
G&A	General and Administrative
G2B	Government to Business
G2G	Government to Government
GAO	General Accounting Office
GB	Gigabyte
GCSS	Global Combat Support System
GFE	Government Furnished Equipment
GIG	Global Information Grid (DoD-OSD)
GIS	Generic Interface System
GISRA	Government Information Security Reform Act (replaced by FISMA)
GMRA	Government Management Reform Act
GNIE	Global Network Information Enterprise
GOSIP	Government Open System Interconnection Protocol
GOTS	Government Off-the-Shelf
GPEA	Government Performance and Results Act
GRM	Government Reference Model
GRM WG	Government Reference Modeling Work Group
GSA	General Services Administration
GSM	Global System for Mobile Communications
GUI	Graphical User Interface
HCI	Human-Computer Interaction; Hardware Configuration Item
HDF	Hierarchical Data Format
HLI	High Level Interface
HTML	Hypertext Markup Language
HTTP	Hypertext Transfer Protocol
IA	Information Assurance
IADEG	Interagency Data Exchange Group—for standards setting
IC	Intellectual Capital; Integrated Circuit
ICAM	Integrated Computer-Aided Manufacturing
I-CASE	Integrated Computer Aided Software Engineering
ICD	Interface Control Document
ICOM	Inputs, Controls, Outputs, and Mechanisms
ICSA	International Computer Security Association
ICWG	Interface Control Working Group
IDBS	Interoperability Database System

IDEA	Interagency Data Exchange Application
IDEF Language	Integrated Computer-Aided Manufacturing (ICAM) Definition
IDEF0	A hierarchical function/activity modeling technique
IDEF1x	A logical data modeling technique
IDEF3	A sequential process modeling technique
IE	Information Engineering
IEM	Information Exchange Matrix
IER	Information Exchange Requirement
IIDD	Information Interchange Design Document
IM	Information Management
IMA	Interactive Media Association
IMMP	Integrated Master Management Plan
IMRB	Internet Management Review Board
IMS	Information Management System
INMS	Integrated Network Management System
IOR	Internet Object References
IP	Internet Protocol
IPT	Integrated Product Team
IRB	Investment Review Board; Institutional Review Board
IRM	Information Resources Management
ISO	International Standards Enterprise
ISO 12083:1994	Electronic manuscript preparation and markup
ISO 23950:1998	Information retrieval (Z39.50) application service definition and protocol specification
ISO 2709:1996	Format for information exchange
ISO 8459-2:1992	Bibliographic data element directory Part 2: Acquisitions applications
ISO 8777:1993	Commands for interactive text searching
ISP	Information Strategy Plan; Internet Service Provider
ISSA	Interservice Support Agreement
ISSO	Information System Security Officer
IT	Information Technology
ITMRA	Information Technology Management Reform Act (Clinger-Cohen)
ITP	Information Technology Plan; Integrated Test Plan
IV&V	Independent Verification and Validation
JAD	Joint Applications Development
JTA	Joint Technical Architecture
JVM	Java Virtual Machine
KB	Kilobyte, Knowledgebase
KB/SQL	Knowledge-Based/Structured Query Language
KBMS	Knowledgebase Management System
KDP	Key Decision Point
KM	Knowledge Management
KPA	Key Practice Area; Key Process Area
LCC	Life Cycle Cost
LCM	Life Cycle Management
LOB	Line of Business
LOINC	Logical Observations, Identifiers, Names, and Codes
LOM	Logical Object Model
MB	Megabyte
MDA	Model Driven Architecture
MDRIC	Metadata Registry Implementers Coalition
MILNET	Military Network
MIL-STD	Military Standard

MIME	Multi-Purpose Internet Mail Extensions
MIP	Managed Internet Protocol
MIPR	Military Interdepartmental Purchase Request
MIS	Management Information System
MOM	Message Oriented Middleware
MOF	Meta Object Facility - OMG's technology for defining metamodels
MOTS	Modified Off-the-Shelf
MOU	Memorandum of Understanding
NAP	Network Application Platform
NIST	National Institute of Standards and Technology.
NIPRNet	Non Secure Internet Protocol Router Network
NPV	Net Present Value
O&M	Operations and Maintenance.
O&S	Operation and Support
OAG	Open Applications Group, Inc.
OASD	Office of the Assistant Secretary of Defense
ODB	Object Database
ODBC	Open Database Connectivity; Open Dual Bus Configuration
ODBMS	Object Database Management System
ODC	Other Direct Charges; Other Direct Costs
ODP	Open Distributed Processing
ODS	Operational Data Store
OEM	Original Equipment Manufacturer
OGP	Office of Government wide Policy
OI	Operating Instructions
OID	Object Interaction Diagram
OIG	Office of the Inspector General
OLAP	Online Analytical Processing
OLE	Object Linking and Embedding
OLTP	Online Transaction Processing
OMA	OMG's Object Management Architecture
OMB	Office of Management and Budget
OMG	Object Management Group
OO	Object Oriented
OOA	Object-Oriented Analysis
OOAD	Object-Oriented Analysis and Design
OOD	Object-Oriented Design
OOPL	Object-Oriented Programming Language
OOPS	Object-Oriented Programming System
OOSE	Object-Oriented Software Engineering
OP	Obsolete Parts
OPM	Office of Personnel Management
ORB	Object Request Broker
ORDBMS	Object-Relational Database Management Systems
ORM	Order Message
OSD	Office of the Secretary of Defense
OSE	Open Systems Environment
OSI	Open Systems Interconnection Standard
PDF	Portable Data File
PIR	Post Implementation Review
PM	Performance Measure; Program Manager
PMA	Policy Management Authority
PMO	Program Management Office
PMP	Program Management Plan
PMR	Program Management Review
PPM	Process Performance Measures

PPTP	Point-to-Point Tunneling Protocol
PR	Peer Review; Purchase Request
PRA	Paperwork Reduction Act
PRAG	Performance Risk Assessment Group
PRM	Performance Reference Model
QA	Quality Assurance
QC	Quality Control
QMB	Quality Management Board
RACS	Reference Architecture and Common Services
RAD	Rapid Application Development
RIM	Reference Information Model
RM	Risk Management; Requirements Management
RM/CM WG	Requirements Management/Configuration Mgmt Working Group
RM/CMB	Requirements Management/Configuration Management Board
RMP	Risk Management Plan
RMWG	Requirements Management Working Group
ROI	Return on Investment; Return on Innovation
ROM	Read-Only Memory
SA&D	Systems Analysis and Design
SEMCI	Single Entry Multiple Carrier Interface
SHADE	Shared Data Environment
SIPRNet	Secure Internet Protocol Router Network
SCRM	Service Component Reference Model
SOA	Service Oriented Architecture
SOAP	Simple Object Access Protocol
SW	Software
TAFIM	Technical Architecture Framework for Information Management
TBQ	Taxonomy-Based Questionnaire
TCP/IP	Transfer Communications Protocol/Internet Protocol
TEAF	Treasury Enterprise Architecture Framework
TISAF	Treasury Information Systems Architecture Framework
TRM	Technical Reference Model
UDDI	Universal Description, Discovery and Integration
UEML	Unified Enterprise Modeling Language
UML	Unified Modeling Language
UMLS	Unified Medical Language System
VEN	Virtual Enterprise Network
VPN	Virtual Private Network
VRML	Virtual Reality Modeling Language
WWW	World Wide Web
W3C	World Wide Web Consortium
WBS	Work Breakdown Structure
WSDL	Web Services Description Language
XLL	Extensible Linking Language
XMI	Extensible Markup Interface; Extensible Metadata Interchange
XML	Extensible Markup Language

Suggested Additional Reading

Allen, Brandt and Andrew Boynton. "Information Architecture: In Search of Efficient Flexibility." *MIS* Quarterly. December 1991.

Boar, Bernard. Constructing Blueprints for Enterprise IT Architectures. John Wiley & Sons, Inc. 1999.

Cook, Melissa. Building Enterprise Information Architectures. Prentice Hall Publishers. 1996.

Federal CIO Council. Federal Enterprise Architecture Framework, Version 1.1. Washington DC. September 1999.

King, Christopher, et al. Security Architecture: Design, Deployment, and Operations. McGraw-Hill. 2001. .

Laartz, Jurgen et al. "The Paris Guide to IT Architecture." *The McKinsey Quarterly*, 2000/3.

National Association of State Chief Information Officers. NASCIO Enterprise Architecture Framework Toolkit, Version 2.0. July 2002. Lexington, Kentucky 40507-1324 www.nascio.org

Nolan, Richard and Dennis Mulryan. "Undertaking an Architecture Program." *Stage by Stage*. Volume 7, Number 2. March/April 1987.

Schekkerman, Jaap. How to survive in the jungle of Enterprise Architecture Frameworks. Trafford, Victoria, BC, Canada. 2004.

Sowell, Kathie and Ann Reedy. "Enterprise Architecture Tools Report." Prepared for the Federal CIO Council, Architecture Working Group, 2001.

Spewak, Steven. Enterprise Architecture Planning: Developing a Blueprint for Data, Applications, and Technology. Wiley & Sons. 1992.

Thomas, Rob et al. A Practical Guide to Federal Enterprise Architecture. Federal CIO Council. 2001. http://cio.gov/documents/bpeaguide.pdf

Zachman, John A. "A Framework for Information Systems Architecture." *IBM Systems Journal*. Volume 26, Number 3, 1989.

Zachman, John and J. Sowa. "Extending and Formalizing the Framework for Information Systems Architecture." *IBM Systems Journal*. Volume 31, Number 3. 1992.

Subject Index

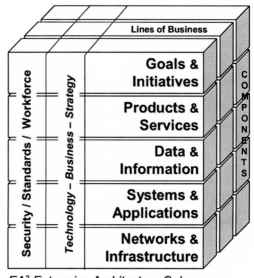

EA³ Enterprise Architecture Cube ™